EXPERIMENTAL CHILD PSYCHOLOGIST:

Essays and Experiments
in Honor of
Charles C. Spiker

PROFESSOR CHARLES C. SPIKER

EXPERIMENTAL CHILD PSYCHOLOGIST:
Essays and Experiments in Honor of Charles C. Spiker

edited by
LEWIS P. LIPSITT
JOAN H. CANTOR

LAWRENCE ERLBAUM ASSOCIATES, PUBLISHERS
1986   Hillsdale, New Jersey   London

Lawrence Erlbaum Associates, Inc., Publishers
365 Broadway
Hillsdale, New Jersey 07642

68124397

Library of Congress Cataloging-in-Publication Data

Experimental Child Psychologist

   "Spiker bibliography": p.
   Includes index.
   1. Child psychology   2. Spiker, Charles C.
I. Lipsitt, Lewis Paeff, 1929–   . II. Cantor,
Joan H.   III. Spiker, Charles C.
BF721.E79   1986   155.4   86-13536
ISBN 0-89859-807-9

Printed in the United States of America
10 9 8 7 6 5 4 3 2 1

For Professor Charles C. Spiker's students

Contents

Preface

"... not by becoming an imitative disciple of mentors, but through penetrating examination of their products and proposals ... "

These words, the essences of Charles C. Spiker's personal contribution to the field of experimental child psychology, were described by the late Howard Meredith, an American dean of physical anthropology, a good friend and colleague, and a long-time professor in the Institute of Child Behavior and Development (formerly the Iowa Child Welfare Research Station).

The words could not have been better chosen for the way in which most of Charlie Spiker's students represent the spirit of this volume. As will be evident, those who have been taught by him are a diverse lot in their origins, and in their eventual life tasks and personal development. Many have moved away from their Iowa roots in important ways—in their research, in their theory, and even in their philosophy of science. Still, we think they agree that their ability to do so successfully and confidently stems directly from the fundamental lessons learned so well from Charlie Spiker.

Charlie is a very special friend, a very special man, a very special teacher, and a very special intellect. He would not necessarily endorse the order in which we have placed these attributes. The fact is that he won his way to our hearts through his intellect. Those who never made it through the first encounters in his classes, or in his laboratory, would have no way whatever of knowing what we are talking about or here celebrating. But, tolerant as he is of the ambiguities of our vocabulary (which he does all he can to improve upon), Charlie has taught us, among other things, that matters of the heart are not so distant from things of the laboratory. Life is what we study. If we have different ways, that too helps to make the whole enterprise worthwhile.

It seems especially fitting, different though the tradition is, that we were able to prevail upon the man we are here honoring to write the showpiece article for the volume! The chapter by Charles Spiker is the best distillation we have seen of the content of the course he has been developing over a period of more than thirty years. We believe, and are sure the reader will agree, that this profound and lucid treatment of the philosophy of science is as edifying a piece of writing as we have ever encountered. The elements of the piece were in the courses we took from Spiker, but here it is packaged as one magnificent chapter. Although we are honoring Professor Spiker with this volume, we are the ones truly honored to have this brilliant tour de force as his gift to us.

Each of the contributions to this volume echoes in its way the proclamation that some of the best lessons learned were from Charlie Spiker. It is not for us to belabor the message here. It is captured differently but exquisitely in several chapters, but most especially in the chapter by Glenn Terrell, Spiker's first doctoral graduate student, and that of V. Alan Spiker, Charles Spiker's son. We have heard it said that fortuitous circumstances are important determinants of life destinies. Not wanting to dispute that, we only wish to add that any young person aspiring to a scholarly way of life in the field of child behavior and development, or some related life destiny, would be fortunate indeed to chance upon Charlie Spiker.

Working on this volume has been for us and, we are sure, for all the authors, a very rewarding, nostalgic experience. Some old friendships have been renewed, and many old memories of graduate school have been revived. We have been provided, too, with the rare opportunity to interrupt the normal flow of our busy professional lives and take a penetrating look backward to our academic roots. Although we have traveled many different roads to get where we now are, the roads lead back in many ways to Charlie Spiker. He not only had a strong hand in shaping the field, but he guided each of us individually in the way we approach our science, the ways we teach, and the ways we think. We hope this volume expresses to Charles Spiker a small measure of our debt to him and the deep appreciation felt by his students and colleagues everywhere.

Lewis P. Lipsitt   Joan H. Cantor
Brown University   The University of Iowa
Providence, Rhode Island 02912   Iowa City, Iowa 52242

October 19, 1986

Foreword

Higher education is nourished by excellence in university teaching, research, and administration. Professor Charles C. Spiker has become distinguished by having excelled in each of these functions. For more than three decades he has served higher education magnificently. At this time in his career, it is fitting that students and colleagues honor him publicly in his roles as scholar, professor, and administrator.

From 1952 to 1972, Charles and I were faculty members in the University of Iowa Institute of Child Behavior and Development (formerly the Iowa Child Welfare Research Station). During this time, he manifested a strong and sustained personal disposition toward scholarly dedication, creativity, and productivity, matched by a persistent fostering of and support for stronger faculty, improved curricular programs, and higher levels of teaching and research in the Institute as a whole.

The Institute had four successive Directors between 1917 and 1960, when Charles became Director. Knowing the teaching commitments and program of research Charles was carrying at the time he became Director, I was surprised (and delighted) with the attention he gave to mastering the history of the Institute, moving ahead on the responsibilities enumerated in its Charter, and especially in working with the full Institute faculty in determining a splendid balance between faculty responsibility in policy

---

*We were saddened by Howard Meredith's death on October 7, 1985. He was a close colleague and friend of Charlie Spiker for many years, and we feel especially fortunate in having Howard's contribution to this volume.

formulation and administrative responsibility for policy implementation. From a background of having served under seven administrators during my professional career, I rank Charles Spiker as the one who worked most vigorously to realize the principles of the American Association of University Professors regarding administrative leadership and faculty participation.

Across all aspects of his professorship, Charles stands high in creativity. In teaching, over the years he has developed (and revised) several quality courses not in the psychology curriculum at the time he was a graduate student. His teaching has been soundly-based, rooted in perspicacity, and directed to provoking student thought on the topics discussed. In research, Charles has amassed a sterling record of original investigations, and he has given stimulative guidance to undergraduate and graduate students in the formulation and execution of innovative studies.

In the 1940s, when Charles was enrolled for graduate study at the University of Iowa, his background in psychology was strengthened through contacts with Professors Orvis Irwin, Beth Wellman, and Don Lewis. Over ensuing substantial periods, he matured professionally through scholarly interchange with Professors Kenneth Spence and Gustav Bergmann. In an exemplary manner, he sought out and responded to these influences, not by becoming an imitative disciple of mentors, but through penetrating examination of their products and proposals in ways that enabled him to achieve insightful extensions of learning theory, and important empirical contributions to the understanding of many facets of learning in children.

Charles is being honored as a conscientious and competent teacher, counselor, investigator, administrator, and editor. During the early 1960s he helped launch and served as co-editor of the important and continuing series titled *Advances in Child Development and Behavior*. Along with others, I benefited on occasions from his concise and pertinent editing proficiencies.

This foreword looks reflectively on the career of an exceptional contributor to psychological knowledge and training. The chapters that follow partly look back, partly represent the present, and partly look ahead. It will be particularly pleasing to Charles that the book includes a chapter by his son. Overall, the assembled expressions of high esteem assuredly comprise a benchmark in the continuing brilliant career of Professor Charles C. Spiker.

Howard V. Meredith
Late of the University of South Carolina

1 Principles in the Philosophy of Science: Applications to Psychology

Charles C. Spiker
University of Iowa

INTRODUCTION

Science as a Method

This chapter deals with the general rules, principles, and procedures that are common to all scientific disciplines. In modern times, this system of information has become known as the philosophy or logic of science. The different scientific disciplines—e.g. physics, chemistry, psychology, physiology, anthropology, sociology, etc.—represent the division of labor that scientists have effected. Each discipline has staked out its own area with relatively little overlap among the several areas. Despite this division of labor, all disciplines use the same general method. It is the common aspects of scientific methodology with which this chapter is concerned. A description of the scientific method describes how scientists obtain, formulate, and organize new knowledge. It does not deal specifically with knowledge that has been obtained by the scientific method.

The goal of science is variously expressed as the explanation, prediction, or understanding of the natural phenomena that surround us. One purpose of this chapter is to discuss the meanings of the words "explanation," "prediction," and "understanding" and to show that the three goals are really the same.

This chapter is an adaptation of one written for J. Hinrichs and I. Levin (Eds.), *Principles of Experimental Psychology,* Chicago, IL, Dorsey Press, and published here with permission.

Science achieves its goal through observations, the careful description of observations, the formulation of laws of nature, and the construction of theories. This chapter explains the criteria that scientists use in relating their observations to descriptive words. It describes the way in which laws are formulated and it displays the anatomy of scientific theories.

Scientists use both inductive and deductive reasoning. This chapter explains in considerable detail what each of these two types of reasoning involves and how they differ. In particular, the nature of deductive reasoning is exposed and the central role of deductive processes in explanation, prediction, and understanding is specified.

Since the time of Isaac Newton, the development of theory has been viewed as one of the highest achievements of scientific effort. This chapter recognizes the importance of theory by providing a careful analysis of its structure, a description of the logic of testing theories, and an example of a relatively simple, comprehensible theory.

Three Kinds of Knowledge

The analysis of the scientific method presented here is based on the idea that all knowledge can be divided into three categories. It is helpful to think of each category as consisting of a very large number of sentences, statements, or propositions. (In this chapter, "sentence," "statement," and "proposition" are used synonymously.) We can tell which category a statement belongs to by noting what we would have to do to determine whether that statement is true or false. In other words, the categories of knowledge are different because the truth or falseness of their statements are determined in different ways. The distinction among the three categories of knowledge should become clearer as we proceed. First, however, we need to clarify the notion of a sentence.

The Characteristics of a Sentence.   In a technical treatment of the scientific method, a great deal would be said about the nature of sentences. Given our more modest purposes, we try to grasp the basic notion of a sentence with a few examples and a liberal use of intuition.

A sentence is a string of words. Not every string of words, however, is a sentence.

Napoleon, first, blue, difficult

The previous string is not a sentence, because it lacks grammar. All words in the string are familiar, meaningful English words. Nevertheless, they obviously do not constitute a sentence.

Spirotes girulate elatically.

This string of words seems to have the necessary grammatical structure. "Spirotes" looks like a plural English noun. "Girulate" has the form of many English verbs and "elatically" resembles an English adverb. Unfortunately, not one of the three words can be found in an English dictionary, and we would not count such a string as a statement.

Seventy-five percent of adult males have smudsy.

This is another string of words that appears to be a sentence; it also seems to have the necessary grammatical structure. There is one word in the sentence, however, whose meaning is unknown. Only if all words in the string are meaningful will we count a string as a sentence because we would otherwise not know how to determine if it is true or false.

There is one other type of word string that must be ruled out of the class of sentences for our present purposes:

Open the door.

Although such a sentence is grammatically correct, it does not make sense to assign a truth value to imperative sentences. So, imperative sentences will also be excluded from the class of sentences that make up the three kinds of knowledge.

In this chapter, "sentence," "statement," or "proposition" will be used to refer to those strings of words that are grammatically correct and contain only meaningful words. Most important, for a string of words to be a sentence, it must make sense to assign a truth value to the string.

The Characteristics of the Three Types of Knowledge.   We can identify the class of knowledge a statement belongs to by considering what must be done in order to determine the truth value of that statement. Consider the following:

It is raining outside Seashore Hall right now.

To determine whether this statement is true, an observation must be made. Now consider this statement:

Either it is raining outside Seashore Hall right now

or it is not raining outside Seashore Hall right now.

Is it necessary to make an observation about the conditions outside Seashore Hall? On the contrary, we know that this statement is true simply because we understand English. The key words in the sentence are "not" and "or." There is nothing to see outside Seashore Hall that could possibly help us to assign a truth value to this statement.

Finally, consider the following statement:

It is very pleasant to walk in the rain.

Everyone knows individuals who would consider this statement false and other individuals who would consider it true. The truth value of the statement varies from person to person; such a statement, therefore, has no interpersonal truth value. It is not possible to assign truth values to such statements except in accord with the personal beliefs or preferences of particular individuals. It would not be reasonable to expect everyone to share these beliefs or preferences. Certainly, we do not expect everyone else to agree with the truth values that we, as individuals, might assign to such statements.

Let us now proceed to assign names to these three classes of knowledge. The first class is variously referred to as empirical, factual, or synthetic knowledge. Its distinguishing feature is that it is necessary to make observations, of something other than the sentence itself, to determine the truth value of the statement. The second class is called logical, formal, structural, or analytic knowledge. The truth of such statements is determined by analyzing the meanings of, and spatial patterns among, certain words that occur in the sentences. The third category is value knowledge. It consists of several subclasses—moral, ethical, esthetic, and societal laws. Statements in this class of knowledge do not have absolute interpersonal truth values. Their truth is relative, in the sense that the alleged truth values vary from society to society, from time to time in the same society, from individual to individual at the same time in the same society, and from one time to another for the same individual.

The foregoing paragraphs are designed to make it intuitively plausible that the distinction among three kinds of knowledge can be maintained. They do not constitute a fundamental, philosophical proof that there are three kinds of knowledge. Not all philosophers would accept the distinctions made here, although most philosophers concerned with the description of the scientific method would agree that these distinctions are highly useful in that description.

Another set of examples provides a test for comprehension of the trichotomy: (1) Ninety-nine percent of U.S. citizens say, "Sunsets are beautiful"; (2) sunsets are beautiful or sunsets are not beautiful; (3) Sunsets are beautiful. The first sentence requires observation to determine its truth value; indeed, a great many observations would be required to determine whether it is true. Hence, it is a statement of fact. Note that it is not necessary to know whether a statement is true before classifying it as factual. The term *factual,* as used here, refers to a statement, either true or false, that must be confirmed or disconfirmed by making observations. No observation beyond looking at the sentence is required to determine that the second statement is true; the meanings of "or" and "not" testify to its truth. Note that the substitution of "ugly" for "not beautiful" in the second sentence does not yield a sentence that is necessarily (logically) true, because there is at least one more category into which sunsets could fall—the mediocre category. The third statement is clearly a statement of value and lacks interpersonal truth value.

The Relation of Science to the Three Types of Knowledge.   How does science relate to the three types of knowledge described previously? In one sense, the answer to this question is spread through the remainder of this chapter, but we can provide a preliminary answer at this point. The scientific method was developed to determine the truth value of statements from the empirical category. Knowledge from the logical category is used by scientists as an indispensable tool, although scientists, qua scientists, do not contribute to this knowledge. Science does not attempt to determine directly the truth value of any statements from the value category.

Science and Values.   At this point, some readers may wonder whether science and value knowledge are really independent. Some may think that science does affect our values in important ways. For example, some of us have smoked cigarettes and have stopped after learning from scientific sources of an alleged relation between smoking cigarettes and several fatal illnesses. Did not science determine values for these reformed smokers? The answer is affirmative, but the effect was indirect. Science did not attempt to determine the truth value of the statement, "It is bad to smoke cigarettes." The attempt was made to determine the truth value of the statement, "Cigarette smoking makes people ill," which is a statement of fact. Individuals who believe the factual statement to be true may very well assign their own personal truth values to the former statement. Science, however, did not. Science does not even assign a truth value to the statement, "It is bad to die before you need to."

If science does not attempt to determine the truth value of statements of value, who does? The answer varies from one society to another, from one segment of a society to another, and from one set of values to another. Thus, religious leaders have considerable influence on matters of morality; legislators and judges greatly affect legal prescriptions; musicians and artists provide important input with respect to esthetics; and the leaders of the various professions help to formulate ethical codes. Whether we like this way of determining values, these statements are a fair description of the way our society is structured with regard to values. Science affects human values only indirectly.

THE NATURE OF FORMAL KNOWLEDGE

To learn to fly an airplane takes many hours of practice. To become an airplane mechanic requires even more hours of study and practice. To design airplanes, one must know nearly everything the pilot knows, most of what the mechanic knows, and much more. Nevertheless, there is no need to become a pilot, a mechanic, or a designer in order to understand why an airplane flies. Similarly, it is not necessary to be a logician or a mathematician to understand the nature of logic.

The Role of Formal Knowledge in Science

Many readers will consider themselves to have a reasonably good grasp of the nature of empirical knowledge and a fair understanding of the scope and nature of value knowledge. At the same time, some of the same readers may hesitate to claim the same degree of comprehension of the nature of formal knowledge. In developing this section on formal knowledge, we show that formal knowledge consists of both logic and mathematics. The purpose, however, is not to provide training in either logic or mathematics, but instead to clarify the nature of this type of knowledge. Indeed, this material would have to be developed with a great deal more rigor to provide training in logic. While reading this section, some readers will discover that they already know a good deal about the rules of logic but still find it difficult to express this knowledge explicitly.

The Role of Logic in Laws and Theories.   A great deal must be said about the nature of logic and mathematics before much can be said about the scientific method. This very fact is a testimony to the central role that formal knowledge plays in science. As we see in a later section of this chapter, laws of nature are formulated through induction. It is not even possible to fully understand the nature of induction without first understanding the nature of deduction—i.e., the nature of the logical process. As we see, a scientific theory is best described as a set of deductively connected empirical laws. So, a good grasp of the nature of deduction is required in order to understand what a theory is.

The Role of Logic in Prediction and Explanation.   Scientists use the highly related terms, *prediction, explanation,* and *understanding,* with relatively restricted meanings. The scientific meanings of all these terms are best explicated by means of deductive (logical) schemata. Once the nature of formal knowledge is understood, a clear grasp of the meanings and implications of these terms is readily obtained. Conversely, vagueness about the nature of the logical process precludes more than a superficial understanding of these important concepts in science.

The Logic of Sentences (Sentential Logic)

Ideally, the words in a language can be divided into two classes—descriptive and logical. Descriptive words refer to things that are in the world, things as concrete as tables and chairs and things as abstract as honor and patriotism. Logical words do not refer to things in the world; rather they are used like glue to stick descriptive words together to form sentences. To study logic is to study the meanings and implications of a handful of these words. Logic is an analytic discipline concerned with the rules for correct reasoning. In contrast to physics, chemistry, or psychology, logic is not an empirical discipline. The next several sections are devoted to clarifying what is involved in analytic thinking.

Logic is divided into two layers. The first is sentential logic that deals with the connectives "and," "or," "if . . . then," and "if, and only if . . . then." The second layer is functional or quantitative logic that deals primarily with "all," "some," and the several meanings of "is." It was functional logic that occupied the minds of the ancient Greeks, who did not realize that sentential logic is the more basic of the two. The discovery that sentential logic is so fundamental was not made until the latter half of the 19th century.

Formal knowledge is hierarchically organized. At the bottom is sentential logic. Built on top of that is functional logic. Next in the hierarchy is the number system, with the rules of arithmetic on top of the number system. Higher mathematics is the top level. In attempting to expose the nature of logical knowledge, we concentrate on the bottom layer, dealing with this level with some rigor. We try only to make it plausible that sentential logic can be developed into functional logic, and that the latter forms the basis for arithmetic.

The Postulates of Sentential Logic.   The starting point for sentential logic can be represented in two postulates. Although neither postulate appears to be of earth-shaking importance, what can be developed from them is truly astonishing.

Postulate 1. There are sentences referred to as p, q, r, s,. . . .
Postulate 2. Each sentence belongs in exactly one of two mutually exclusive and exhaustive categories, called true (T) and false (F).

These postulates, which can be stated in various ways, introduce three primitive terms, *sentence, true,* and *false,* which are not further defined. Although we have already given some discussion to the notion of a sentence, the meanings of the truth categories are not defined in terms of other words. Postulate 2 announces that the categories are mutually exclusive and exhaustive; that is, no sentence can be put in more than one of the two categories, and the two categories are the only ones available. In short, every sentence must be either true or false, but no sentence can be both true and false. Anyone who understands the meanings of the three primitive concepts will be able to follow the next steps.

The Meaning of "Not."   An attempt to define the word "not" constitutes a major problem for anyone who has not been exposed to formal logic. We understand the word, of course, but to define "not" without using more complex words (e.g., "negate," "negation," "denial") seems difficult. Logicians make use of a device called the truth table that, although not necessary, greatly simplifies the definitions of several of the logical words for beginning students. The postulates indicate that all possible sentences can be placed into either the *T* category or the *F* category; that is, any arbitrarily selected sentence, *p,* must be either true or false. The definition of "not" can then be given by the following pattern:

p	not p
T	F
F	T

In English, this pattern says that placing "not" before a sentence creates a new sentence and that the new sentence has a truth value opposite to that of the original sentence. In ordinary speech, of course, we do not put "not" before a sentence; rather, we place it inside the sentence to create a smoother pattern. Thus, we say, "I am not going to the game" rather than "Not I am going to the game."

The Meaning of "And."   Given the truth-table device and the example of defining "not," the definition of other terms becomes manageable. Consider now the English word "and." Everyone has taken true–false tests in which there were some "double-barreled" questions; that is, there were some questions that consisted of two sentences hooked together with "and." We believed one part to be true and the other part false. How should we answer such questions? The correct strategy is to give the answer, "true," only if both parts are true. Otherwise we respond with "false." This meaning of "and" can also be expressed by means of the truth table following.

If we consider all possible pairs of sentences, they could be classified into exactly four categories with respect to their truth values:

p	q
T	T
T	F
F	T
F	F

that is, both sentences may be true; both may be false; the first may be true and the second false; or the first may be false and the second true. There are no other possibilities. Now "and" can be defined in much the same way as "not."

p	q	p and q
T	T	T
T	F	F
F	T	F
F	F	F

This pattern says that "p and q" will be true only if "p" is true and "q" is true.

The strategy is to make a compound sentence of two simpler sentences by connecting the two component sentences by "and." The truth value of the compound sentence is a function of the truth values of the two component sentences. Therefore, the "and" function has been expressly defined and it means exactly what it does in English.

Implications of "Not" and "And."   What are some of the implications of the two postulates and the two definitions? Consider any arbitrary statement, *p,* and its negation, not *p.* Suppose that we connect two such statements by "and," so that we assert, "p and not p." Let us examine the possible truth values of the compound statement using the truth-table device:

p	not p	p and not p
T	F	F
F	T	F

Note that the final column contains only Fs. What does this imply? The answer is: No matter what statement we substitute for "p" in the statement form, "p and not p," the resulting statement cannot be true. (Technically, such statements are called contradictions.) This answer is a sweeping generality; there are no qualifications and there is no need to try out a few examples. We can be absolutely certain. What is the source of such certainty? Given the meanings that we assigned to "not" and to "and," no statement having the form, "p and not p," can be true. Had we assigned a different meaning to "and," then the truth table for "p and not p" would have been different. For much the same reason, if we were to agree to use the word "fawn" to refer only to baby chickens, the statement, "Fawns are baby deer," would no longer be true. One of the logical implications of the two postulates and our two definitions is that any statement of the form "p and not p" must be false.. There are other implications, however.

The Meaning of "Or."   Consider next the word, "or." As some readers are aware, the English "or" is an ambiguous word. For this reason, the construction, "and/or," is often used in legalistic documents to indicate that either of two conditions or both conditions may be required. (For example, the deposit will not be refunded if the book is lost and/or damaged.) The following truth table gives the definition of "and/or:"

p	q	p and/or q
T	T	T
T	F	T
F	T	T
F	F	F

The ambiguity of "or" appears in the first row. On the one hand, if someone were to say, "I will buy a Ford or a Chevrolet," we would understand "or" to mean one or the other but not both. For this meaning of "or," the first row of the truth table would contain *F.* On the other hand, if the head master were to announce, "Lying or cheating will be punished," we would be astonished if the student who lied was punished, the student who cheated was punished, but the student who lied *and* cheated went scot-free. In this usage of "or," the "and/or" meaning is intended and the entry in the first row of the truth table would contain a *T.*

Logicians, of course, are unwilling to tolerate the ambiguity of the English word and have selected the "and/or" meaning, symbolizing it more concisely by "V." The "and/or" meaning is referred to as the inclusive "or," whereas the other meaning is called the exclusive "or." (The exclusive "or" can be rendered as, "(p V q) and not (p and q).")

Further Implications.   We have now stated two postulates and defined three logical words. Although the logician's definition of "not" is identical to the English meaning, it is usually symbolized by "-" for brevity. Similarly, the logical "and" is the same as the English "and," but it is often assigned "."

for a symbol. We again take time to examine some of the implications of the postulates and definitions up to this point. Consider the following table:

p	-p	p V -p
T	F	T
F	T	T

The table says that if any statement and its negation are connected by "V," the result is a statement that must be true. (Note that the same table would have been obtained had we used the exclusive "or" rather than "V.") Thus, "It is raining or it is not raining (right here and right now)" is true by virtue of logic and not by virtue of the current weather. Once again, we can make one of those sweeping generalizations—all statements of the form, "p V -p" are true. Compound statements that are true irrespective of the truth of their component statements are called tautologies. Therefore, "It is raining or it is not raining," is a tautology.

There are two other implications of these postulates and definitions. They are concerned with the relations between the "." function and the "V" function. Given the meanings of these two connectives, is it possible to say with one of them what can be said with the other? The truth tables offer us a means of determining an answer to this question. If the answer is negative, then both connectives are needed; if the answer is positive, perhaps we can get by with only one.

Consider the following table:

p	q	-p	-q	(-p V -q)	-(-p V -q)	p . q
T	T	F	F	F	T	T
T	F	F	T	T	F	F
F	T	T	F	T	F	F
F	F	T	T	T	F	F

The third and fourth columns were obtained merely by reversing the truth values of each of the first two columns. The fifth column was obtained by connecting the statement forms heading the third and fourth columns with "V." The sixth column was obtained by negating the statement form over the fifth column. Finally, the seventh column was obtained by connecting the statement forms over the first and second columns with the "." symbol.

Note that the corresponding truth values shown in the last two columns are identical. This means that whenever the statement form "p . q" is true, the statement form "-(-p V -q)" is also true, and whenever the first is false, the second will also be false. It is clear, then, that whatever can be said with

"." could also be said with "V" and "-", at least in principle. The qualification, "in principle," is in recognition of the psychological difficulty that we have in processing multiple negatives. An instance of the statement form shown at the top of the sixth column in the preceding table is the following: "It is not the case that it is not raining or the sun is not shining." It is difficult to see that this statement expresses, "It is raining and the sun is shining," and this difficulty is largely due to the multiple negatives.

The following table shows that "V" can be expressed in terms of "." and "-."

p	q	-p	-q	(-p .-q)	-(-p . -q)	p V q
T	T	F	F	F	T	T
T	F	F	T	F	T	T
F	T	T	F	F	T	T
F	F	T	T	T	F	F

This table was constructed in the same manner as the preceding one. It shows that the statement form, "p V q," has the same truth column as does "-(-p . -q)." The former could be substituted for the latter on any occasion.

Although it was shown that anything said with "." can be said with "V" and "-," and that anything said with "V" can be said with "." and "-," the difficulty that we have in processing the double negatives indicates that both connectives are *psychologically* necessary even though they are *logically redundant.* (Incidentally, computers do not find it difficult to process multiple negatives; for them, having two connectives is both logically and "psychologically" redundant.)

In the process of showing the relation between the "." function and the "V" function, two rules of logic have been uncovered. The first states that anytime a statement has the form, "-(-p V -q)," a statement of the form, "p .q," can be substituted for it with neither a change nor a loss in meaning. The second rule states that anytime a statement has the form, "-(-p . -q)," a statement of the form, "p V q," can be substituted for it, also without any change in meaning. These two rules are both true by virtue of the meanings that have been assigned to "not," "and," and "or." Both rules are tautologies.

Two Additional Connectives.   In the usual systems of sentential logic, two additional connectives are defined. The first is similar to the English "if . . . then," and the second is identical to the English "if and only if . . . then." The following table gives the definition of both connectives:

p	q	p ⊃ q	p ≡ q
T	T	T	T
T	F	F	F
F	T	T	F
F	F	T	T

The first connective is called the conditional and the second is the biconditional. "If... then" can usually be expressed by the conditional, although there are some important differences. Consider the campaign slogan, "If I am elected president, then I will negotiate a disarmament treaty." When we attempt to evaluate the truthfulness of the campaign promise, we have no difficulty if the candidate is elected: The promise was true if he negotiated a disarmament treaty and it was not true if he did not negotiate a disarmament treaty. The problem arises if the candidate does not get elected. Was his campaign promise truthful? Our response is a shrug of the shoulders. Who knows? Thus, if we were to substitute "if... then" for the horseshoe in the preceding table, we would not know what truth values to put in the last two rows. Once again, the logicians must have unambiguous connectives and they arbitrarily assign "T" to both rows. The resulting connective proves to be very useful. It is important to remember, however, that there is a difference between the horseshoe and "if... then."

The biconditional means exactly what "if and only if... then" means. Notice that the compound biconditional is true if the component statements have identical truth values. This fact makes the biconditional very convenient in the expression of certain kinds of tautologies, as is seen next.

The Sufficiency of Four Connectives.   Logicians claim that the four connectives are entirely adequate *logically*. By this they mean that everything that can be expressed using any English connective can be expressed using one or more of the four connectives just defined. It should be pointed out that some connectives, in English as well as in other languages, have nonlogical functions. The word, "although," for example, has an empirical connotation that goes beyond the meaning of any of the four connectives. In the sentence, "He obtained a job as a bank teller, although he was once convicted for embezzlement," the "although" is used to express the *fact* that such appointments are unusual for individuals who have been convicted for embezzlement. A sentence such as "He obtained a job as a bank teller and he was once convicted as an embezzler and that is most unusual" would be required to replace the "although." It is important to see that an additional statement of fact is required, not an additional *logical* notion. Other English connectives such as, "despite," "nevertheless," "because," "since," etc. all have some empirical, nonlogical connotations but can be replaced with one or more of the four connectives and some additional factual information.

Not only are the four connectives logically adequate, but we could in principle get by with only one of them and "not." For example, all that would be *logically* required is "not" and "and" or "not" and "or." Either pair could be used to say everything that can be said using all four connectives. If this claim is true, then there must be some rules, similar to those we found for the "." function and the "V" function, that tell us how to translate from one connective to the others. Such rules do indeed exist, although it would take us too far afield to list and explore them. The rules for translating from one connective to others constitute several of the rules of inference in sentential logic.

Logical Rules as Tautologies.   Let us return to the relation between "." and "V," using the biconditional to show that the translation rule is a tautology. Consider the following table:

p	q	p . q	-(-p V -q)	(p . q) ≡ [-(-p V -q)]
T	T	T	T	T
T	F	F	F	T
F	T	F	F	T
F	F	F	F	T

The truth tables for "p . q" and "-(-p V -q)" were constructed in preceding tables. In this table, the truth columns for the two compound statement forms are used to construct the truth table for "(p . q) ≡ [-(-p V -q)]." Note that the truth column for this statement form consists entirely of Ts. We have again encountered a tautology, a statement whose truth value is independent of the truth values of the component statements (i.e., of the truth values of the statements that "p" and "q" represent.) The statement can be read, " '(p . q)' means the same as '[-(-p V -q)]'." A statement of either form can be freely substituted for a statement of the other form.

The preceding paragraph constitutes the derivation of a rule of inference in sentential logic. The rule is tautologically true, as are all logical rules. The certainty of this truth lies in the definitions of the five logical words as developed earlier in this section. Given the meanings assigned these words, it is not possible for the rule of inference to be false. All of the rules of inference in sentential logic are tautologies and all can be demonstrated to be tautologies by means of the truth tables, although such demonstrations are sometimes quite tedious.

Some of the rules of inference consist of the translation rules among the four connectives, analogous to the one just derived. Others are sentential representations of simple arguments. Thus, the simple argument,

$$\frac{\begin{array}{l} p \supset q \\ p \end{array}}{q}$$

can be represented in statement form, "[(p ⊃ q) . p] ⊃ q." An example of such a statement is, "If it is the case that if it is raining then the streets are wet and It is raining, then the streets are wet." It is not difficult to see why such statements are always true—they do not say anything about the way the world is. Rather, they are true by virtue of some verbal agreements about the way logical words are to be used.

Introductory textbooks in symbolic logic contain a list of the rules of sentential inference. The length of the list varies from textbook to textbook, because some can be derived from others. All are tautologies, however, and are true by virtue of the definitions given the four connectives and "not." These definitions were in turn based on the two postulates.

Functional Logic

The Meanings of "All" and "Some." We have been considering the logic of intact sentences—the logic of the connectives. We have seen that the truth of certain sentences depends on their structure and not on conditions in the world. Conditions in the pantry are irrelevant to the truth of, "If we had some ham, then we would have ham and eggs, if we had some eggs." The sentence is certainly true; the price of the certainty is factual vacuity. It tells us nothing about the state of the pantry.

The next step is to make it plausible that the same kind of certainty and empirical emptiness is true of higher forms of logic and, indeed, of arithmetic and mathematics. The discussion proceeds less formally. To proceed with even a moderate degree of rigor and formality would take us well beyond the scope of the projected discussion. Those interested in such matters should pursue courses in formal logic and mathematics.

Functional logic is concerned, at least in part, with the meanings of the words "all" and "some." These two words are closely related in the sense that anything that can be said with one can be said with the other and "not." Thus, "All things are green," means the same thing as, "It is not the case that some things are not green." Or, "Not all things are green," means the same as, "Some things are not green." "It is not the case that something is green," means the same as "All things are not-green." Finally, "It is not the case that all things are not-green," means the same as "Some things are green." From these examples, it is clear that one of the two words could be defined in terms of the other, just as we found was true for "and" and "or." The four examples in this paragraph, properly formalized, are rules of inference in functional logic which specify how to translate between "all" and "some."

The English word "some" is rather ambiguous. How many students must miss a class to permit us to state correctly that "some members" were not there? Logicians, again, require unambiguous concepts and they define a symbol, similar to the English "some," that means "at least one." Thus, the statement, "Some class members were absent," would be interpreted as, "There was at least one member of the class absent." The logically equivalent statement for the English statement, "Something is green," is the rather quaint expression, "There is at least one x such that x is green." The logical equivalent for "All things are green," is "For all x, x is green." There are special symbols for both "all" and "some" with which we need not bother. To define "all" in terms of "some," we can make the following statement: "For all x, x is green" means the same as "it is not the case that there is at least one x such that x is not-green."

If "all" and "some" can be related to notions developed in sentential logic, then it becomes plausible that they are also logical words of the same general sort as are "not" and the connectives. We can see intuitively, without proving, that the general ideas involved in these words are already present in sentential logic. Under what conditions will statements of the following form be true?

$$p_1 \lor p_2 \lor p_3 \lor \ldots \lor p_n$$

Generalizing from the definition of "$\lor$," the answer is that any such statement will be true if *at least one* of the component statements is true. Hence, the notion of *at least one* is already implicit in sentential logic and, therefore, the logician's notion of "some" is implicit in that level of logic. Similarly, under what conditions would any such statement be false? The answer is that it will be false if *all* the component statements are false. Thus, the notion of "all," at least for finite sets, is also implicitly contained in sentential logic.

The two levels of logic can be combined to produce a powerful and flexible language. The following statement serves as an illustration of the combination: There is an x such that (x is green $\cdot$ x is square). In this statement form, "x is green" is an instance of "p" and "x is square" is an instance of "q." The statement, of course, means simply, "There is at least one green square." The following statement represents an important form called the universal statement: For all x [(x is a wall) $\supset$ (x is green)]. Literally, the statement says, "For any x, if x is a wall, then x is green." More colloquially, it says, "All walls are green," and it is a false statement of universal fact. The form is important because all laws of nature can be stated in this form.

The "Is" of Identity.   It is conceivable that two billiard balls could be manufactured so that they were indistinguishable at any given moment except for their positions. All their properties would be identical except for their positional coordinates. Yet, we would still speak of two things. The Leibnitz principle states that if "two" things, *A* and *B,* have exactly the same properties, including the same spatio–temporal coordinates, then there are not two things but only one thing; that is, *A* is *B.* The sentence, "The owner of the Green Dragon Tavern is the mayor of the town," uses the same "is" of identity. The word has the same meaning as the " = " of ordinary arithmetic and can be defined using only logical words, without reference to any descriptive term. It is therefore a logical word like "not," "all," "and," etc. It is one of the words whose meaning is made explicit in functional logic.

The Bridge between Logic and Arithmetic

We have seen that the notion of "at least one" is already contained in sentential and functional logic; therefore, the notion of "one" is there. Consider the following statement form: $p_1 \lor p_2 \lor \ldots \lor p_n$. Under what conditions would any such statement be false? The answer is, only if *none* of the component statements is true. Hence, we see that the notion of "none" (zero) is a logical notion. (The same point can be made by noting that "none" is the case when "not some" is the case.)

We have already noted that " = " is defined in purely logical terms. Given the logical words "0," "1," and " = ," consider what would be possible if " + " were available as a logical word. Using nothing but logical words, we could create the positive integers. Thus, as a series of definitions, we could write:

$$2 = 1 + 1 \text{ def}$$
$$3 = 2 + 1 \text{ def}$$
$$4 = 2 + 2 \text{ def}$$

  etc.

Logicians specializing in mathematical logic have demonstrated that the arithmetic " + " can be defined in purely logical terms. Hence, the positive integers are also logical creatures. Given the idea of addition, it is not difficult to define subtraction in terms of the addition of negative numbers. Because multiplication is successive addition, and because division is successive subtraction, these two operations are readily specified as well.

What we have tried to do, without technical proofs, is to make it intuitively plausible that the number system and arithmetic are built on top of the lower logical systems. The rules of arithmetic and mathematics are tautologies in exactly the same way that the rules of sentential and functional logic are tautologies. These rules do not say anything about the empirical world. They are merely reflections of agreements on how certain words are going to be used. The definitions of these words were in one sense arbitrary but in another sense, the meanings were chosen so that the words defined would be highly useful in logical deduction.

The Utility of Formal Knowledge

We have said a good deal about what logic is, but not much about how it is used. A problem in logic begins with some premises, whether statements that we know to be true or statements that we assume to be true. The rules of logic are then used to justify conclusions that are drawn from these premises. In formal deductions, each conclusion is justified by citing the relevant premises and the pertinent logical rules that permit that conclusion. Most readers have become familiar with this process, either in mathematics or in geometry.

The rules of logic and mathematics have been constructed in such a way that false conclusions cannot be drawn from true premises. The rules guarantee that true premises will yield only true conclusions. The converse, however, is not the case; the correct use of logical rules does not guarantee that the premises are true if the conclusions are true. False premises may yield conclusions that are either true or false. For example,

All fish play the piano.

All piano players swim.

Therefore, all fish swim.

The first two statements are premises and both are false. The third statement is true and it clearly follows from the first two. If a false conclusion is derived from a set of premises, however, then at least one of the premises must be false.

The correct use of the rules of logic guarantees that *if* the premises are true, the conclusions will also be true. The rules do not guarantee the conclusions to be true, however. It is especially important to remember that the truth of the conclusions does not imply the truth of the premises. As we see later, this characteristic of logical knowledge is important in testing scientific theories.

The Vacuity of Logical Knowledge

The rules of logic are all tautologies and therefore say nothing about the nature of the empirical world. There is still another sense in which logical knowledge is factually empty. This idea is probably more difficult to grasp. The notion is stated in abstract terms and then illustrated with a specific example.

Suppose we have several premises and we use the rules of logic to deduce some conclusions from them. There is a sense in which the conclusions say nothing that is new; everything that they state was already implicit in the premises. We cannot create new empirical knowledge by using the rules of logic. Yet, we may deduce statements that we did not previously know to be true. We often seem to need the logical rules in order to understand what the premises truly say.

To illustrate this characteristic of logical knowledge, consider the following pair of statements:

$$3x + 4y = 10$$

$$x - y = ?$$

It is not possible to find a unique pair of values for x and y that will satisfy the first equation. The second statement, being incomplete, does not help. From the moment we substitute a real value for "?," however, the values of x and y are uniquely determined, whether or not we "see" what those values are. No manipulations performed with the rules of algebra will change those values. All that such operations can do is to find out what those values are. If we set "?" to "1," then we can use the tautological rules of algebra to discover that x is 2 and y is 1.

It may seem strange, at first, to say that the conclusions are always implicit in the premises when it sometimes requires the genius of a Newton or an Einstein to "see" which conclusions the premises contain. Nevertheless, this is simply a reflection of how difficult and complex logical deductions can become.

THE NATURE OF DEFINITIONS IN SCIENCE

The Need for New Words in Science

The distinction between logical and descriptive words has been noted and the nature of logical words has been discussed in considerable detail. In this section, the descriptive words that scientists use are considered, as well as the criteria by which scientists evaluate the meaningfulness and usefulness of descriptive terms.

Scientists have a special need for new descriptive words. Because they make observations that other persons have not made, they will observe phenomena that have no names because others have never seen them. They will study phenomena that have never been named because other persons have never paid any attention to these phenomena. Scientists use telescopes and microscopes that are not available to the casual observer. Not only do they make observations that nonscientists have not made, but they must describe their observations and findings to their colleagues. This communication requires careful definition of words so that the observations of one scientist can be repeated and confirmed (or disconfirmed) by colleagues. Science is indeed a social enterprise.

Let us consider an example from the history of physics. In the late sixteenth century, Galileo Galilei, an Italian physicist, began to study the behavior of free-falling bodies. He soon found that the fall was so quick that he could not observe exactly what was happening. To slow down the process, he constructed an inclined plane that could be tilted at several different angles. He obtained some perfectly smooth spheres and began to measure the time that it took them to roll down the plane when it was set at various angles. He found some regular relations between the speeds of the spheres and the angles of inclination. He became even more interested in the *rate of change* in the speeds. He called this rate of change in speed, *acceleration,* a term that was subsequently found to enter into a great many laws of mechanics.

Now, Galileo was certainly not the first person to notice that bodies change their speeds. In the context of his observations of the speeds of the rolling spheres, however, he recognized the importance of the rate of change in speed. A similar story could be told about Pavlov, the Russian physiologist who studied the salivary behavior of dogs. Pavlov was certainly not the first person to observe dogs salivate in anticipation of being fed. In the context of his careful experimentation, however, he saw the significance of the development of the anticipatory salivation and called it *conditioning.* Conditioning is now discussed, as a basic process, in every introductory textbook of scientific psychology.

Where did Galileo and Pavlov find their new words? Did they look in a dictionary? The dictionaries of the times would not have contained either *acceleration* or *conditioning,* at least not in the sense that they used these words. The scientists selected the words (symbols) and then told other scientists what the words meant. This process of assigning meaning to a symbol is called giving a definition of the symbol. Constructing proper definitions is a very important aspect of scientific work. Scientists must make certain that their colleagues understand precisely what the new word is intended to mean.

Some Properties of Definitions

The Arbitrariness of Definitions.   A little reflection shows that there is no necessary connection between a word and its referent. That the same objects have different names in different languages shows that only historical accidents have determined which words go with which objects. The word "dog" would have served just as well as the term for the animal that says "meow" as it does for the one that says "bow-wow." Despite the obviousness of this point, it is difficult to keep it clearly in mind at all times.

In the present context, "definition" refers to one or more statements that tell how a word is going to be used. Accordingly, definitions are always considered verbal; pointing at instances of what a word refers to does not constitute a definition. Thus, the word "automobile" is not defined by pointing at numerous automobiles. Rather, we make one or more statements that specify what kinds of objects are to be referred to by the symbol "automobile."

The Content of Definitions.   What should be included in a definition? Two quite different answers have been considered. The first view is that a definition should include everything that we know about the word's referent. Thus, to define "elephant," we would have to say everything that is known about elephants. Adhering to this view would certainly produce some very cumbersome definitions, but there are even more serious problems with it. First, we must ask, "Everything *who* knows about elephants?" The typical psychologist's knowledge of elephants is probably quite limited compared to that of any zoologist. A child's definition might be briefer still. Secondly, this view would seem to require the redefinition of each word whenever something new is learned about its referent. A serious attempt to follow the stipulations of this view of definitions would require that we spend an inordinate amount of time in reformulating definitions in order to keep up with extensions in knowledge.

The other view is that a definition need contain only as much information as is necessary to permit anyone who knows and understands the definition to identify the referent. The additional information that we now have about elephants would be stated, not in the definition, but in ordinary factual statements. Thus, if we were to define "elephant" as a large mammal with a proboscis (trunk), then other information we have about elephants would be carried in factual statements such as, "Elephants have two ivory tusks," "Nearly all elephants are gray in color," "Elephants are the most intelligent of subprimate, land-living mammals," etc.

One important implication of the second and more reasonable view is that definitions have a very large arbitrary component. For example, elephants have a number of unique characteristics and it would matter little which of these unique properties we select for the definition of the word "elephant." All other properties of elephants would be described in ordinary statements of fact. This implication is entirely consistent with our earlier observation that the relation between words and their referents is arbitrary.

Because definitions are arbitrary, it is not possible to make a "wrong" definition. Stated another way, it is not possible for a definitional statement to be false. At first glance, this conclusion seems to be incorrect; surely everyone has encountered wrong definitions. Consider the following definition: "Elephant" refers to a mammal that wags its tail and says, "bow-wow." Is not this surely a false statement and therefore, if offered as a definition, an instance of a false definitional statement? The answer is that the statement is not false. It seems false because we implicitly insert some words into the sentence that are not there. We mistakenly translate the preceding statement into the following: *The English word,* "elephant," refers to a mammal that wags its tail and says, "bow-wow." This sentence is a false empirical statement, because the English word, "elephant," does not mean what the statement says it means. The statement, therefore, is not a false definition; rather, it is a false factual statement about the way an English word is used by English-speaking people.

The Set of Primitive Words

Circular Definitions.   Many readers have had experience with small, vest-pocket dictionaries. The use of such dictionaries can be quite frustrating. A typical, though hypothetical, encounter is the following. We wish to learn the meaning of "paregoric," using our vest-pocket dictionary. We find, "Paregoric is a camphorated tincture of opium." Suppose that we know the meanings of all the words in the definition except "camphorated." We look for the meaning of the latter and we find, "putting camphor on." We look up "camphor," finding, "Camphor is a derivative of terpenes." We look for "terpenes" and find that, "Terpene is an isomeric hydrocarbon." Next we find that "hydrocarbon" is "a compound such as methane." Finally, we find that "Methane is a gaseous hydrocarbon often used in paregorics." We have come full circle. In the chain of statements that is supposed to constitute the definition of "paregoric," we find the word "paregoric" itself. We still do not know what "paregoric" means; we have learned that a certain set of words are related in meaning, some of them synonyms for each other, but we do not know what any one of them means.

This is the problem of circular definitions and it is frequently encountered in using the tiny dictionaries. The definition is often in the form of an equation, for example, "Hard-hearted, adj. pitiless." If we are fortunate enough to know what "pitiless" means, we are enlightened. If we have to look up the meaning of "pitiless," however, we are likely to run into the circle. The problem of circular definitions is by no means unique to small dictionaries. Instances can also be found in larger dictionaries, although not so frequently.

A Strategy for Avoiding Circular Definitions.   Suppose that we wish to construct a dictionary in such a way that circular definitions cannot occur.

We might remember the admonitions of our elementary school teachers who taught us never to define a word by using that word or one of its derivatives in the definition. For example, we were not allowed to say that "Hunger is the state of being hungry," because whoever does not know the meaning of "hunger" is not likely to know what "hungry" means either. This advice, however, is only a partial solution to the problem of preventing circular definitions.

A seemingly promising strategy is the following. First, define the simplest words so that these can be used in the definition of more complex words. Then the simple and fairly complex words can be used to define still more complex words. In short, we proceed to build an inverted pyramid—a vertical structure with the simplest words on the bottom layer, and with increasingly more complex words at each succeeding level. Each word is defined in terms of words from lower layers, never in terms of words from the same or a higher level. If the users have to look up the meanings of any of the words that occur in a definition, they will be sent to lower layers, ultimately descending to the lowest level that contains the simplest words.

This strategy seems quite promising until we try to write the definition of the first word. What do we use for descriptive words in the first definition? At this point, it becomes clear that *no* language could be constructed in which the meaning of every descriptive word could be stated verbally. We now realize that not every word can be defined because there are no words to use in the definition of the first word. Nevertheless, the general strategy seems sound, if only the "first word" problem can be solved.

If there were a group of words that all users of the dictionary already knew the meanings of, and if these words were adequate to define all other words, then we would have the words necessary for the first definitions. Such a list of words would serve as the primitive words in the language. This idea of primitive words was first met in our discussion of the postulates of sentential logic, where we found "sentence," "true," and "false" to be the primitive words used in the definitions of other logical words.

Criterion for the Set of Primitive Terms.   There are two requirements for the list of primitive words: (1) the words must be adequate to define all other words, and (2) all users of the dictionary must know the meanings of the words. The idea involved in the first criterion can best be explicated by describing a hypothetical game in which we construct a language. The rules permit us free use of all the logical words in the language. For descriptive words, however, we are permitted only the names of the 12 semitones of the chromatic musical scale and a descriptive relational word such as "at the same time as" or "simultaneously." Imagine the kinds of descriptive words we could define. Students who know the theory of harmony realize that we could define all the musical chords, simply by saying "C-major means C, E, and G simultaneously," or "D-major means D, F-sharp, and A simultaneously." We could proceed in this manner with the definition of all the musical chords.

Despite our potential success with the definition of musical chords, we would be able to define only words whose referents were musical tones or temporally simultaneous combinations of musical tones. Therefore, the names of the 12 tones would not be adequate for the definition of *all* other words in the language. Clearly, a much more extensive list would be required. How extensive the list needs to be depends on what we wish to say in the hypothetical language. For example, if we do not intend to talk about music, the names of the 12 semitones would not be needed.

The second criterion for the list of primitive terms is that they are understood by all users of the dictionary. Reflection indicates that there are at least two ways in which we can learn the meaning of a word. We can learn the meaning of a word by repeatedly observing its referent, each time reading the word or hearing it spoken. We can also learn the meanings of (some) words by reading or listening to their definitions. (We can also learn the meaning of a word from the contexts in which the word is used. This method is really a variant of the first method mentioned earlier and is not separately discussed.) It seems likely that the list of words that every user would understand without definition would be words whose meanings were learned by having experienced or having been directly acquainted with their referents.

Words that are most likely to satisfy both criteria will have relatively simple referents. They will refer to things that are readily observed. Consider one of the color words—"green," for example. Is it likely that everyone knows the meaning of "green"? Some readers will immediately think of individuals who are color-blind. Does someone who is color-blind know what "green" means? Because they cannot have been directly acquainted with the referent of the word, they would have had to learn its meaning through definition. Consider a possible definition for "green." We can say, " 'green' refers to color, as 'blue' does, except that 'green' refers to a different color." Somehow that does not seem very helpful. What does the dictionary say? One standard dictionary states that " 'green' is the color of growing grass." That is not very helpful, either, to the person who has never been able to observe a green color.

The previous discussion sets the stage for an important insight into language. We saw earlier that it is not possible to define all the words in a language, because we have no words to define the first word. Now we discover that there are some words that cannot be defined at all; to understand their meanings, we *must* be acquainted with their referents.

It will occur to some readers that the meaning of "green" might be obtained through the context in which it is used. It is probably true that children learn the meanings of many such words from context, but it would be impossible for them to learn the meaning of "green" in this way without being able to see the color. Color-blind individuals would not be able to acquire the meaning in this way.

Some readers will consider giving color-blind individuals a meter, marking off a section of the meter, and instructing them that they are in the presence of green whenever the meter needle enters the marked region. In principle, color-blind individuals would be able to respond correctly with the word "green" whenever they were in its presence. It would be patently false, however, to say that they have the same meaning for "green" as do persons with normal vision. We can always assign a new meaning to a symbol. The problem is that the *conventional* meaning of "green" cannot be expressed in one or more statements.

The difficulty of defining "green" extends to other simple visual properties of objects. Problems exist for each of the senses. We would be no more successful in defining "sweet" or "sour." The tactile words, "rough" or "smooth," would also be troublesome. Simple relational words, such as "above," "below," "to the left of," "between," etc. would also be intractable with respect to satisfactory definitions of their conventional meanings.

The hypothetical problem of constructing a dictionary without circular definitions has provided us with some important insights into the nature of the descriptive words in a language. We now return to a discussion of the language of science to determine how scientists safeguard their definitions. In this analysis, we draw heavily on the work of philosophers of science.

Primitive Predicates in the Language of Science

The Role of Philosophers of Science.   Philosophers of science study the writings of scientists and then formulate an abstract description of what scientists do. For example, they state the rules that scientists follow in constructing definitions; they state what scientists mean when they use such words as "explain," "predict," "law of nature," and "theory;" and they describe the structure of scientific theories and models.

Philosophers of science *describe* what they observe scientists doing. They do not *prescribe* a set of rules that scientists are supposed to follow. Rather, their work resembles that of the grammarian who describes the rules that the speakers of a language follow. Some members of the language community break many of the rules; hardly any one follows all the rules. Nevertheless, most members of a language community would agree that the rules represent ideals that the majority of speakers try to follow. The philosophers of science describe the rules that scientists try to follow as ideals, although some individual scientists may break many rules and nearly every scientist inadvertently breaks a rule from time to time.

The Characteristics of Primitive Terms in the Scientific Language.   Philosophers of science tell us that there is a basic set of terms that scientists never attempt to define. Nevertheless, these terms are used freely in the definitions of other words. The basic words refer to simple properties of, and simple relations among, physical objects and events. The terms are known technically as *primitive predicates,* because they are the *first* words and they refer to properties and relations that are *predicated* about physical objects and events. Thus, "green" refers to a property that we predicate about growing grass, the leaves of trees, and four-leaf clover.

Philosophers of science do not provide us with a list of these words but characterize them instead. The words refer to objects of sense data, rather than to sense data itself. For example, the term, *rough,* refers to a property of a physical object, not to the sensation the scientist has when feeling a rough object. If all words in a language were defined in terms of such words, then the referents of all defined words, in principle, would be observable.

One of the reasons that a complete list of primitive predicates is not provided is that there are actually many different lists that could serve equally well. For example, consider the words "above" and "below." Either word can easily be defined in terms of the other, but neither can be defined except in terms of the other. If "above" is counted among the primitive terms, then "below" can be defined as follows: "A is below B" means the same as "B is above A." Conversely, if "below" is included among the primitive predicates, then "above" can be introduced by the definition: "A is above B" means the same as "B is below A." An analogous relation exists between "left" and "right." Thus, considering only these four words, four different lists of primitive predicates could be specified—one that includes "above" and "left;" one with "above," and "right;" one with "below" and "left;" and one with "below" and "right." In fact, there are many other instances that could be cited and the number of possible sets of primitive predicates is very large indeed.

The Empiricist Meaning Criterion

The Definition in Use.   The criteria that scientists use in defining their descriptive words can best be explicated by means of a device known as the definition in use, a definitional form favored by logicians. This form of a definition resembles the more familiar equational form, except that two statements rather than two words are balanced. The statement on the left is the simplest statement in which the new word can be used. The statement on the right is ordinarily a complex statement of the "if . . . then" form. The left-hand and right-hand statements are connected by "means the same as." Consider the following: "This rat is hungry" means the same as "If food is placed before this rat, then it eats." Assuming that every word in the right-hand statement is understood, we now understand the new word "hunger" well enough to determine whether any rat is in this state. If food is placed before the rat and it eats, then the statement, "This rat is hungry," is true. If food is placed before the rat and it does not eat, then "This rat is hungry" is false. If no food is placed before the rat, then the truth of the statement is indeterminate.

Some readers may judge this definition to be inadequate or inappropriate, either because it is nonquantitative, because it does not consider all possible reasons why a rat may not eat, or possibly because they know that such a concept of hunger has not proved to be very useful. Although these objections are reasonable ones, our previous discussion of definitions reminds us that no such consideration renders the definition *false*.

The Meaning Criterion.   It is now possible to state the criterion that scientists use for meaning. Philosophers of science indicate that scientists hold, as an ideal for definitions, that no word should appear on the right-hand side of the definition unless it is either a primitive predicate, or a word that has already been defined in terms of primitive predicates. This criterion is commonly referred to as the *Empiricist Meaning Criterion.*

A careful study of the Empiricist Meaning Criterion shows that it provides for exactly the hierarchical structure of words necessary and desirable to construct the noncircular dictionary. At the bottom of the hierarchy is the list of primitive terms. With them, and with them alone, we could define a second tier of concepts. Using primitive predicates, and terms from the second tier, we could define a third tier of words. In defining the fourth tier, we could use primitive terms and words from the second and third tiers. We could continue on up the hierarchical structure as far as necessary and convenient.

Readers who are familiar with physics will recognize the preceding paragraph as a realistic description of the hierarchical character of the concepts in, say, mechanics. To illustrate, begin with the concepts of "time," "mass," and "distance" rather than with primitive predicates. All three of these concepts are already quite high in the hierarchy, relative to primitive predicates. First, "velocity" or "speed" is defined using "distance" and "time." Next, "acceleration" is defined using "speed" and "time." "Force" is defined in terms of "acceleration" and "mass." Then, "work" is defined in terms of "force" and "distance." Finally, "power" is defined in terms of "work" and "time."

Exemplification of Referents.   If primitive predicates refer to observable properties and relations of physical objects and events, and if all other words are defined in terms of them, then, in principle, the referents of all defined words would be observable also. Why is it necessary to use the qualifier, "in principle"? The problem is with the word, "observable." It is no more difficult to define "mermaid" than it is to define "cow." "Cow" clearly refers to something observable; it is not immediately clear whether "mermaid" refers to something observable. Because the mermaid class cannot be exemplified, some might deny that mermaids are observable. Nevertheless, there is a sense in which the referent of "mermaid" is observable. If a mermaid were somehow placed before us, we would surely recognize it. It might be better to say that "mermaid" refers to a property that is unobserved (not *unobservable*), but potentially observable. "Spirit" or "ghost," in their usual meanings, refer to unobservables.

Even though a term has been defined in accord with the empiricist meaning criterion, that criterion does not guarantee that the referent of the term will be exemplifiable. In somewhat more familiar language, though less precisely, scientists may inadvertently define words whose referents do not exist. As is explained later, it is possible to define words that meet the empiricist meaning criterion that are scientifically useless. Thus, a word is not guaranteed a place in the language of science simply because its definition meets the empiricist meaning criterion. As we see later, it must also meet a significance, or usefulness, criterion. The word must also occur in scientific laws and theories; if scientists do not find laws in which the word occurs, sooner or later it is dropped from the scientific vocabulary. The significance criterion is explained in a later section.

Operational Definitions.   Some scientists, particularly some psychologists, speak of the operational definition of their concepts. This phrase refers to the practice of specifying the meaning of a concept by stating the manner in which that concept is measured. Thus, one can define "weight" by describing the procedures for measuring the weight of objects. Clearly, any such description of the measuring process would also meet the empiricist meaning criterion. Thus, it would be proper to say that operational definitions constitute a subclass of those definitions that meet the empiricist meaning criterion. Because many scientific concepts, especially in psychology, are not yet quantified, the empiricist meaning criterion serves as a more general statement of the definitional criterion.

Primitive Terms in Psychology.   The empiricist meaning criterion seems entirely appropriate for the physical sciences, where the focal point is the study of the properties and relations among physical objects and events. But is it obvious that such a criterion would be appropriate for psychology, which includes the study of sensory and perceptual phenomena? Will not psychologists wish some of their primitive terms to refer to properties and relations among the sensory data?

The answers to these questions bring out a major distinction between nineteenth century and modern psychology. The experimental psychologists of the nineteenth and early twentieth centuries were concerned with the study of consciousness as revealed through analytical introspection, a form of self-observation. They conceived the problem of psychology to be the analysis of all possible states of consciousness into basic mental elements that would resist all further analysis. Thus, they included among their primitive predicates some that referred to these mental elements and their attributes. Color words referring to properties of mental experiences, tactile words referring to certain sensory characteristics, gustatory words referring to sensations of sweet and sour, all these and many more were required among the primitive terms of the classical psychologists.

Their experiments attempted to reduce such complex states as perceptions, ideas, thoughts, images, and emotions to irreducible elements, such as various attributes of sensation, feeling states, and thought elements. Unfortunately, psychologists from different schools did not agree well on either the type or number of the irreducible elements. Because each psychologist was observing a different set of data, his or her own consciousness, the source of the disagreements could not be ascertained. The disagreements might be the result of one or more of the following three conditions: (1) differences in the phenomena being observed, (2) differences in the meanings the psychologists had for the primitive words referring to the mental elements, or (3) varying degrees of competence among the psychologists as observers.

It was in response to these unresolved disagreements that John B. Watson formulated his behavioristic doctrine. Although he did not use the terminology established in this chapter, his primary principle was that psychologists should adopt the same primitive predicates that the physical scientists had found to be entirely adequate. The mentalistic primitive terms should be discarded. If mentalistic-sounding terms were to be used at all, they would first have to be defined. This principle of Watsonian Behaviorism has come to be known as "methodological behaviorism."

The Empiricist Meaning Criterion as an Ideal.   Some readers probably have been wondering about the feasibility of defining words solely in terms of primitive predicates. Because these words refer to simple properties and relations, would it really be practical to describe, say, a table using as descriptive terms only primitive predicates. The answer is certainly not! To do so would be both terribly tedious and pointless. Neither has anyone ever counted to infinity, and for much the same reason. We can satisfy ourselves that we can count indefinitely without actually doing so. In this case, we know the rule that tells us how to make the next number no matter how high we are in the series. Describing an individual table or chair using only primitive predicates would be no less onerous, although there is no reason to doubt that, in principle, it could be done.

In practice, the words that scientists use in their definitions may include some primitive predicates, but they will typically also include words considerably higher in the hierarchy. Sometimes scientists make mistakes in judgment and misunderstandings develop. For example, from the days of Newton, physicists considered the term *simultaneous* to be entirely meaningful. There is no problem about what is meant by saying that two events occurred simultaneously, if they occurred contiguously in space. "Local simultaneity" is among the primitive predicates and need not be defined. One of the achievements of Einstein, however, was the recognition that if two events are widely separated in space, determination of their simultaneity becomes a complex matter. "Nonlocal simultaneity" must be defined.

Two Kinds of Meaning

The proper definition of a term does not guarantee that it will be a useful term. For a word to be accepted into the scientific language, it must have a clear definition and it must ultimately be used in the formulation of laws. In our everyday language, the "meaning" of a word includes both its definition and everything else we know about the word. It is helpful to separate these two components of meaning. Thus, the philosopher, Gustav Bergmann, has referred to the definitional meaning of a word as Meaning 1 and to the other things we know about the referent of the word as Meaning 2.

We are entirely free to formulate the definition of a word in any way we wish. Having constructed the definition, however, whether the word will enter into laws of nature, or even whether the referent of the word can be exemplified, is no longer up to us. Although we are free to create definitions, we are not free to create their referents. We are free to define "mermaid," "centaur," and "witch," but we cannot create mermaids, centaurs, and witches. Another way to say the same thing is that we are free to formulate definitions in any arbitrary way that we wish, but we do not have the same freedom with respect to giving the new terms significance. Whether any newly defined word will enter into laws of nature depends on nature, not on the scientist who formulated the definition.

The assignment of Meaning 1 to a term is arbitrary, under control of the person who is making the definition. Whether the term, thus defined, will ever have any Meaning 2, and exactly what the Meaning 2 will be, depends on the way the world is. Meaning 2 cannot be fully appreciated until we understand exactly what determines the significance of a concept. This requires a discussion and an analysis of the nature of scientific laws.

THE NATURE OF SCIENTIFIC LAWS

The Meaning of Induction

Imagine a primitive physicist sitting in his cave next to a burning fire. On the floor of the cave is a hollow rock filled with water. The physicist places the rock on the fire without spilling the water. He notices soon that the water in the rock container begins to bubble. He scrawls on the cave wall the equivalent of the following sentence, "There was water and it was heated and it bubbled." Let us abbreviate this sentence in the following way, "W . H. B." The physicist takes more water, heats it and again observes the bubbling phenomenon. Once again, the sequence is recorded. The physicist repeats the series of actions n times with the same outcome (bubbling) on each occasion. He records his observations after each experiment. These n statements may be represented as follows:

$$W_1 \quad . \quad H_1 \quad . \quad B_1$$
$$W_2 \quad . \quad H_2 \quad . \quad B_2$$
$$. \qquad . \qquad .$$
$$. \qquad . \qquad .$$
$$\underline{W_n \quad . \quad H_n \quad . \quad B_n}$$

The subscripts represent the number of times that the sequence was observed.

The line at the bottom of the series of statements designates the end of what might be considered a set of premises. Each of the n statements above the line is a statement of individual fact, as opposed to a statement of universal fact. Given his observations, the physicist would assign the truth value, T, to each of the statements. What logical implications are contained in these n statements? The physicist would like to be able to conclude: "Water always boils if heated." The rules of logic guarantee that the conclusions will be true if the premises are true. If the physicist knows the rules of logic, however, he will realize that the statements above the line may all be true and yet the conclusion could be false; that is, no matter how large the value of n, the $n + 1$ parcel of heated water might not boil. The most general statement that is deducible from the n statements above the line is, "Water was heated n times and each time it boiled." This statement, which can be expressed in English in several different ways, is a summary of what was observed and nothing more. It is also a statement of individual fact, rather than of universal fact.

Our scientist, however, wants to write the statement of universal fact, "If water is heated, then it boils." Because there are no qualifications, not even about air pressure and a specific temperature, such a statement is universal. It covers all instances of water being heated, including those in the past, present, and future. It claims far more than deductive logic would permit, given the finite number of premises. The physicist wishes to generalize beyond the evidence that was obtained.

All laws in science can be expressed as statements of universal fact. Even quantitative laws can be placed in the "if, then" format. The primitive physicist wishes to state a law about the boiling of heated water. To do so, however, he must go beyond the certainty of logical deduction; he must risk being in error. (As was noted in the section on functional logic, a more complete form of the statement of universal fact just considered is the following: "For any x, if x is water and x is being heated, then x boils." In the present context, the more complex form of the statement does not add a great deal; hence, we continue to use the simpler form, "If water is heated then it boils.")

David Hume (1711–1776) is credited with being the first to realize that scientific laws cannot be given a logical justification. Because the conclusion (the universal statement) says more than is said jointly by all the premises (statements of individual fact), the conclusion is not *logically* justified. How large would n have to be to warrant the generalization? The answer is that no finite number of statements above the line would *logically* justify the conclusion.

There is a logical gap between the statements above the line and the conclusion that the scientist wishes to draw. To bridge the gap, it is necessary to make a generalization. The process of generalizing from evidence to a scientific law, that is, to a universal statement, is called "induction." Deduction is governed by strict rules of inference—the tautologies of logic and mathematics. Induction does not seem to have any hard and fast rules. One scientist is willing to generalize on the basis of evidence that another scientist would consider inadequate. No matter how certain scientists might be of the truth of each statement above the line, they must be less certain of the truth of the universal statement that is written below the line. Despite this hazard of induction, scientists insist on making the inductive leap. We may well ask why.

The answer is not hard to find. Consider the following pair of premises:

1. On *n* different occasions, water was heated and it boiled.

2. This (n + 1) parcel of water is being heated.

For any finite value of *n,* these two statements do not permit the deduction of the statement, "This (n + 1) parcel of water will boil." Now consider these two premises:

1. If water is heated, then it boils.

2. This water is heated.

These two statements jointly imply, "This water will boil." From the first pair of premises, we cannot deduce what will happen. With the second pair, we can predict that the water will boil. We may not have any more information when we write the second pair of statements than when we wrote the first pair, but the second pair of statements permits us to draw upon the tautological rules in the logico–mathematical storehouse. In the simple case we are considering, the fruits are not terribly impressive and the achievement may appear trivial. With increasing complexity, the apparent triviality disappears.

The Hazard of Induction

Disconfirmation of Statements of Law.   The preceding discussion indicates that the truth of a scientific law is not logically certain. Induction does not lead infallibly to true conclusions (generalizations). In fact, if we kept track of the successes and failures of attempts at induction, we would probably find that attempts fail far more frequently than they succeed. Although statements of universal fact cannot be proved to be true beyond all question, they may be proved false with a single unqualified exception. The statement, "If water is heated, then it boils," is shown to be false if there is a *single* instance in which water is heated without boiling. As everyone knows, the statement *is* false, because we often heat water without its boiling.

Modification of Statements of Law.   The following is the description of a fairly typical sequence of events that would occur in the course of scientific progress. Suppose that our primitive physicist lived at an altitude of some eight or ten thousand feet on a mountain. After having made the initial generalization, based on *n* instances of having heated water and observed its boiling, the physicist discovers that on one occasion, the water fails to boil when heated. (We know, of course, although he does not, that the water failed to boil because it was not raised to a high enough temperature.) With the aid of a thermometer, he eventually discovers that the water does not boil unless heated to about 195 degrees Fahrenheit.

How are we now to interpret the truth of the original statement, "If water is heated, then it boils"? Are we to consider it to have been true in the light of the earlier evidence, although it has now become false? Recall that the logical system is based on the premise (postulate) that every sentence is either true or false but not both. Because water does not always boil when heated, the statement *is* false and *was* false when it was originally formulated. Moreover, were the physicist now to say, "If water is heated to 195 degrees Fahrenheit, then it boils," this statement would also be false. As soon as the scientist attempted to heat water at sea level, where the temperature must be approximately 212 degrees Fahrenheit before water boils, the generalization will fail.

Scientific progress often moves forward as a result of such steps. After the identification of each new relevant variable, scientists attempt to formulate a new statement of universal fact that will accord with the existing evidence. Sometimes scientists talk about the boundary conditions within which a law holds. Thus, the law about the boiling of water might be said to have as a boundary condition that the water be heated on a mountain. Psychologists who have found generalities in a laboratory animal may specify as a boundary condition that the subjects be, say, rats. In the case of a well-known theory of discrimination learning, among the boundary conditions was the stipulation that the theory held only for inarticulate organisms. In a strict sense, the boundary conditions are part of the law. Any reformulation of the boundary conditions is a reformulation of the law itself.

References to boundary conditions are attempts to keep the record straight with regard to the truth of the laws. To think of the earlier statements as "partially true," or true under some "unknown conditions," can only result in confusion. Such statements were false, even though the scientists who formulated them thought they were true at the time.

Confirmation of Statements of Law. Although scientists cannot be *logically* certain of the truth of their laws, they can and do assemble overwhelming evidence for many laws. The law of freely falling bodies can scarcely be doubted by any sane individual. Induction does not have a logical justification, but it has the practical (pragmatic) justification that it often works. In principle, however, all scientific laws are subject to the hazard of induction. Scientists simply take their established laws as "true until further notice."

Prediction, Explanation, and Understanding

It is not possible to comprehend fully what scientists mean by "explanation," "prediction," and "understanding" without also having a good grasp of the nature of scientific theories. A first installment on a more complete comprehension, however, can be made within the context of scientific laws. The lowest level of explanation occurs when individual phenomena are explained by means of one or more scientific laws. In a later section, scientific theories are shown to explain the laws themselves.

Explanation and the Deductive Schema.   Let us examine what the word "explanation" refers to in everyday usage. Suppose that a child sees a pot of water boiling and asks, "Why does that water bubble?" We would be likely to answer, "Because it is being heated." If the questioner then asked, "What does the heating have to do with it?" we would respond, "Water always bubbles if it is heated." Examination of this sequence of questions and answers reveals the possibility of forming a deductive pattern. We would eventually provide the questioner with enough information that the statement, "This water bubbles," could be deduced from statements summarizing that information. Thus, the information could be placed in the following deductive schema:

> If water is heated, then it bubbles.
>
> This is water and it is being heated.
> _____
>
> This water bubbles.

In our everyday explanations outside the laboratory, we recognize the deductive schema as a satisfactory explanatory device. To explain a phenomenon, we may provide a set of statements from which we can deduce a statement that describes that phenomenon. Note that what is deduced is a *statement* that describes the phenomenon; we cannot deduce the *phenomenon* itself. In science, the deductive schema is the only device that is recognized as truly explanatory. The scientist explains a phenomenon by deducing from a set of premises a statement that describes that phenomenon. Moreover, at least one of the premises must be a scientific law—a statement of universal fact.

Prediction and the Deductive Schema.   It is interesting that the same deductive schema that was used to clarify the notion of explanation can also be used in scientific predictions. Consider the premises of the argument presented before:

> If water is heated, then it boils.
>
> This is water and it is being heated.
> _____

They permit the deduction, "This water will boil." This statement is a prediction about what will happen, given that the premises are true. In scientific prediction, we deduce from available premises a statement that describes what is going to happen. In scientific explanation, it is necessary to provide the premises that permit the deduction of a statement that describes that which is to be explained. The deductive schemata for explanation and prediction differ primarily in the tense of the verb in the conclusion. The prediction is ordinarily couched in the future tense and the explanation in the past or present tense.

Checks on the Correctness of Explanations.   If there is only one phenomenon to be explained, it is very easy to make up a set of statements that permit the deduction of a statement describing that phenomenon. Consider the phenomenon of the boiling water:

> If it is water, then it contains invisible homunculi.
>
> If it is a homunculus, then it has tender feet.
>
> If water is heated, then the feet of the homunculi get hot.
>
> If their feet get hot, then homunculi jump up and down.
>
> If homunculi jump up and down, then the water bubbles.
>
> This is water and it is being heated.
> _____

It is clear that the statement, "This water bubbles," can be deduced from the set of statements listed above the line. These statements, therefore, would seem to qualify as an explanation for the boiling of water. Yet, scarcely anyone would accept this argument as a good explanation because we do not accept the truth of most of the statements above the line. Indeed, some would argue that not all the statements are even meaningful. Hence, the correctness of the deductive schema, while necessary, is not sufficient to determine that an explanation will be scientifically acceptable.

It is much more difficult to make up an explanation that will permit the deduction of statements that describe many different phenomena. For this reason, scientists prefer those explanations that have a very considerable scope. In the same vein, scientists do not place much credence in an explanatory system that does not also permit correct predictions. In a real sense, scientists use the prediction criterion to keep their explanations honest.

Understanding.   Having said so much about prediction and explanation, very little needs to be said about understanding. Speaking as we ordinarily do, we claim to understand phenomena when we can explain them. (We may sometimes claim to understand when we cannot explain. Such claims are of dubious validity; certainly they are difficult to check.) Scientists also claim understanding when they can give explanations that are supported by correct predictions.

The Relation between Laws and Causes

Some readers may be surprised that a discussion of explanation and prediction has been completed without "cause" or "causation" having been mentioned. Do we not explain phenomena by stating the causes of those phenomena?

The modern view of causation, often referred to as the neo-Humean view, is that knowing laws and knowing about causes is the same thing. The word "cause" does not seem to add anything to our understanding of the fundamental logic of science. Let us examine that view in more detail. A scientific law typically relates a dependent variable to one or more independent variables—i.e., to a set of relevant variables. For example, the pressure of a gas is related to the temperature and volume of the gas. Thus, the temperature and volume of the gas can be considered relevant variables determining the pressure of the gas. As another example, the current in an electric circuit is related to the voltage and resistance in the circuit. Hence, voltage and resistance in a circuit are relevant variables in the determination of the current in the circuit. The neo-Humean view treats causes as virtually synonymous with the relevant variables that the laws mention. When we know laws that explicitly state the relevant variables, we know causes.

It is important to understand that the argument is not that the word "cause" should not be used. On the contrary, experimenters in scientific laboratories freely use a most convenient cause–effect terminology, including "partial cause," "alternate cause," "sufficient cause," "necessary and sufficient cause," etc. There is no reason for scientists to give up their customary use of such terms. The argument is only that analysis of "cause" does not add to our understanding of the logic of the scientific method.

Scientifically Unacceptable Explanatory Formats

The deductive schema provides the format for scientific explanation. The same schema constitutes an acceptable format for explanations outside science, even among primitive peoples. Although the deductive schema is the only acceptable explanatory format within science, it is not the only type of explanation that occurs outside science.

Teleological Explanation.   The bones of birds are much lighter than those of earthbound animals. If we were asked why birds have light bones, the answer that comes immediately to mind is, "So that they can fly well." This answer has an apparent soundness that is deceptive. The same kind of question could also be asked about an exceptionally tall man who also plays basketball. "Why is this man so tall?" "So that he can play basketball well."

The *man* might do a number of things to improve *his* basketball playing; he might practice extensively, do calisthenics, quit smoking, or jog. But to say that he is tall in order to play basketball implies that *something* or *someone,* capable of determining the height of adult humans, *and* sufficiently interested in basketball, had a hand in the affair. In the case of the light bones of the bird, the answer just given suggests the existence of a guiding intelligence whose intentions we know about and who intervened in the evolution of birds.

The kind of explanation illustrated in the preceding paragraph is called *teleological explanation.* It is an attempt to explain what is presently occurring in terms of some final goal. Thus, the guiding intelligence gave the bird light bones because it wanted the birds to be able to fly. A scientifically acceptable explanation for the existence of birds with light bones would mention laws of nature that specify conditions under which birds with light bones evolve on planets like our own. It would also state that those conditions actually occurred on our earth prior to the evolution of birds.

Empathic Understanding.   We have indicated earlier that scientists do not take explanations too seriously that do not also permit correct predictions. An explanatory schema that does not permit correct prediction is either incorrect or incomplete. A particularly seductive type of explanation that often occurs in psychological contexts is illustrated in the following hypothetical account. A mother arranges a consultation with a child psychologist concerning her son's behavior. She tells the psychologist that on the preceding Saturday afternoon, her son went to his room, cut up the pillows and mattress with his Scout knife, and scattered the stuffings around his room. The mother wants an explanation for such an unusual and offensive behavior. The psychologist queries her further and learns that, as a punishment, the child had been denied permission to attend his customary Saturday movie. The psychologist informs the mother, "When you denied your son's request to attend the movies, you frustrated him. We know that frustration produces aggression. Your son's aggression took the form of destroying his mattress and pillows."

This explanation appears to be informative. We learn from the psychologist something that was not contained in the mother's initial statement. The child's behavior makes "more sense" after we find out about the punishment. The explanation would scarcely stand the prediction test, however, because only a small fraction of children would respond to comparable frustration by destroying their pillows and mattresses. The sense of "understanding" that we experience is called "empathic" understanding. We can well imagine that we might do something "comparable," given a frustration such as the child experienced.

Empathic understanding may still be somewhat satisfying in our understanding of the behavior of other humans, or even that of higher level infrahumans. Although it was at one time considered of value in understanding the behavior of inanimate objects, we no longer consider it helpful. Empathic understanding probably underlies most of our tendencies to attribute human form and personality to infrahumans (anthropomorphism). Scientific psychology, like other scientific disciplines, does not accept empathic explanations. Rather, it insists upon an understanding based on the deductive schema and tested by the difficult taskmaster, prediction.

Naming Versus Explanation.   We sometimes seem to be satisfied with an "explanation" that only assigns a name to the phenomenon for which an explanation was sought. Thus, if we ask why the subjects in an experiment learned a second list of words faster than they learned the first list, we may settle for the response, "That's an instance of learning to learn." If we ask why the subjects make the conditioned response on the day after it had been thoroughly extinguished, we may accept, "That's spontaneous recovery." In these examples, the responses do not constitute explanations; they merely name the phenomenon to be explained. They are at best mere fragments of what would constitute satisfactory explanations. In the first example, a more complete explanation would include, at a minimum, a statement of law about learning to learn, as well as a statement of some initial conditions. The requirements for an explanation in the second example are similar.

Statistical Laws

The schema for laws that has been presented thus far is a bit too narrow, because it does not explicitly include the possibility of statistical lawfulness. Because statistical laws are presently quite common in psychology, we should make sure that our conception of laws is sufficiently broad to include those whose character is statistical. In order to clarify the relevant notions as simply as possible, let us return to the case of the boiling water; afterward the basic ideas are extended to psychology.

The Form of Statistical Laws.   Suppose that the primitive physicist had a heating device that, unknown to him, varied irregularly in the amount of heat that was actually generated. To make the example concrete, let us suppose that the device was capable of generating a temperature equal to or greater than 212 degrees Fahrenheit only about 85% of the time, with the successes and failures occurring in an irregular, unpredictable manner. Our physicist would be faced with a rather different set of statements above the line of inference. After, say, 100 attempts, only *approximately* 85 would have resulted in successfully bringing the water to boil. Moreover, if additional sets of 100 trials were attempted, the physicist would obtain several different percentages that would be scattered rather closely, but irregularly, around 85%.

The question now arises as to the conclusion that can appropriately be made on the basis of the statements that describe the results of the hundreds of experiments. The statement, "If water is heated, then it boils," is patently false on the face of the existing evidence. (It would be an error in logic to say that this statement is true 85% of the time, because the basic logical system dictates that a statement be either true or false but not both.) It is still possible to make a statement of universal fact that is consistent with the set of statements of individual fact that describe the existing evidence: "If water is heated, then it boils 85% of the time." This is a generalization, because the universe consists of all the water, past, present, and future. It is also consistent with the statements above the line, because the percentage is consistent with the evidence.

Confirmation and Disconfirmation of Statistical Laws.   The preceding generalization is an instance of a statistical law. The law says that in any collection of trials in which water is heated, the water will boil on 85% of the trials. Like the nonstatistical laws we have considered, it cannot be completely confirmed. It differs from nonstatistical laws, however, in how it is disconfirmed. A nonstatistical law is disconfirmed by a single exception. In this case, if the physicist found only 80% success in a certain collection of trials, this would not be considered a disconfirmation of the statistical law because, even if the law were true, the percentage is expected to vary around 85% from one set of trials to another. A statistical law would be considered disconfirmed only if the percentage of successes obtained, on each of several sets of observations, deviated in the same direction from the percentage specified in the original law. In other words, the *disconfirmation* of a statistical law requires the accumulation of evidence in much the same manner that is required for *confirmation* of either a statistical law or a nonstatistical one. The confirmation and disconfirmation of statistical laws are both inductive in nature; both are subject to the hazards of induction.

Predicting with Statistical Laws.   The statistical law permits prediction about a collection of individuals, but not about any specific individual. Although it makes sense to ask what will happen in a particular instance (c.g., "Will this container of water boil?"), the statistical law provides no basis for answering such questions. It would be a mistake, however, to consider statistical laws as inferior for this reason. What is to be considered as an individual and what is to be considered as a group of individuals is a relative matter. For the psychologist, a human being is an individual and a group of individuals is a collection. To the cellular biologist, however, the human being is a collection of individuals.

Statistical Laws in Psychology.   Many of the laws of psychology are statistical. Some of these laws state that if some set of conditions is experimentally realized for a group of individuals, then some unspecified percentage of the individuals will behave in a certain way. In other statistical laws a percentage may be stated, but it is usually bounded by a standard deviation or standard error; rarely is a statistical law stated as a flat, unqualified proportion. It is common in psychological writing to state statistical laws in a nonstatistical format, leaving the context to supply the information that the law is statistical. Thus, we may state that the administration of classical conditioning trials results in the development of a conditioned response, without stating explicitly that the procedures will fail for a certain small fraction of subjects. Strictly speaking, such statements are false; practically, it is doubtful that any harm stems from these convenient expressions. In psychology, we do not yet know whether any or all of the statistical laws will ultimately be replaced with nonstatistical laws. This is an empirical question that can not be answered until we have tried and either succeeded or failed.

SCIENTIFIC THEORY

Given the background that we have now acquired with respect to definitions, logic, and laws, we can characterize scientific theory in a very brief, although preliminary, way. A scientific theory is a group of laws that are deductively connected. The final section of this chapter provides details that expand on this provisional statement.

Some Common Meanings of "Theory"

In ordinary speech, the word "theory" is used with several different, though related, meanings. Most of these meanings ascribe to the term a connotation of speculation or of factual falseness. For example, one may hear, "Theoretically, Event A should have happened, but of course Event B happened instead." The connotation in this context is that anything theoretical is probably factually incorrect. Another example is the use of "theory" to refer to the detective's guess as to who murdered the victim and where the body was buried. Here the connotation is that anything theoretical is speculative and untested. An alleged distinction is often made between theoretical and applied research. Usually, applied research is characterized as practical and useful, whereas theoretical research is impractical and of no value.

In the following pages, it becomes apparent why "theory" has come to be used in these ways. We see that scientific theory *need* not be incorrect, speculative, impractical, or useless, although instances of scientific theories could be found that exemplify one or more of these properties. Most extant scientific theories, however, particularly those in the more mature sciences, are well grounded in research, are apparently correct, and are highly useful.

The Structure of Scientific Theories

A scientific theory consists of a set of empirical laws, from one subset of which all the remaining laws can be deduced. The first subset of laws are called "axioms," a term which many readers have already encountered in their study of geometry. The laws that are deduced from the axioms are called "theorems," another term from geometry. (Because Euclidean geometry, in its empirical interpretation, is historically the first instance of a scientific theory, it is not surprising that these terms have been borrowed for the description of all scientific theories.) The way that "theory" is ordinarily used within science, it also includes certain critical definitions as well as the proofs that the theorems follow deductively from the axioms.

The preceding description of theory does not characterize the axioms as speculative, except in the sense that all laws are inductive and their truth is therefore uncertain. The axioms of Euclidean geometry were for many years entirely noncontroversial; geometricians considered them to be "self-evident truths." Nevertheless, when first formulated, many scientific theories have included axioms that were speculative and untested. This fact has led to the common use of the term, outside science, to refer to propositions for whose truths there is little or no evidence.

The importance of the deductive connections between the axioms and the theorems cannot be overemphasized, as the following hypothetical story illustrates. Imagine that in a certain scientific field there is a set of 100 laws that are organized into a theory with 10 axioms and 90 theorems. Thus, from 10 of these 100 laws, the remaining 90 can be strictly deduced according to the rules of logic and mathematics. Suppose further that a theoretical scientist in that area demonstrates that among the 100 laws, there is a subset of five that permits the deduction of the remaining 95. (The new set of five axioms may have been drawn from the old axioms, the old theorems, or both.) Scientists in the field would consider the work of the theoretical scientist to be a great achievement and they would consider the field to have been significantly advanced, even though no new laws were thereby discovered.

Theoretical Explanation.   To understand the reason for the scientific rejoicing, the context of scientific explanation should be recalled. From the discussion of scientific laws, it is remembered that scientists claim to explain a phenomenon when they can provide the premises from which they can deduce a statement describing that phenomenon. To explain an individual phenomenon, one of those premises must be an empirical law. Thus, laws are used to explain individual phenomena. In the present context of scientific theories, we note that the theorems are deduced from the axioms. Will scientists also claim that they have explained the theorems? Indeed they do, provided that the axioms are correct in predicting that the theorems will pass the experimental test. (There is no more merit in explaining a false law than there is in explaining a phenomenon that never happens. The rigorous requirement that explanation must permit correct prediction, therefore, holds for theories as well as for laws.)

Laws are used to explain statements of individual fact (i.e., statements describing individual phenomena) and theories (i.e., sets of axioms) are used to explain laws (i.e., theorems). No theory can be used to explain its own axioms, although the axioms of one theory may be explained by (i.e., deduced from) some other, more general, theory. The following observation is instructive. If we were given only the axioms of a theory, we could, at least in principle, construct the entire theory. The theorems are implicit in the axioms and the entire logical and mathematical storehouse of rules is available to help in proving the theorems to be deductive consequences of the axioms. In practice, this reconstruction probably would be quite difficult, and especially so if we did not know in advance what the theorems were. Nevertheless, there is a clear sense in which a complete theory can be equated with its axioms.

Levels of Explanation.   In any deductive argument, it is likely that certain conclusions must be drawn first because they will be needed in the deduction of the others. The same situation exists for theorems: Certain theorems are required for the proofs of other theorems. As a consequence, there are levels of explanation within a theory. As a simple example, consider the explanation for the boiling of water. At the lowest level of explanation, the premises state that this water is being heated and that water boils if heated. If one asks, however, why water boils when heated, the explanation might include a statement about what happens to liquids as a result of temperature changes, together with a statement that water is a liquid. Nor is this the final level. The law that describes changes in the state of liquids with changes in temperature can also be derived from more general laws in the theory of physics.

It is often necessary to make choices among different levels of explanation, adjusting the level to the capabilities and backgrounds of those for whom the explanation is provided. If a 5-year-old asks why it thunders, we are likely to answer that it always thunders when there is lightning. An 8-year-old child is more likely to ask why it always thunders when there is lightning. In this event, a more complex answer is required, one in which we describe the development of electrical charges and the effect that electrical discharges have on the surrounding air.

Although there are different levels of explanation, at any given time there is a final explanation. When we begin the explanation by stating the axioms of the most comprehensive theory in the field, we are offering the highest level of explanation possible at the moment. In a different sense, though, there is no final explanation. The future may bring a new theory that will permit the deduction of the axioms of today's most advanced theory, thereby providing a still higher level of explanation.

Competing Explanations.   In science, there are sometimes competing theories, and therefore competing explanations. This is especially likely to be true in the younger sciences. Such theories may coexist for long periods of time. The most famous, as well as the longest, competition is that between the corpuscular theory of light and the wave theory of light. These two theories date back to the seventeenth century and Isaac Newton. At the present time, both are still necessary. Some phenomena can be explained only by the particle theory; others can be explained only by the wave theory; a great many phenomena can be explained equally well by either theory. As a general rule, however, scientists prefer a single, unified theory that can be used to explain all phenomena in the field.

Axioms versus Theorems

The Indiscriminability of Axioms and Theorems. Is it possible, simply by looking at a law, to decide whether it should be an axiom rather than a theorem? Are there some distinctive characteristics that can be used to identify and correctly classify the two types of laws? The axioms of the most comprehensive theory in a field are often referred to as the most fundamental laws of that field. Is there any way to recognize the fundamental character of the axiom?

Unfortunately, the answers to all these questions are negative. There is no grammatical mark on an axiom that permits us to distinguish it from a theorem. Axioms are not necessarily more plausible than theorems. When an axiom is called a "fundamental" law, it is its position in the theory that is being referred to; i.e., it is the axioms that serve as premises in the deduction of theorems and not the other way around. Indeed, after additional knowledge has been obtained, some of the axioms and theorems of an older theory may be interchanged in a newer version of the theory. The only criterion for a law to be an axiom in a theory is that it be able to function as an axiom in the deduction of theorems that stand the test of experience and experiment. If even one of the theorems deduced from a set of axioms turns out to be false, then there is at least one of the axioms that is false. We learned from our study of logic that it is not possible to deduce false conclusions from true premises.

The Indirect Testing of Axioms. Scientific theories often have one or more axioms that cannot be directly tested for one reason or another. The impossibility of deducing false conclusions from true premises provides a means of indirectly testing such axioms. If theorems that can be directly tested can be deduced from the axioms, then it is possible to test the axioms indirectly by testing the theorems directly. If any of the deduced theorems turn out to be false when tested by observation and experiment, then some of the axioms must also be false. If a theorem survives the experimental test, however, this does not prove the axioms to be true, because true conclusions can be deduced from false premises. Nevertheless, confidence in the truth of the axioms increases with an increase in the number of theorems that survive the test of experiment. There is no definite number of true theorems that proves the axioms to be true, just as there is no definite number of observations that can prove a law to be true. Both are instances of induction. The use of scientific theory in this way has been a major component in the scientific method since the time of Newton.

An Illustrative Theory

One of the simplest theories to understand, at least in a nonquantitative way, is the theory that Newton proposed in 1686. There are only five axioms, four of which can be stated in ordinary English, without resort to mathematics. The fifth law is the vector addition of forces, familiar to anyone who has been introduced to analytic geometry. Of course it is not possible to derive the theorems from the axioms when stated in a nonquantitative form. Instead, examples of axioms and theorems are given and the process of indirectly testing the axioms of a theory is illustrated.

The Newtonian Axioms.   The five axioms consist of the three laws of motion, the law of universal gravitation, and the law of vector composition — the vector addition of forces.

1. A body remains at rest or, if in motion, remains in uniform motion in a straight line, unless acted upon by an external force.
2. The acceleration produced in the motion of a body is directly proportional to the magnitude of the force acting on that body.
3. Whenever one body exerts a force in a given direction on a second body, the second body exerts an equal force on the first body, but in the opposite direction.
4. Every particle in the universe attracts every other particle with a force that is directly proportional to the product of their masses and inversely proportional to the square of the distance between their centers of gravity.
5. (The law of vector addition, which specifies the manner in which vectors can be combined and decomposed.)

Terrestrial and Celestial Mechanics.   First, we examine Newton's application of his theory to terrestrial bodies. Using these axioms in quantitative form, Newton deduced the law that Galileo had found for the inclined plane. He also deduced the law of free falling bodies, a special case of the law of the inclined plane.

Newton applied the theory to celestial bodies, too. Using the same axioms, he deduced the three Kepler laws that describe the motion of planets and predicted the times at which they would arrive at any point along their paths. These two applications demonstrated that the theory had great scope, because it included both terrestrial and celestial applications. The successful prediction of the planetary orbits especially impressed many of his colleagues. Newton also made successful predictions concerning the acceleration that the earth imposed on the moon and the effect of the moon on the tides.

Indirect Confirmation of Axioms. The theory was not immediately accepted by all of Newton's contemporaries, however. The first law of motion was contrary to the teachings of Aristotle, who had taught that the motion of a body could be maintained only by force. The law of universal gravitation was especially difficult for many to accept, because it seemed to defy common sense, given that objects do not ordinarily jump at each other. Moreover, Newton could not "explain" why it should be true, and several influential scientists and philosophers of the day questioned the value of deducing statements from other statements whose truth could not be confirmed. Without using the law of universal gravitation as a premise (axiom), however, none of the impressive deductions could be made. Within 100 years, after many more deductions from the Newtonian axioms, the truth of all the axioms was unquestioned by virtually all physicists. A direct, laboratory test of the law of universal gravitation was not achieved until the beginning of the nineteenth century, by which time no informed person doubted its truth. This is a clear instance in which an axiom, which for technical reasons could not be directly tested at the time, was indirectly confirmed to the satisfaction of nearly everyone.

Composition Laws. We should take special note of the fifth axiom— vector addition. This law was also absolutely essential to Newton's derivations. Analysis of this law indicates that it instructs the scientist how to conceptually analyze complex situations (i.e., those with many bodies) into elementary situations (i.e., those with only two bodies) so that the laws of elementary situations can be applied. Conversely, the law also instructs the scientist how to combine the values of variables that are computed for elementary situations so as to yield the values of variables for the complex situation. Philosophers of science call such laws "composition laws." Composition laws are the source of much of the scope of a theory, and it seems to be the case that every theory with noteworthy scope has at least one such law.

Models as Theories

A strategy for the construction and development of theories that has become quite pervasive in the field of psychology has also been used from time to time in the physical sciences. It involves the use of a theoretical structure from one area as a model for another area. There are really several different classes of such theories, ranging all the way from crude analogies to the use of highly articulate models with axioms, theorems, and well-developed proofs. To do more than give the flavor of these kinds of theories would take us well beyond the scope of this chapter.

The Simple Analogue. In the sixteenth century, there was some mystery as to why a suction pump could bring up water from no more than about 34 feet below the surface. An Italian scientist named Torricelli, a student of the famous Galileo, suggested that an explanation could be found if the air were conceived as analogous to a sea of water. This analogy, however, was really limited to the idea that air, like water, is spread evenly through space and has weight. Torricelli did not intend that air should be conceived as having *all* the properties of water. For example, he did not think that air could be drunk instead of water, or that one could wash one's laundry in it.

With the sea-of-air conception, Torricelli explained the limitation of the suction pump in the following way. The pump acts to remove air from the pipe. The weight of the air on the surface of the pool of water surrounding the pipe is then able to push the water up into the pipe, because there was no air in the pipe pushing back, and on out the spout. The limit of 34 feet is a measure of the pressure exerted on the water by the weight of the air column.

Use of this analogy led to several other developments. A mercury barometer was constructed in which a glass tube, open at one end and closed at the other, was filled with mercury, rapidly turned over, and the open end was placed in a reservoir of mercury. This action created a vacuum in the glass tube at the closed end. As predicted by the sea-of-air model, mercury was pushed well up into the tube. Because mercury is about 14 times heavier than water, it should extend up into the tube only one-fourteenth as far as water—i.e., only about 34/14 feet. This was found to be the case.

The deeper one goes in a pool of water, the heavier the weight of the water. Is the same thing true of air? A mercury barometer was taken to the top of a mountain and another was kept at the base of the mountain. If the sea-of-air model is correct, the height of the mercury column at the top of the mountain should be lower than that at the bottom. Because a difference of several inches in the appropriate direction was observed, this prediction was also confirmed.

Other predictions were made and confirmed. Removal of air from metal containers was found to cause them to collapse, presumably crushed by the pressure of air on the outside. The sea-of-air model led Boyle to the idea of the constancy of the product of the pressure and volume of a gas. Although the sea analogy for air is simple, it proved to be a highly useful conception. It is important to remember that some terms that would be used in any formulation about water would not occur in a formulation about air. The analogy does not have to be complete in order to be useful.

Use of One Theory as a Model for Another Field.   There have been a few instances in the physical sciences in which a theory for a well-developed area has been taken over as a model for another less developed field. One instance that is often cited was the use of the theory of mechanics as a model for thermodynamics. The laws of mechanics are about the masses, spatial locations, and temporal properties and relations of physical bodies. The laws of thermodynamics are about temperature, pressure, volume, etc. The connection between these two sets of terms is the kinetic theory of heat, which aids in the reduction of thermodynamics to mechanics. This reduction is achieved by two assumptions. First, wherever there appears to be a continuous medium such as a gas or a liquid, there are actually millions of invisible particles. Secondly, these particles move about according to the laws of motion as stated in the theory of mechanics.

For the theory of mechanics to serve as a model for thermodynamics, some connections must be established between the concepts of the model and the descriptive concepts of thermodynamics. In this case, statistical functions of properties of the invisible particles are coordinated to descriptive concepts of thermodynamics. For example, the heating of the gas or liquid causes the particles to move with greater speed, thereby increasing the average kinetic energy (a function of mass and velocity). Moreover, the average kinetic energy is coordinated to the concept of "pressure." There are, however, no concepts from thermodynamics coordinated to any properties of the individual particles, which remain uninterpreted. Thus, the mechanical model is only partially coordinated, partially interpreted. (Remember that the sea-of-air model did not insist that all properties of the sea were to be found in the air.)

Models in Psychology

For many years, psychologists have used simple analogies in their attempts to explain psychological phenomena. Several of these analogies were concerned with the nervous system. Thus, Descartes believed that the peripheral nerves were hollow tubes through which animal spirits flowed, thereby developing his "pathway" theory of the nervous system. David Hartley, an eighteenth-century physician, likened the transmissions in the peripheral nerves to the vibration of physical particles. Perhaps the best known of all analogies in psychology is Helmholtz's representation of the nervous system as a telegraph system, with the brain as a switchboard. Probably none of these simple analogies has been as useful as Torricelli's sea-of-air model. Some of the more recent models may be more promising.

Statistical Learning Theories. The first influential model in modern psychology was one published by William K. Estes in 1950. This model was based on statistical principles and was originally designed to predict and explain phenomena manifested in some relatively simple learning tasks. A population or set of elements in the model was coordinated to the potential stimulating conditions on a set of learning trials. Moreover, the ratio of the numbers of two different classes of elements in the model was coordinated to the relative frequency with which the subject would make a designated response. Given certain principles about sampling theory that were stated as axioms in the statistical model, theorems could be mathematically derived that could be translated, by virtue of the coordinating statements, into predictions about the changes in behavior of the subject as a function of learning trials.

The Estes model was followed by a large number of similar or related models during the succeeding decades. The mathematical sophistication of the models generally increased over the years. It is probably correct to say, however, that no one model was ever demonstrated to have a great deal of scope. Nevertheless, in certain instances, a group of related models, taken together, have been used to explain and predict quite a large range of phenomena.

Information Processing and Cognitive Models.   Reflection indicates that the source of the model is of no importance. The use of a well-developed theory from a mature area as a model for another area will by no means guarantee that a useful theory will be constructed for the new area. What is important logically is that the model be internally consistent and what is important empirically is that there be relational correspondence (isomorphism) between the model and the phenomena to which it is to be applied. For example, if certain psychologists believe that there are important similarities between the way computers process information and the way humans process information, then they may attempt to use the principles governing computer operation as the model for the human information processing. This task requires that some useful coordinating statements be found that will connect certain aspects of the computer model to informational input to, and to behavioral output from, the human subject.

Psychologists did in fact begin to construct and test information-processing models in the late 1950s. In some instances, models of this kind have also been supplemented with axioms that probably were suggested by the theorists' introspections on their own cognitive processing. Not all psychologists at the present time look favorably on the statistical, mathematical, and information-processing models. Although one may question the potential usefulness of any such model for a particular area, the methodological legitimacy of these kinds of models has already been established. They have been used successfully in the physical sciences for many years.

Testing and Modifying Theories

The Confirmation of a Theory.   A theory has two different aspects—the logical and the empirical. If uniform substitution of meaningless symbols were made for all the descriptive words in the theory, it would still be possible for an expert mathematician to show that the denuded theorems follow deductively from the denuded axioms. In other words, the mathematician could still provide proofs for the theorems, although both the axioms and the theorems would be devoid of any empirical meaning. This feat is possible because logical deduction depends only on logical words and not on descriptive words. Thus, it is possible to confirm that a theory is *logically* correct.

We saw that an empirical law cannot be completely confirmed. A theory consists of axioms and theorems, both of which are empirical laws. It is not possible, therefore, to completely confirm a theory for the same reason that it is not possible to completely confirm a law. Our confidence in a theory may increase over time as a result of its providing only correct predictions, but we must recognize that, in the future, new predictions from the theory may turn out to be false.

Disconfirmation of a Theory.   If any theorem deduced from the axioms turns out to be false, then at least one of the axioms is also false. Moreover, if there is a single exception to any axiom or to any theorem, then the theory is disconfirmed. Thus, we have the same condition for theories as for nonstatistical laws—although they cannot be completely confirmed, they may be disconfirmed with a single contrary observation. One may well marvel that any law, much less a whole set of laws (i.e., a theory), can meet such a rigorous criterion.

Modification of Theories.   Technically, a theory is disconfirmed if a single contrary observation is obtained. Practically, scientists attempt to modify the theory by changing one or more axioms in such a way that the "exceptions" are predicted. Just as the primitive physicist described in an earlier section attempted to save the law of boiling water by incorporating the temperature and pressure variables into it, scientists attempt to save their theories by making whatever modifications in the axioms are necessary. Usually, scientists are not willing to relinquish a theory until a better theory is at hand. Characteristically, the new theory will not only explain phenomena that the old theory could not explain, but it will also explain why the old theory succeeded as long as it did and why it ultimately failed.

SUMMARY

Three Kinds of Knowledge

There are three kinds of knowledge distinguished by the way in which truth values are determined for sentences in each class. For sentences in the *empirical* category, truth values are determined after pertinent observations have been made. Truth values for sentences in the *logical* category are determined after analysis of the meanings of, and patterns among, certain key (structure) words. No truth values are assigned to sentences in the *value* category, because there are no interpersonal truth values for such statements.

The scientific method was developed to determine the truth value of statements from the empirical category. Scientists use knowledge from the logical category as a tool in the design of experiments, the reduction of data, and the development of theories. Scientists make no attempt to determine the truth value of statements from the value category, although the results of scientific investigations may indirectly affect the values of individuals in profound ways.

Formal Knowledge

Formal knowledge is a hierarchical structure consisting of sentential and functional logic, the number system, arithmetic, and higher mathematics. At the ground level is sentential logic, within which the basic connectives are defined in terms of "sentence," "true," and "false." The rules of sentential logic result from these definitions and are tautologies, i.e., compound statement forms which are true irrespective of the truth of component statement forms. At the next level is functional logic, which is concerned with the meanings of "all," "some," the several meanings of "is," and "the." Functional logic rests upon sentential logic. The number system sits on top of functional logic, with arithmetic next. Mathematics is then a generalization of the rules of arithmetic.

What is important to grasp in connection with formal knowledge is that all the rules of inference, in both logic and mathematics, are tautologies. The rules are true by virtue of the definitions that have been given the logical words introduced at each of the various levels. The rules of logic have been so developed that if they are correctly applied in making deductions, the conclusions drawn must necessarily be true if the premises are. That is all that these rules guarantee.

Definitions

In defining new concepts, scientists generally conform to the empiricist meaning criterion. This principle ideally would require the definition of any new word to be ultimately reducible to a statement, or a series of statements, that contains only primitive predicates. Primitive predicates are words that refer to simple properties of, and simple relations among, physical objects and events. Strict adherence to the empiricist meaning criterion would constrain scientific discourse to the discussion of characters, properties, and relations that are readily observable.

Scientists do not adhere strictly to the empiricist criterion in two respects. First, they do not insist that the definitions of all new words be reduced to the level of primitive predicates. Rather, they push their definitions down toward the primitive predicates only as far as they judge necessary to avoid ambiguity and misunderstanding. There have been occasional misjudgments in the past and there will undoubtedly be more in the future. Secondly, scientists do admit some new terms into the scientific language by other than a definitional route. In some of the models that have been employed in the construction of theory, there are some terms that are not directly coordinated with empirical phenomena but serve only as intervening calculational entities.

Statements that specify the manner in which a variable (concept) can be measured have been called "operational definitions." It is probably best to consider operational definitions as a subclass of scientific definitions. Clearly, operational definitions also restrict the use of the language of science to the discussion of observable properties and relations. The empiricist meaning criterion, however, is both clearer and more general.

Laws

Laws are statements of universal fact and are arrived at by induction. The general form is, "For any x, if x has the property A then x has the property B." Because the universe of such statements includes the past, present, and future, no finite number of observations can ever serve as a logical justification for the statement of law. The justification for induction is a pragmatic one—it often works. Thus, scientists consider their laws true "until further notice."

Laws are critical for scientific prediction, explanation, and understanding. Explanation and prediction both require a deductive schema (argument). The premises of the argument consist of, at a minimum, a statement of law and a statement of individual fact describing some initial conditions. The conclusion of the argument follows logically from the premises. In the case of prediction, the conclusion will describe what is going to happen. In the case of explanation, the conclusion will describe the phenomenon to be explained. Within science, those explanatory schemata that also permit correct predictions are most highly valued. Understanding is claimed when explanatory schemata can be provided that also permit correct prediction.

Theory

A scientific theory consists of a relatively small set of laws (axioms), from which a larger set of laws (theorems) can be derived, and proofs that the theorems follow deductively from the axioms. At least one of the axioms of any theory with reasonable scope will be a composition law. A composition law provides instructions as to how complex situations can be conceptually analyzed into all possible elementary systems so that the laws of the elementary system can be applied. In addition, the composition law provides instructions as to how the values of variables computed for the elementary systems can be combined to obtain values for the variables of the complex system.

Because the theorems are deduced from axioms, scientific theories are said to explain the theorems. Thus, just as laws are used to explain individual phenomena, theories are used to explain laws. No theory can explain its own axioms, although some other theory is said to explain the first theory if the axioms of the first theory can be derived from the second theory.

The use of analogue models as theories has been much favored in psychology in recent years. These theories have typically been statistical, mathematical, or information-processing models. The model consists of a set of statements that are deductively connected but which either pertain to some other empirical field or are purely formal (i.e., factually empty). Coordinating statements are formulated that connect (some) terms from the model to empirical terms in the field for which the theory is being constructed. As a consequence of the coordination, predictions about what should happen in the empirical field are immediately available.

A law cannot be completely confirmed, and a theory consists of a group of laws. It is not surprising, therefore, that a theory cannot be completely confirmed. A theory can be disconfirmed, however, in the same way that a law can be disconfirmed. If an exception is found to any theorem in the theory, then at least one of the axioms of the theory is false. Generally, scientists will attempt to modify the axioms of the theory in such a way that correct predictions are obtained. Because the theory of a field represents most of the explanatory power in that field, scientists are reluctant to give up a theory until an alternative is available.

ACKNOWLEDGMENT

My views on the philosophy of science and the methodological problems of psychology have been greatly influenced by the teachings of Gustav Bergmann. It is a great privilege to have been one of his colleagues at the University of Iowa for many years and to have benefited from his lectures as well as from his writings. Readers who are familiar with Professor Bergmann's works will recognize in the preceding pages the immeasurable debt that I owe to him. I am pleased to acknowledge that debt, although I cannot guarantee that I have faithfully represented his viewpoints in all respects.

2 The Spiker Influence

Glenn Terrell
Washington State University

Charles C. Spiker has been a major influence in the development of behavioral science for the past thirty years. His theory-based research, in its precision of design, is one evidence. Furthermore, the excellent work of Spiker's numerous students, associates, and those stimulated by Spiker's ideas, clearly indicates his remarkable impact on experimental psychology. The most important sources of information for assessing Spiker's contributions and impact are the opinions of his former students and peers regarding the quality of his work and his influence on the development of their careers. Accordingly, in delineating the Spiker influence, I shall rely heavily on perspectives provided me by former students and associates in numerous conversations and letters. Some came to me many years ago; others came in recent years.

Since my doctoral dissertation was the first directed by Charlie Spiker thirty-three years ago, I write from a background that spans the full length of his influence on the discipline of psychology. Never mind that many of my own recollections are over thirty years old—Spiker has a way of creating unforgettable impressions on his students! Never mind that after ten years of fairly productive life as a researcher in the Spiker mold, I changed from a life of doing important things in the academic community to the more volatile and conflict-ridden world of administration that began with the chairmanship of the Department of Psychology at the University of Colorado and has continued for almost eighteen years in the presidency of one of Washington State's research universities. The point is that throughout these past thirty years, I have experienced the "Spiker Effect" in teaching, research, and administration. As a matter of fact, as I write this paper, I can see Charlie looking over my shoulder, observing both the content and the style of my writing. I find the specter of his presence as I write both amusing and impressive, yet somewhat disturbing. I am amused that, even after 32 years and the hard knocks I have experienced, I remain intimidated by him—I am impressed because of the persistence of his influence on my standards of performance—and I am somewhat disturbed because of the difficulty I experienced in getting started on this chapter. After numerous starts at writing the introductory pages, I remain dissatisfied. Knowing that both editors of this volume, Lewis Lipsitt and Joan Cantor, also heavily influenced by Spiker, will have the final say on this piece is comforting.

What is this thing I refer to as the "Spiker effect"? It is described by his former students in various ways, of course, but there is a common thread in most of our descriptions. Simply stated, Charlie made all of us think. One way or another, he made us think about what we were saying and why, what we were writing and why, and, even on occasion, what we were doing and why. He did this, and he still does whatever he has to do, within the bounds of honesty, to produce in his students a highly disciplined and thoughtful approach to psychology. Always the standards of performance for himself and for his students were extraordinarily high. They still are.

A cornerstone of his philosophy of the social sciences is that behavioral science is not different, theoretically, from the physical sciences—more complex to be sure, and therefore more difficult methodologically. This philosophy, heavily influenced by the logical positivists, placed a premium on the application of logic and mathematics in the development of theory and research in psychology. Charlie is a genius in presenting this approach to his students. Furthermore, whether or not his students remain faithful to Charlie's philosophy of science as applied to theory and research in psychology, they consistently acknowledge that their general approach to problem-solving in teaching, research, and clinical applications of psychology still distinctly bear the mark of the Spiker influence—a deep respect for scientific precision and accuracy.

It would seem appropriate, then, that I include descriptions of Spiker's influence on his students' teaching, research, and administration with additional observations about his impact (undoubtedly mostly unintended by Spiker) on their clinical practice.

But first, as a preface for these comments, I believe a rather brief character sketch of Charlie Spiker, the man, will be helpful. Spiker is a complex person with strong personal attributes. Similar to many scholarly, interesting people, he possesses traits that are contradictory in the usual sense of the word. For example, although he is brilliant of intellect, he is willing nevertheless, unlike many gifted people, to accept the limitations of those less talented than he, and to work at great length to get the most out of their abilities. His excellence is enhanced by his patience and his dedication.

Spiker's capacity for work is extraordinary. Students remember seeing him in his office early in the morning, late at night, and on weekends. It is obvious to all who have been closely associated with him that he is a driven man, not unhappily so, but rather driven by a profound professional and personal commitment to his discipline, to his department, to his peers, and especially to his students. Still, with this rare dedication, he is able to relax on occasion, and he has a few somewhat offbeat hobbies—for example, he took up flying and motorcycling at different stages of his career, the former since abandoned, I believe. It is interesting that this shy, introspective, consummate scholar did dangerous things to retreat from the intense, intellectually strenuous life that regularly consumed eighty hours of his week.

As in the system of experimental child psychology which he so ably professes, Spiker himself tends to be somewhat difficult to bend on certain attitudes. For example, in the early years of his career, he had difficulty coming to grips with the problems created by women students who were more likely to interrupt their careers by marriage, either temporarily or permanently. Yet, there is not a trace of bias in him regarding sexual equality, nor was there any difference whatsoever in the amount or quality of time he would devote to his students, regardless of his predictions about the duration of their careers in psychology or, for that matter, their productivity.

Although I cannot personally vouch for the accuracy of the assertion, at least one of Spiker's former students contends that Spiker had some rather definite ideas about what is and is not considered acceptable behavior by graduate students. For example, students were not to call faculty members by their first names (not an uncommon expectation); they were expected to keep regular office hours, day and night; sharp departures from generally accepted patterns of personal behavior, including dress at the office and at social functions, were alleged to be noted and used in the overall evaluation of students. Some former students interpreted these expectations as unnecessarily authoritative, even unnecessarily rigid.

My opinion is different. Having since observed faculty evaluations for many years, I regard the expectations of Spiker in the personal behavior of students to be a reasonable part of his program of preparing students for the realities of membership in the academic community. Certainly, every department and institution I have ever been affiliated with applies its own unique code of social and moral standards to evaluating the performance of its members when critically important decisions such as appointment, reappointment, tenure, promotion, and salary increases are at issue. While it is correct to say that, in the early years, Spiker and many of the Iowa

group insisted on an extraordinarily rigorous philosophical and methodological system for theory and research in the behavioral sciences, I believe
that their expectations for standards of personal and ethical behavior were
entirely appropriate.

Paradoxically, and even more important, Spiker is one of the most
constructively supportive faculty members I have ever seen. Many of his
former students agree that, just when everything in their lives as graduate
students seemed to be going adversely, Charlie would find the time and
some legitimate reasons to encourage and assist them. Of course, this trait
requires both flexibility and compassion, which leads me to another observation about Spiker, the person. To most students, Charlie Spiker has been
regarded as an awesome figure. Clearly, he is regarded as one of the most
demanding of the faculty members in the department. In short, he is tough,
and that is just the way he wants to be. This trait is in large measure
responsible for the fact that many of the best students have chosen Spiker
as their major professor or as the director of their dissertation. At the same
time, he recognizes that students vary in ability; he accepts this as a fact of
life; and he dedicates much of his time to bringing out the best he can in his
students. Thus, as mentioned above, he is both an intensely demanding
person and a most compassionate person.

Finally, part of Spiker's complexity is due to the fact that his extraordinarily serious commitment to the discipline sometimes obscures a subtle
sense of humor. As a result, he is occasionally misinterpreted because, as
he speaks on a topic, the twinkle in his eye or the subtle change of tone of
his voice goes unnoticed. Those of us who are fortunate enough to know
him well have enjoyed immensely his fun-loving nature and his delightful
sense of humor.

A character sketch of Spiker would not be complete without a special
reference to his honesty. This trait is most apparent in the way he gives to
others all the credit for the formulation of ideas. In the continuous interchange of ideas that takes place in graduate school between faculty and
students, it is sometimes difficult to identify just where the basic insights
originate and to whom credit for the subtle refinement in ideas should be
given. Spiker never seemed to concern himself with such things. Rather, his
concern was with creating an environment that would produce ideas. The
constant challenging, questioning, listening, and searching that take place
between Spiker and his colleagues, faculty and students alike, create the
environment for producing ideas that he is so fond of and to which he is so
strongly committed. Oh, I do remember Charlie had a way of jokingly
"claiming" credit for an idea that a student or faculty associate may have
generated, but which Spiker himself may have extended, saying with tongue
in cheek, "that's one of my better ideas."

Of one thing I am sure, the idea behind my dissertation in discrimination learning was basically from Spiker's earlier model. There was never any discussion about where the fundamental notion for my thesis originated. It simply evolved from the environment that Spiker created, but Spiker never claimed credit for it. He never seemed to need that recognition.

Spiker's unyielding insistence on precision of the written and the spoken word, his high standards, and his sometimes seemingly contradictory personal traits form the backdrop for what is to follow regarding his influence on teaching, research, clinical, and administrative careers.

Charlie Spiker has been one of the most effective teachers at Iowa for the past thirty years. Lewis Lipsitt refers to him as "my finest teacher." All of his former students with whom I have communicated offer this strongly expressed opinion. All of them comment on his high expectations for his students and on his precisely organized and prepared presentations. He also obviously enjoyed the give-and-take of informal discussions that frequently took place in his classes and the one-on-one exchanges with students outside class. He was deeply concerned that his students understand the material he presented, and he would work tirelessly, if necessary, in reformulating his explanations of difficult concepts to ensure their understanding.

Spiker was a master at helping the student distinguish good ideas from poor ones. He constantly challenged students, not infrequently to the point of irritating them, in an effort to teach them how to think and to write more rigorously.

Winifred Shepard's chapter in this book, "On the Teaching of Teaching," has particularly strong praise for Spiker's skill as a teacher. She contends that Spiker's course on Research Methodology, required of all new graduate students in the Institute, was the "most important and valuable course" she ever had. One extraordinarily powerful statement Shepard makes regarding Spiker's course on Research Methodology follows:

> Clear and devoid of obfuscating embroidery, the ideas Charlie communicated in that introduction to graduate training have withstood the test of time—transcending changes in subject-matter preference and the particulars of the individual research and teaching careers of his students.

The foregoing statement by Shepard dramatizes what I initially referred to as the Spiker Influence—he taught his students how to think and write clearly, how to frame meaningful questions, and how to go about the scientific business of finding answers to these questions. Spiker did this by example in his own research and, as Shepard puts it, he did it by teaching his students how to teach others. Clearly then, Spiker, known primarily as a theoretician and experimenter at one of the nation's distinguished research universities, nevertheless is remembered some thirty years later most vividly for his teaching skills by former students such as Shepard.

Lipsitt describes Spiker, the professor, in somewhat different terms:

> Most important about Charlie Spiker as professor is his enormous talent to teach, both in the classroom and in scholarly advisory situations, as when directing a dissertation. Gentle, patient, articulate, but demanding, Charlie is persuasive as he leads you around to the only possible way to look at an issue profitably, even as he rewards you for your contributions to the progression of his own thought. Rather intolerant of intellectual fuzziness, especially the introduction of arguments or issues not entirely germane to the discussion at hand, Charlie leaves you, after a vigorous discussion or classroom lecture, feeling completely clear.

Another former student, Frances Degen Horowitz, described Spiker's teaching performance in vivid language:

> Classes were intellectual journeys guided by the clarity of Charlie's analyses. It often seemed that only a few minutes had passed when, in fact, an hour or more had gone by. I remember, more than once, emerging from a class with an overwhelming sense that I had learned a great deal. But more exciting, perhaps, was the frequent experience of being pulled along to an understanding that had the powers of insight. Charlie did this by almost literally grabbing at the students' thought patterns and leading them along an unexplored path toward the sense of really knowing and understanding. The result was a kind of intellectual exhilaration that I always hoped I might impart to my students.

David Palermo puts it similarly:

> Charlie is an inspiring teacher. He creates an atmosphere in which the student is caught up in the thrill of new theoretical ideas and the excitement of creating an empirical test of those ideas.

Charlie Spiker has been the driving force behind the experimental child psychology movement at Iowa. Prior to his appearance on the scene in the early 1950's, developmental psychology was dominated by research on children of a descriptive nature. Spiker, heavily influenced by Hull, Spence, and the logical positivists, began to insist that research with children be theory-based and philosophically and methodologically sophisticated. An examination of the literature clearly reveals this impact of Spiker on the research in experimental child psychology during the past thirty years. Many of his students have continued research in learning theory, while others have made their contribution in such varied areas as infant development, preschool education, cognition, parent-sibling relationships, memory, and language development. Among Spiker's doctoral students and others who benefited from his teaching, some of the more productive include Lewis Lipsitt, Brown University; Sheldon White, Harvard University; Frances Degen Horowitz, University of Kansas; Kathryn Norcross Black, Purdue University; Joan Cantor, University of Iowa; Gordon Cantor, University of Iowa; Hayne Reese, West Virginia University; David Palermo, Pennsylvania State University; Langdon Longstreth, University of Southern California; Michael Rabinowitz, University of Newfoundland; Shirley Moore, University of Minnesota; Barry Gholson, Memphis State University; Akira Kobasigawa, University of Windsor; and Thomas Ryan, Carleton University.

Spiker's own research in discrimination learning sparks disagreement among his peers and his former students. Some believe that Spiker's work, derived from the Hullian framework, will not in the long run be of great importance in understanding child behavior. Some of his most productive former students contend that his brand of experimental child psychology was too narrow in its scope, dealt with problems that were too simple and even irrelevant, and was aligned with a psychology of science that was unduly restrictive in terms of the type of behavior it encompassed. Many others, myself included, disagree. Throughout my relatively brief research career, I shared Spiker's view that we cannot expect to predict complex social behavior until we understand precisely how simple learning takes place. I happen to believe that there is a need for research at all levels of complexity, and who is to say that any behavior is irrelevant? The important elements of research are conception and methodological soundness. In these terms, Spiker has few peers. How significant Spiker's research will prove to be in creating major breakthroughs is a question of fact that only the future can answer. Without question, his work has already stimulated the thinking and research of others in experimental psychology as few of his generation have done.

Unquestionably, Spiker will long be remembered as one of the giants in the history of experimental psychology in terms of his pioneer work in what a former student, Michael Rabinowitz, calls "bringing the child to the experiment." Rabinowitz further states that "as a methodologist and statistician, he probably did more to change the course of North American research in child development than anyone else."

Lipsitt has this to say regarding Spiker's talents:

Charlie Spiker is a remarkable hypothetico-deductive theorist. The history of his contributions to the field and his continuing work attest to this. He is also great at implementing deduced hypotheses. Some of the experimental procedures that he has set up during his career, in the fields of discrimination learning and verbal mediation, for example, are truly ingenious. One can teach some of these methods that he was using thirty years ago today, doll them up with a contemporary cognitive vocabulary, and the studies sound as though they were done yesterday.

Particularly noteworthy among Lipsitt's comments is his claim that Spiker's work transcends the changes that have taken place in theory and research in psychology in the past thirty years.

Spiker's influence on the careers of those who chose clinical psychology is more difficult to assess for at least two reasons. First, there are few who were brave enough to defy Charlie in such a seriously obvious way by focusing his career on clinical psychology. Second, I question that Spiker ever intended that his brand of psychology would have immediate clinical applications. But intended by him or not, it did in at least two ways. Whether a clinician uses a social learning theory or the more current cognitive behavior modification as a conceptual framework for therapy, he finds that both are heavily influenced by the learning model. The phenomenon of "self talk" as discussed by Albert Ellis, or the "automatic thoughts" of Aaron Beck, which can cause emotional disorders, are believed by cognitive therapists to be learned possibly through the same processes through which Spiker's subjects learned much simpler discriminations.

Clinical psychologists who have studied with Spiker also credit him with their critical reasoning skills and express deep feelings of concern for measuring up to Spiker's standards. Dr. June Hoyt puts it this way:

I think Charlie's discipline is there in the background. There is some validation for this hypothesis. Often when things are not going well and I'm fretting about some issue or other, I have a dream, always permeated with anxiety, in which I'm back in school trying to measure up to some standard with Charlie in command. I guess what I'm really talking about, when I reflect on his influence on my professional career, is "learning set" or "non-specific transfer." I'd almost forgotten about those terms.

Obviously, Spiker's learning model, never intended to apply to clinical settings, is being used by some of his former students in clinical settings with apparent success.

Not many of Spiker's peers or former students think of him as an administrator, but, for many years, he directed the Iowa Child Welfare Research Station (later known as the Institute) in a very effective manner. Spiker, the administrator, created an excellent environment for faculty and students to perform their teaching and research responsibilities. He did this by persuading the central administration to support the Institute at a high level, which in turn relieved the faculty members of the many tedious tasks that are required of faculty in all too many departments; he provided them with work loads that allowed the ideal combination of teaching and research opportunities; he made available for faculty and students resources necessary for their work (e.g., equipment, library resources, technical assistance, etc.); and he sought salaries that were competitive with leading research universities.

Spiker was also an effective academic leader—constantly placing before the faculty ideas for discussion that were designed to clarify goals and improve the quality of teaching and research. I am indebted to Joan Cantor, for more than twenty years a faculty colleague of Spiker, for much of the information on his administrative style.

Perhaps the most important trait Spiker possessed as an administrator is described by Joan Cantor in the following way:

> Charlie has always brought out the best in those around him. In part he does this by being such an outstanding role model as a professor. He brings his great intellect and motivation to bear in each new situation, and he does so with great personal dignity and a keen sense of humor. But he also brings out the best in people by expecting so much of them. I think Charlie's students and colleagues universally have the feeling that they just can't let him down; they have to prove that they are as good as he thinks they are.

My career as an administrator, as a department chair, as an arts and sciences dean, and then as President, has been filled with examples of Spiker's influence. I believe the single most important skill of the administrator is his or her judgment—of people, programs, and ideas. In these terms, Spiker was the most influential person during my student years—undergraduate or graduate. Sometimes, when the academic world bombards administrators in their role as decision-makers, I think specifically of how Charlie would suggest that I approach the evaluation of complex events. Most of the time, however, his influence is just there—a part of me. To observe Spiker from the perspective of a student—developing ideas, sharpening, expanding, expressing, and testing with others—was a great lesson in both generating ideas and weaving the ideas of others into one's own thinking. Without these skills, an administrator is ineffective in performing such necessary responsibilities as faculty and staff recruiting and development, program development and evaluation, and securing support from off-campus constituencies such as alumni, legislators, and business and professional groups. The rigorous standards for developing ideas in both teaching and research settings that Spiker set for me during my student days easily transfer to the responsibilities of the university administrator.

For a person of Charlie Spiker's stature and influence, only a few words of summary are necessary. I return to the theme of the initial paragraphs of this statement of Spiker's influence. Spiker's own superb theory-based, skillfully designed research, the productivity of his students, his enormous effectiveness as a teacher, his integrity, the power of his personality, the force of his desire for perfection, and his willingness to spend whatever amount of time was necessary to help his associates develop ideas—all these mark him as a truly extraordinary teacher, scientist, and administrator. Add to the above his personal charm, wit, and loyalty to his family, friends, and associates, and you have an extraordinary person—one to whom his friends, associates, and other behavioral scientists everywhere owe more than he has ever fully recognized.

3

Three Decades of Research on Children's Learning: Contributions by Charles C. Spiker

Joan H. Cantor
University of Iowa

INTRODUCTION

Charles C. Spiker played a major role in the birth and development of the field of experimental child psychology as we know it today. When he completed his graduate training and assumed his professorial duties at the Iowa Child Welfare Research Station (ICWRS) in 1951, one of his first priorities was the establishment of a doctoral training program in Experimental Child Psychology. In establishing the program, Spiker worked closely with Boyd R. McCandless, who was then director of the ICWRS. The program began in 1952 and was officially announced by the ICWRS in 1954. Although there are many examples of experimental studies done with children prior to that time, they represented a relatively small portion of the total field known as child development. Similarly, little work was being done with children in the mainstream of general experimental psychology. Most of the earlier researchers in the field of child development had concentrated on asking questions about how behavior in children changes with age, and they had amassed a considerable body of knowledge about such developmental milestones. Spiker saw a need to go beyond these developmental laws and seek out explanations for the observed changes with age. Spiker and McCandless emphasized the importance of prediction and explanation in science, and they argued forcefully that the key to understanding children's behavior lies in the experimental manipulation of variables that may be important determinants of the behavior of interest (McCandless & Spiker, 1955; Spiker & McCandless, 1954).

Spiker and his students began a succession of experiments on children's learning that has been ongoing for more than three decades, providing an illustration of programmatic research at its best. The research has been guided throughout by theoretical issues, and Spiker has continued to modify, expand, and quantify the theories to improve their explanatory power. The result is a body of research and theory that represents a major contribution to our understanding of human discrimination learning.

The purpose of this chapter is to provide an overview of this program of research by describing the major questions of interest concerning children's learning and the answers provided by Spiker, his students, and others in the field. Space will not permit consideration of all the research, nor is an attempt made to summarize the findings in any comprehensive way. (Theses and dissertations directed by Spiker and a complete list of his publications may be found in the Appendix.) Rather, the major lines of inquiry are traced by discussing them within the theoretical framework in which they were embedded. My intent is to demonstrate that, although there have been many changes in the specific learning paradigms used over the three decades, there has been a rather remarkable continuity in the questions being asked and in the basic theoretical issues that motivated the research.

THE FIRST DECADE

Empirical Tests of Hull-Spence Theory

In his early writings, Spiker repeatedly made the point that the child should not be viewed as a unique subject, but rather as an appropriate subject for answering specific questions. He considered the child to be an ideal subject for studying many aspects of the basic processes of learning. He argued further that research with children should contribute to general behavior theory, rather than to special theories of child behavior (Spiker, 1956a). His view was that an important contribution to general behavior theory could be made by studying children to test the limits of theories based on infrahuman data, making appropriate modifications in these theories (Spiker, 1960a). One of the two main lines of investigation during the first decade in Spiker's laboratory included a series of experiments designed to test the applicability to children of some of the basic principles of Hull's theory (1943, 1952) and of Spence's discrimination learning theory (1936, 1937).

Reinforcement Effects. Various aspects of reinforcement variables were investigated in a number of studies with preschool children that Spiker conducted in collaboration with his students. In one of the earliest, G. Cantor and Spiker (1954) confirmed Spence's (1936) assumption that nonreinforcement plays an important role over and above that of reinforcement in simultaneous discrimination learning. Spiker and S. White (1959) demonstrated that two variables that improve discrimination performance in a differential conditioning task may operate quite differently, one tending to increase responding to the reinforced stimulus, and the other tending to decrease responding to the nonreinforced stimulus. They concluded that it is therefore important to maintain a separate theoretical analysis of response tendencies to the positive and negative stimuli, even in more complex situations where only a single choice response can be directly observed. A different aspect of reinforcement was investigated in a dissertation by Holton (1956, 1961), showing that cessation of reinforcement produces frustration effects that are positively related to amount of prior reinforcement and proximity to the goal. The Holton study, together with an earlier one by Hancr and Brown (1955), marked the beginning of the growth of an extensive literature in which Amsel's theory of frustration (1958, 1962) was tested with young children (see Ryan & Watson, 1968, for a review).

Stimulus Generalization. Stimulus similarity is a variable of central importance in discrimination learning, according to Hull–Spence theory, and one that Spiker continued to investigate for two decades. Several of the early studies with preschool children (Spiker, 1956b, 1959) illustrate not only the effects of this variable on learning, but also the identification of other factors that must be considered with young children. The design of these studies made it possible to conclude that stimulus similarity affects learning in part through the mechanism of stimulus generalization and in part through the operation of motivational and attentional factors.

More direct tests of the Hull–Spence assumptions regarding the development of stimulus generalization gradients were made in an important series of studies which, together with some work from other laboratories on spatial generalization (e.g., Mednick & Lehtinen, 1957; Tempone, 1965), constitute the majority of evidence we have on primary generalization in children. The theoretical questions concerned the identification of variables affecting generalization of habit strength and the steepness of the gradients. These questions are important from both theoretical and empirical points of view, because the generalization of habit and inhibition between the positive and negative stimuli is presumed to be inherent in the learning of all types of discrimination problems.

The generalization studies were conducted using a simple instrumental task in which preschool children were rewarded with a marble for each lever pull in the presence of the conditioned stimulus (a light of several seconds duration). Following the training, test trials were introduced using lights differing from the conditioned stimulus in brightness or hue. In the first study, Spiker (1956c) found support for the basic assumption in Hull-Spence theory that the strength of the generalized response is directly related to the number of reinforced trials. Once again, young children proved to be different from other subject populations in an important respect. They tend to generalize broadly across the whole range of test stimuli instead of showing the gradients typically found. To counter this tendency, Spiker (1956d) used differential conditioning in a subsequent study designed to manipulate the steepness of such gradients. The results were consistent with the prediction, based on Hull's principle of stimulus dynamism, that generalization gradients along an intensity dimension are steeper when the CS is more intense than the test stimuli, and flatter when the CS is less intense than the test stimuli. Also, steeper gradients were obtained with a large amount of training than with a small amount of training, as predicted by the theory.

Other studies of primary stimulus generalization were conducted by White, who showed in his doctoral dissertation (White, 1958) that there is less generalization when the test stimuli differ from the CS on two, as opposed to only one dimension. He also collaborated with Spiker (S. White & Spiker, 1960) in demonstrating that generalization is greater with variable CS's than with a single CS. Both of these sets of results are explained in terms of habit summation within Hull's theory.

Verbal Factors in Children's Learning

In keeping with his goal of extending existing theory to encompass the unique aspects of human behavior, Spiker has for three decades been concerned with the effects of children's verbalizations on learning. He and his students were in the mainstream of a widespread search during the 1950s for an understanding of the effects of verbal labels for stimuli on discrimination learning by both children and adults. The theoretical controversies that were the trademark of this research area during the decade of the 50's centered on an issue that is still with us today. What is the relative importance of verbal (mediational) and perceptual (attentional) factors in selective learning?

Verbal Pretraining. This question was extensively debated in "verbal pretraining" studies, in which the subject first learned verbal labels for stimuli (e.g., colors, shapes, faces) and then was either tested for generalization or given a discrimination task using the same stimuli. The pretraining was generally designed to show either increased generalization or improved discrimination performance, relative to controls for warm-up and learning-to-learn. The predicted results were obtained in a wide variety of specific paradigms. What was at issue was not the effectiveness of the verbal pretraining, but rather the theoretical explanation given for the pretraining effects.

One explanation can be traced to the early theorizing of Hull (1930), who postulated that responses produce stimulus feedback to the organism, and that these response-produced stimuli can in turn become conditioned to new responses. Response-produced stimuli (cues) were widely used as explanatory mechanisms by S-R psychologists in the 1950s and 1960s. Miller's (1948) hypotheses of acquired distinctiveness of cues (ADC) and acquired equivalence of cues (AEC) provide examples of such mechanisms. According to the ADC hypothesis, if the subject learns distinctive labels for similar stimuli, the naming responses add distinctive response-produced cues to the stimulus complexes, thereby reducing stimulus generalization. Analogously, according to the AEC hypothesis, learning common labels for distinctive stimuli adds equivalent response-produced cues to the stimulus complexes, thereby increasing stimulus generalization. Spiker (1956e) added the rehearsal hypothesis, arguing that the labels also provide the subject with a means of rehearsing the correct choices between trials in the criterion task. For all three hypotheses, verbal cues play a central role in accounting for the transfer effects observed.

A different type of explanation of the positive transfer effects of verbal pretraining was offered by Gagné and Baker (1950), based on principles of perceptual learning proposed by Gibson (1950) and later elaborated by Gibson and Gibson (1955). According to this view, the facilitation is produced by "stimulus predifferentiation," that is, by increased perceptual differentiation of the stimuli to be discriminated. The verbal learning is considered to play only an indirect role in requiring the subject to accomplish the differentiation. Kurtz (1955) offered a similar interpretation by hypothesizing that the subject learns "observing responses" to the distinctive features of the stimuli during pretraining.

Spiker and his students conducted an integrated set of nearly a dozen experiments designed to test predictions based on the hypothesized roles of the verbal response-produced cues. Since several reviews of this literature are available (e.g., Cantor, 1965; Spiker, 1956a, 1963a), only a few representative studies will be mentioned here to illustrate the thrust of the research. Using a design similar to that introduced by Birge (1941), Shepard (1953) provided one of the first demonstrations of secondary or "mediated" generalization in preschool children, a result predicted by the AEC hypothesis. These and later studies on mediated generalization added considerably to our knowledge of the "ontogeny of mediational deficiency" in young children (Kendler, 1972). Norcross and Spiker (1958) also did pioneering work in the verbal learning area by demonstrating both positive and negative transfer effects of mediated associations in kindergarten and first-grade children, using the now-familiar A-B, B-C, A-C verbal paired-associate learning paradigm.

In a series of verbal pretraining studies with preschool children (G. Cantor, 1955; Norcross & Spiker, 1957; Spiker & Norcross, 1962), special attentional control groups were devised to help separate the effects of verbal and perceptual factors. Although the superior performance of verbal pretraining groups over attention groups was consistent with the ADC hypothesis, the interpretation of the results remained open to debate. In two important dissertations (Norcross, 1958; Reese, 1961), the issue was clarified by using designs in which the similarity of the verbal labels was varied on a within-subject basis. In both cases, there was clear evidence of the importance of verbal cues over and above the effects of perceptual factors. In spite of these successes, the difficulty of separating the verbal and perceptual effects is probably responsible for the abandonment of the verbal pretraining paradigm. We will see later that the basic questions endured and continued to be investigated in the new paradigms that emerged in the next decade.

Associative Transfer.   Spiker and his students made a number of important contributions in a series of eight studies dealing with associative transfer in both motor and verbal paired-associative learning. Spiker and Holton (1958) used the classical A-B, A-C paradigm in four studies of associative interference in motor paired-associate learning with children in the upper elementary grades. They varied amount of first-task practice, and they also developed a within-subject control for nonspecific transfer by mixing D-C pairs in the second task. With this design, they provided the first demonstration that interference is an increasing function of amount of first-task practice. White, Spiker, and Holton (1960) shed additional light on the nature of the interference by increasing the length of the anticipation interval in the second task. They found that the interference disappeared with the longer anticipation interval. However, the latencies of the correct responses became longer as the amount of first-task practice increased, suggesting that subjects who have strong A-B associations from Task 1 take longer to suppress these potentially interfering intrusions during the learning of the criterion task.

Spiker (1960b) also studied associative transfer in verbal paired-associate tasks, using pictures of common objects as both stimuli and responses. Once again he pioneered techniques that were later widely adopted by other investigators of children's learning. In the first of three studies with fifth and sixth graders, the results mirrored those found in the earlier motor paired-associate studies; that is, greater associative interference was found with a larger amount of first-task practice, as measured by the differences between A-C and D-C performance. Surprisingly, the greater interference was attributable to better performance on the D-C control pairs, rather than to poorer performance on the A-C experimental pairs.

In the remaining two studies, Spiker tested his hypothesis that the improved control performance in the initial study reflected the development of new strategies. Instructions, rather than amount of first-task practice, were manipulated. In one of the studies, half the children were instructed to rehearse the correct associations between trials. In the other study, half were instructed to form visual images relating the stimulus and response items. In both cases, the instructions had strong positive effects on D–C performance and no effects on A–C performance, just as had the larger amount of first-task practice in the first study. Spiker concluded that the greater associative interference produced by a large amount of first-task practice might best be explained by the spontaneous development of such strategies. The importance of strategies involving the use of rehearsal and imagery has of course been widely investigated by child psychologists in more recent years.

THE SECOND DECADE

During the second decade, Spiker and his students conducted an intensive program of research on discrimination learning in children. The period is notable in two respects: first in terms of Spiker's major extensions of Hull–Spence discrimination learning theory, and second in terms of the accumulation of a sizeable body of knowledge concerning children's learning in simultaneous, successive, conditional, and oddity discrimination problems. As we have seen, Spiker's early research was concerned with testing various aspects of Hull–Spence theory. As he began to focus his attention on discrimination learning, he became particularly interested in determining the extent to which Spence's discrimination learning theory (1936, 1937), originally developed to explain learning in infrahumans, could be successfully applied to the learning of children.

The Spiker Discrimination Learning Theory
(1963b, 1970)

Need for Modification of the Spence Theory. Spence's theory had achieved a considerable degree of success in explaining many of the known phenomena in discrimination learning (Spiker, 1973), particularly those dealing with simultaneous discrimination learning. Spence analyzed the sensations experienced by the subjects into their dimensional components and assumed that these components acquire habit strength and inhibition based on their reinforcement history. For example, in a simultaneous black–white discrimination with position irrelevant and black as the positive cue, a choice of black is always reinforced, a choice of white is never reinforced, and choices of left and right positions are equally often reinforced and nonreinforced. The prediction of learning depends on the development of a strong excitatory tendency (habit minus inhibition) for approaching black, relative to that for the other dimensional components.

In spite of these successes, the Spence theory ran into serious difficulty in explaining learning in a class of problems that requires the consistent choice of particular stimulus *compounds,* rather than the choice of a particular stimulus *component.* For example, in a successive black–white discrimination, the solution might be to pick the left position when both stimuli are black and the right position when both are white. Another example is provided by the conditional discrimination, for which the solution might be to choose the circle when both stimuli are red and the square when both are blue. It became clear that both infrahuman and human subjects are capable of learning problems that require such "stimulus compounding." Because all the dimensional components in these compounding problems are equally often reinforced across trials, the original Spence theory could not predict that these problems would be learned.

Spence (1952) attempted to solve this theoretical problem by assuming that habit and inhibition develop to compounds rather than to components only in problems in which no single dimensional component is consistently reinforced. Spence's assumption was not supported by results obtained by Birch and Vandenberg (1955), who demonstrated that compounding occurs even in a simultaneous problem, where there *is* a single reinforced component. They concluded that habit and inhibition develop to both components and compounds in the same problem. Spiker's dissatisfaction with the complexity of such two-level (i.e., component and compound) theories led him to search for a theoretical solution that would preserve the component nature of the Spence theory, while increasing its scope to include the empirical phenomenon of stimulus compounding. The result was one of his major theoretical contributions in the form of an important new axiom in the theory: the principle of stimulus interaction.

The Principle of Stimulus Interaction (Spiker, 1963b).   The principle of stimulus interaction specifies how directly conditioned habit and inhibition generalize across compounds in a given problem. Briefly, the principle states that the amount of generalization from one dimensional component to another (e.g., from black to white) is an increasing function of the *overall similarity* of the two compounds containing the components in question. Thus, the generalization from black to white is relatively great when both are presented in the same spatial location, since black–left and white–left are similar compounds. There is relatively little generalization, on the other hand, when black and white are presented in different locations, since black–left and white–right are dissimilar compounds. According to the original Spence (1936, 1937) theory, the generalization from black to white is the same for all compounds in the problem, regardless of the overall similarities of the compounds. The basic notion of stimulus interaction was contained in Hull's (1943) principle of afferent neural interaction, which was a general schema for an explanation of compounding phenomena in classical conditioning. Spiker elaborated and quantified the principle, leading to empirical predictions that could be used to test the explanatory power of this principle relative to other assumptions about stimulus generalization.

The principle of stimulus interaction increases the scope of the theory in two important respects (Spiker, 1963b, 1970, 1973). First, as noted previously, stimulus interaction provides an explanation of the empirical phenomenon of stimulus compounding totally within the context of a component learning theory. Thus, the theory predicts learning of the successive and conditional discrimination problems, along with a variety of other problems that require the subject to choose on the basis of stimulus compounds, rather than stimulus components. Second, stimulus interaction provides an explanation of the profound effects produced by the introduction of irrelevant dimensions in many discrimination tasks. For example, stimulus interaction predicts that the number of irrelevant dimensions and the similarity of the cues on these dimensions are both important variables in simultaneous tasks. Some of the overwhelming evidence supporting these predictions is described in a later section.

Prediction Equations for Discrimination Tasks. Another major theoretical contribution was the high degree of quantification of Spiker's discrimination learning theory (1963b, 1970, 1971). Spiker derived a general equation for the predicted difference in excitatory tendencies between the correct and incorrect discriminanda in any two-choice discrimination learning problem (Spiker, 1970, p. 501, Equation 6). Furthermore, he derived specific prediction equations for a variety of discrimination tasks, including the simultaneous, successive, and conditional discrimination problems. These equations specify the exact manner in which task difficulty is predicted to depend upon the number of trials administered and the distinctiveness of cues on the relevant and irrelevant dimensions in the task. It thus became possible to make predictions of differential task difficulty over a wide range of tasks and stimulus conditions.

The Role of Response-produced Cues. As noted earlier, response-produced stimuli played an important role in S–R explanations of more complex forms of human learning, and many of the paradigms used involved discrimination learning. The scope of the Spiker theory was therefore considerably increased when he showed how the effects of verbal labeling could be incorporated into the basic prediction equations. Cue-producing responses of any type (e.g., verbal, motor, perceptual) are assumed to add cues that provide added stimulus dimensions in the task. These response-produced-cue dimensions function in the prediction equations in the same way as do all other stimulus dimensions. In this manner, facilitative effects of distinctive verbal labels, previously explained by the ADC hypothesis, are easily predicted within the Spiker theory through the addition of a relevant (response-produced) stimulus dimension in the prediction equation. Spiker (1971, 1973) also specified a set of working hypotheses about the conditions under which cue-producing responses are assumed to occur, which proved very useful in applications of the theory.

Transfer of Training.   Spiker (1971) took a further theoretical step forward with his derivation of equations for predicting performance in transfer tasks. These equations permit the prediction of differential rates of acquisition in the second task that reflect either positive or negative transfer from the first task. Particularly noteworthy is the theory's prediction of differential performance on the various settings in the transfer task. The "subproblem analysis" by Tighe and Tighe (1972) of such setting differences in nonreversal-shift tasks sparked a controversy that stimulated considerable research and led to some important theoretical modifications (Zeaman & House, 1974). As we shall see later, the prediction of setting differences plays a major role in the success of Spiker's theory in explaining results in the major discrimination-shift paradigms.

Quantitative Estimates of Parameters in the Theory.   The final step in the quantification of the theory was the development of procedures for estimating the stimulus and learning parameters that appear in the prediction equations. Building on earlier Hull–Spence assumptions concerning the relationship between excitatory potential and the subject's choice behavior, Spiker developed methods for obtaining both least-squares and maximum-likelihood estimates of the parameters (Spiker, 1970, 1971, 1977a). For example, in an experiment in which simultaneous discrimination problems are used with stimuli varying in size and color and with subgroups of subjects labeling the stimuli on each of these dimensions, parameters are estimated for the rate of learning and for the distinctiveness of the size cues, the color cues, the response-produced cues on the size dimension, and the response-produced cues on the color dimension. These parameter estimates are then used to generate theoretical learning curves for each group of subjects in the experiment. Comparison of the theoretical learning curves with the actual performance curves permits a determination of the percentage of the observed variability that is accounted for by the theory. The remarkable success of the theory in making such predictions in a wide variety of discrimination tasks is evident in the next section, where the empirical tests of the theory are reviewed.

Empirical Tests of the Spiker Theory

Throughout this period of theoretical development, Spiker and his students and colleagues were actively engaged in designing and conducting experiments to test predictions derived from the theory. Again, no attempt is made to give an exhaustive account of this large body of research; rather, the major lines of investigation are described using representative studies as illustrations. The reader can perhaps best appreciate the scope of this research by referring to the titles of the M.A. theses and Ph.D. dissertations conducted during this period (see Appendix).

Stimulus Interaction. At the time that the principle of stimulus interaction was introduced, thus permitting the prediction of stimulus compounding, relatively little was known about the occurrence of such compounding phenomena in children. In order to learn more about the occurrence of compounding in children, and to test the large number of predictions flowing from the hypothesis of stimulus interaction, over a dozen studies were performed in Spiker's laboratory during the first half of the decade.

In one of the earliest studies, B. White and Spiker (1960) worked with preschool children, using the same basic paradigm Birch and Vandenberg had used in demonstrating that rats respond on the basis of cue-position (e.g., black–left) compounds in simultaneous problems. White and Spiker found that young children do respond on the basis of cue-position compounds, and that the theory correctly predicts that such compounding increases as the similarity of stimuli within settings is increased. Using a related paradigm, Lubker (1962) demonstrated cue-position compounding in kindergarten children and confirmed the further prediction that compounding increases as the amount of training is increased.

Additional tests of the compounding predictions involved conditional and successive discrimination learning problems. Recall that Spence's (1936, 1937) theory was unable to predict learning in these problems. In two experiments with preschool and kindergarten children, Hoyt (1960, 1962) showed that young children can learn a conditional discrimination, and that learning is faster when the conditional cues are made more distinctive. Lubker (1969a) demonstrated that performance in the successive problem is an increasing function of the number of relevant dimensions used.

In two additional studies, comparisons were made between performance in simultaneous and successive problems. The theory predicts that the simultaneous problem is the easier of the two and, furthermore, that confounding distinctive cues with position in these problems makes the simultaneous problem harder and the successive problem easier. In the first study, Price and Spiker (1967) confirmed these predictions with preschool children. Spiker later estimated four parameters in the appropriate prediction equations for this study, and demonstrated that the theory could account for 90% of the variability among the 36 data points in the group learning curves (nine blocks of trials for each of four groups). The average absolute deviation between predicted and observed proportions of correct responses was only .038.

In the second study, Spiker and Lubker (1965) varied the similarity of the spatial and nonspatial cues in simultaneous and successive problems, using third and fourth-grade children. The successive problem was more difficult, as expected, but the similarity differences were nonsignificant. Nevertheless, with only five parameters estimated, the theory was able to predict an amazing 96% of the variability among the 56 data points in the learning curves for the eight groups, with a mean absolute deviation between predicted and observed proportions of only .025 (Spiker, 1971).

An important series of studies involving critical tests of the stimulus interaction hypothesis was conducted by Spiker and Lubker (1964), using specially designed mixed simultaneous-successive problems. These were simple simultaneous problems, to which a dimension was added that provided a successive solution. For example, the simultaneous solution might be to choose the large stimulus consistently, whereas the successive solution might be to choose the left stimulus when both are black and the right stimulus when both are white. On the basis of stimulus interaction, problems of this type (Problem A) are predicted to be easy to learn, relative to a problem (Problem B) in which the same stimuli are rearranged in such a way that the second dimension (brightness) is irrelevant. Additional implications of stimulus interaction were tested by manipulating the similarity of cues on both dimensions. The results of several experiments (Spiker, 1971; Spiker & Lubker, 1964) were, for the most part, in agreement with these predictions. The theory accounted for between 80 and 91% of the variability of the observed trial-block means in these studies, with mean absolute deviations ranging between .040 and .056.

Response-produced Cues.   In the studies cited previously, the theory was successful in making good predictions without consideration of response-produced-cue dimensions. The results of one experiment (Spiker & Lubker, 1964, Experiment IV), however, were poorly predicted by the theory. In this study, an irrelevant dimension was made to vary either within settings or between settings in simultaneous problems, and the similarity of both relevant and irrelevant cues was varied. The results with kindergarten and first-grade children demonstrated the fact, now well known, that within-setting irrelevant dimensions produce much greater interference than do between-setting irrelevant dimensions. The prediction equations, however, are the same regardless of how the irrelevant values are varied; thus, the theory could not predict the observed differences. The incorporation of assumptions regarding the differential use of cue-producing responses under these two conditions not only explained this set of results, but also the results of many later experiments. Specifically, Spiker (1971) assumed that subjects tend to make cue-producing responses (e.g., attentional or verbal) to the most distinctive dimension varying within settings (trials), and that they do not tend to make cue-producing responses to any irrelevant dimensions that vary between settings. By introducing appropriate response-produced-cue dimensions into the prediction equations on the basis of these assumptions, the percentage of variability accounted for in the Spiker–Lubker study increased from 58% (without cues) to 84% (with cues).

Additional tests of the predictive power of response-produced-cue dimensions were made in a series of experiments in which verbal pretraining procedures were used to experimentally manipulate the cue-producing responses (Spiker, 1971). In these studies, some of the children were taught to label the values of a dimension that would become relevant in the subsequent discrimination task, some labeled values of a dimension that would become irrelevant, and others labeled values of a dimension that would not vary.

Spiker's working assumptions about the subject's use of cue-producing responses in the criterion task were used to add appropriate response-produced-cue dimensions into the prediction equations. The resulting predictions were tested for children in preschool through first grade, using simultaneous problems of varying degrees of complexity. The effects of pretraining on discrimination performance were generally quite strong, with relevant verbal labels producing facilitation, and irrelevant verbal labels producing interference, relative to the control condition. In four separate theoretical fits to the data involving a total of 234 data points, the percentages of variance accounted for by the theory ranged from 82 to 94%, with mean absolute deviations between predicted and observed proportions ranging from .021 to .056.

In the applications discussed thus far, the theory was fit to group learning curves. An even more ambitious theoretical undertaking was the fitting of individual subjects' learning curves in a study with kindergarten children in which cue-producing responses were assigned on the basis of the child's own verbalizations (Spiker & Cantor, 1977). Following each block of eight trials in a simultaneous problem with two irrelevant dimensions, the experimenter asked for the child's current hypothesis concerning the solution. A separate prediction equation was provided for each child on each of six trial-blocks. For each equation, an appropriate response-produced-cue dimension was assigned on the basis of the dimension mentioned in the child's hypothesis. A total of 648 data points were fit, using estimates of only six stimulus parameters (three representing the distinctiveness of color, form, and size cues, and the other three representing the distinctiveness of the response-produced cues on these same dimensions). When the child's verbalization was used to predict performance on the *next* trial-block, 53% of all the individual-subject variability in discrimination performance was accounted for by the theory. If, on the other hand, the child's verbalization was used to predict performance on the *previous* trial-block, an even more impressive 65% of the variability was accounted for. It is interesting and perhaps instructive to note that the children's verbalizations reflected their previous behavior better than their future behavior.

Cue-producing responses were manipulated not only in discrimination tasks, but also in multidimensional generalization tasks (Spiker, Croll, & Miller, 1972). Kindergarten children were pretrained to label stimulus compounds on the basis of one of three varying dimensions. Subsequently, one compound was displayed, and the children were asked to classify a large set of compounds in terms of whether or not they "looked like" the display. Prediction equations were derived from the theory for these generalization tasks, including appropriate response-produced-cue dimensions. As predicted, the children tended to classify the stimuli on the basis of the dimension for which they were using verbal labels. With estimates of seven parameters, the theory accounted for 90% of the variability among 192 subgroup means, with an average absolute deviation between predicted and obtained means of .078.

Transfer of Training.   Spiker (1971) first illustrated the theory's ability to predict transfer performance in a study conducted by Bigelow (1970). Kindergarten children initially learned a simultaneous task with two redundant relevant dimensions, using labels for the stimuli on just one of the dimensions. In a subsequent transfer task, the dimension labeled in the first task was made either relevant, irrelevant, or nonvarying. As predicted by the theory, transfer performance was best for the children previously required to label values of the relevant dimension, and worst for those required to label values of the irrelevant dimension. Also predicted by the theory were differences in performance found for two types of settings in the transfer task. With seven parameter estimates, the theory accounted for 93% of the variability among the 72 trial-block means in the transfer task. The mean absolute deviation between predicted and obtained means was .03.

Discrimination Shifts.   During the decade beginning with the mid-1960s, a great deal of theoretical work centered on transfer of training in discrimination-shift paradigms, including reversal and nonreversal shifts, intradimensional and extradimensional shifts, and optional shifts (e.g., Campione & Brown, 1974; Kendler & Kendler, 1962, 1968; Shepp & Turrisi, 1966; Spiker & Cantor, 1973; L. Tighe & T. Tighe, 1966; T. Tighe & L. Tighe, 1972; Zeaman & House, 1963, 1974). A very large literature developed involving children's performance in these paradigms (for a review, see Esposito, 1975).

Most shift paradigms have an original learning task consisting of a simultaneous problem with one irrelevant dimension. The paradigms differ with respect to the nature of the subsequent transfer (shift) task. Some shift tasks require the subject to learn to choose a different value on the previously relevant dimension (the reversal and intradimensional shifts). Others require the subject to choose on the basis of the previously irrelevant dimension (the nonreversal and extradimensional shifts). The optional shift can be learned on the basis of either the formerly relevant or formerly irrelevant dimension.

These paradigms were developed to expose the nature of the discrimination learning process indirectly through comparisons of performance in the various shift tasks. In particular, comparisons were made to identify developmental changes in the relative importance of instrumental transfer (e.g., transfer of a tendency to approach triangles) and dimensional transfer (e.g., transfer of the tendency to pay attention to shape).

One of the major findings to emerge from this large literature is the unmistakable evidence of a developmental increase in the importance of dimensional transfer. Thus, a successful discrimination learning theory must provide a mechanism to explain such dimensional responding. Once again, as in the 1950s, we find that some theoretical explanations depend on mediating or cue-producing responses. For example, Kendler & Kendler (1962, 1968) postulated that children develop dimensional representations that are mediational (though not necessarily verbal) in nature. Other explanations still depend on attentional mechanisms. For example, Zeaman and House (1963) attribute dimensional responding to perceptual observing responses that selectively focus attention on a particular dimension, and Tighe and Tighe (1966) explain such dimensional responding on the basis of a process of perceptual differentiation. As we have seen, Spiker generally explains dimensional responding by incorporating response-produced-cue dimensions in his prediction equations. Nevertheless, he demonstrated that an alternative attentional mechanism can be introduced into the prediction equations with no change in the mathematical consequences (Spiker & Cantor, 1973).

Spiker and the author (Spiker & Cantor, 1973) provided the derivations of the prediction equations for a number of the major shift paradigms, together with theoretical fits to the data of several experiments conducted in our laboratories. In one study (Cantor & Spiker, 1976), verbal labeling was manipulated in a reversal-shift paradigm with kindergarten children. The results confirmed theoretical predictions of differences in shift performance on four different types of settings within tasks, differences in performance for the relevant and irrelevant labeling groups, and larger setting differences in the irrelevant labeling groups. Eight parameters were estimated in the theoretical fit to these data (Spiker & Cantor, 1973), which accounted for 82% of the variability among 216 data points (six trial-block means for four setting types in each of nine subgroups). The mean absolute deviation between predicted and observed means was .062.

In a doctoral dissertation conducted in Spiker's laboratory, Guldmann (1972) manipulated dimensional labeling in both nonreversal and reversal-shift tasks. The results confirmed theoretical predictions concerning the effects of labeling on both types of shifts. The theory also correctly predicted setting differences in the nonreversal shift, as well as differential effects of relevant and irrelevant labeling on these setting differences. The theoretical fit with eight parameter estimates accounted for 88% of the variability among 96 means, with an average absolute deviation of .053 (Spiker & Cantor, 1973).

Dimensional labeling was also manipulated in an optional-shift paradigm by Lundback (1971), using second-grade children. For half the children, labeling on the reversal dimension was required during the shift task, and for the other half, labeling on the nonreversal dimension was required. Test settings were interspersed with the shift settings to determine which type of shift was being learned. As predicted by the theoretical equations, the labeling had profound effects on shift and test performance. Most of the children labeling on the reversal dimension made reversal shifts, whereas most of those labeling on the nonreversal dimension made nonreversal shifts. With estimates of only eight parameters, the theory accounted for 95% of the variability among the 60 trial-block means for the shift and test settings. The mean absolute deviation between predicted and obtained means was .052.

THE THIRD DECADE

Spiker's theory is clearly highly successful in making quantitative predictions for children's performance in a wide variety of discrimination tasks. Nevertheless, it became clear, particularly in the context of transfer performance, that parameters estimated from the data do not always account well for the rapid learning that occurs during the early trials under some conditions. (Spiker & Cantor, 1973). Thus, it appears that at least some children may be learning such tasks rapidly in a more adult-like mode, perhaps using hypothesis-testing strategies.

Hypothesis Testing in Young Children

Theoretical Considerations.   Hypothesis-testing theories that were developed during the 1960s (e.g., Bower & Trabasso, 1964; Levine, 1963; Restle, 1962) are quite successful in predicting adult performance in discrimination and concept learning tasks. At that time, theorists working predominantly with younger children (e.g., H. Kendler & T. Kendler, 1962, 1968; Spiker, 1970, 1971; L. Tighe & T. Tighe, 1966; T. Tighe & L. Tighe, 1972; Zeaman & House, 1963, 1974) did not find the need to postulate the use of such strategies. During the 1970s, theorists working at both ends of the age continuum began to ask the next obvious questions: When do children begin to use systematic strategies and how do these strategies develop? During the past decade, a considerable body of data has been collected to help answer these questions. Furthermore, some initial attempts have been made to develop theories applicable to hypothesis-testing in children (e.g., Gholson & Beilin, 1979; Kemler, 1978; T. Kendler, 1979; Spiker & Cantor, 1979a). Although Spiker and Cantor (1979a) presented the general outline of an associationistic hypothesis-testing theory applicable to children, they also expressed the view that a great deal more empirical information was needed, and they conducted over a dozen experiments to learn more about children as hypothesis testers (Spiker & Cantor, 1982, 1983a).

Methodological Considerations.   One of the first questions of interest to Spiker and Cantor was whether children as young as kindergarten age show any signs of using hypothesis-testing strategies, either spontaneously or in response to special training. Early results reported by Gholson, Levine, and Phillips (1972) were discouraging, showing mainly stereotypic responding and little learning among kindergarten children. However, their use of blank-trial probes and difficult learning tasks raised some metholodological questions concerning what conditions are most appropriate for assessing hypothesis-testing capabilities at younger ages.

The first such question concerns the method used to monitor the child's hypotheses. Levine (1963) successfully used blank-trial probes and later introtact probes (Karpf & Levine, 1971) for this purpose with adult subjects. A blank-trial probe is a series of trials given without feedback and arranged in such a manner that the sequence of positional responses can be used to infer the subject's current hypothesis. For example, three choices on the left followed by one on the right might signal a consistent choice of red stimuli, from which it is inferred that the subject is testing red as a potential solution. An introtact probe is simply a request for the subject to state a current hypothesis, usually just prior to each choice response. On the basis of Phillips' (1974) finding that introtact probes facilitated learning in second graders, whereas blank-trial probes interfered, Spiker and Cantor selected introtact probes for use with kindergarten children.

A second question concerns the nature of the discrimination task. Spiker and Cantor were interested in determining what method the child uses to reach solution; thus, it was important to select a task that most of the children could solve. Because it is well established that irrelevant dimensions varying within settings greatly increase the difficulty of simultaneous tasks for children (e.g., Lubker, 1967, 1969b), relatively simple tasks were chosen.

A third question concerns a special problem that younger children appear to have in multidimensional discrimination tasks. They have a strong tendency to limit their hypotheses to the values of their initially preferred dimension, even when that dimension is irrelevant. This apparent attentional rigidity is referred to as "dimensional fixation" by Cantor and Spiker (1977) and as "attribute perseveration" by Kemler (1978). In order to prevent the dimensional fixation from masking any hypothesis-testing skills in younger children, an attempt was made to minimize its effects. Toward that end, Spiker and Cantor developed special tasks in which relevant and irrelevant "pseudodimensions" are constituted entirely from values of a single dimension. For example, red and green might serve as the relevant dimension, and blue and yellow might serve as the irrelevant dimension. Whereas in a conventional problem, the child might choose between a red square and a green triangle, here the child would choose between a red + blue combination and a green + yellow combination. On other trials, the choice would be between red + yellow and green + blue. The child can therefore learn to choose the positive cue (e.g., red) without being required to shift attention among dimensions.

A Simple Strategy. For use with younger children, Spiker and Cantor devised the "sequential hypothesis-testing strategy," which is defined by adherence to the win–stay, lose–shift, and valid-hypothesis rules. According to these rules, the subject maintains the current hypothesis following positive feedback, shifts to a new hypothesis following negative feedback, and tests only valid hypotheses, that is, hypotheses that have not been previously tested and disconfirmed. A series of studies was run to determine the ability of kindergarten and first-grade children to use this strategy.

Pretraining Effects. Cantor and Spiker (1978) used kindergarten and first-grade children to study the effects of instruction in the use of the sequential hypothesis-testing strategy. Introtact probes were used in pseudodimensional tasks with one irrelevant dimension. The children were always trained against their initial dimensional preference; that is, the pseudodimension named in their initial introtact response was made irrelevant. At each age level, a hypothesis-training group (Group HYP) was given instruction in using the strategy in three preliminary tasks prior to the criterion task; a learning-to-learn group (Group LTL) received the same three preliminary tasks without instruction; and a control group (Group CON) received no preliminary training. Group LTL was given an opportunity to solve each pretraining task and then provided with the solution if necessary. Group HYP was guided and prompted during the pretraining tasks in such a way that the rules of the strategy were made explicit, and each problem was solved with no strategic errors.

The groups showed marked differences in performance in terms of indices of learning as well as indices of strategy. Not only did most of the children given hypothesis training learn rapidly, but in addition, 58% made no errors in using the strategy, and 82% made fewer than four strategy errors. At the other extreme, only 20% of the control children learned, and 40% of them were dimensionally fixated on the irrelevant pseudodimension. There was no evidence of the use of the strategy in this group. The performance of the learning-to-learn group was intermediate, with 65% learning. Considering that they had no training on the strategy, the LTL children did surprisingly well, with 30% making no strategy errors and 48% making fewer than four strategy errors. No differences were found between kindergarten and first-grade performance. These results clearly demonstrate that most kindergarten children are capable of learning a strategy, and that many will adopt such a strategy on their own after some successful experience in solving the tasks.

Given these encouraging results, Spiker and Cantor (1979b) set out to determine what aspects of the pretraining are responsible for its dramatic effects. Five groups of kindergarten children were trained under conditions that differed in type and amount of preliminary experience, ranging from no experience to complete training in hypothesis testing. Two experimental sessions were used to determine whether the children could transfer their new skills from pseudodimensional tasks (all forms) on Day 1 to conventional tasks (color-form compounds) on Day 2. The results pointed to the importance of providing the child with (1) an understanding that the tasks are indeed solvable, (2) practice in shifting attention among dimensions, and (3) explicit training in use of the strategy. With pseudodimensional tasks (Day 1), all three factors played a significant role in overall performance. When tasks with genuine dimensions were used (Day 2), the children tended to revert in sizeable numbers to being dimensionally fixated unless they had received explicit training in shifting dimensions. Strategic performance tended to fall off somewhat in the more difficult tasks, with one important exception. The children given explicit training in using the strategy continued to perform at the same high levels even in the tasks with genuine dimensions.

Six additional studies (Spiker & Cantor, 1982, Experiments 2–5, 7–8) were conducted, in which the pretraining effects were assessed for tasks of varying degrees of complexity. Of particular interest was the question of whether any type of pretraining would prepare the children to use the strategy in genuine-dimensional criterion tasks. The answer seems to be that at least some pretraining with genuine dimensions is needed; pseudo-dimensional pretraining by itself does little to prevent dimensional fixation in younger children when they attempt to solve tasks with genuine dimensions.

Age differences appeared in two of the studies, with first graders showing consistently better performance than the kindergarten children. Only one study provided data for older children. Second and third graders were given a mixture of pseudodimensional and genuine-dimensional pretraining, followed by a difficult criterion task with two irrelevant genuine dimensions. The results were interesting on two counts. On the one hand, dimensional fixation appeared even at this age in over half the children who did not receive any pretraining. On the other hand, those given hypothesis pretraining performed surprisingly well: Only 8% were fixated and nearly half were perfect in using the strategy.

Probe Effects.   In two studies (Cantor & Spiker, 1977, 1979), performance in groups receiving introtact probes was compared with that in groups who were not probed. The probes interfered with the performance of unpretrained kindergarten children in the first study but had no effect on their performance in the second study. In the first study, 71% of the introtact group became dimensionally fixated, suggesting that the introtacts may have contributed to this problem. The failure to find probe effects even in pretrained groups in the second study is consistent with results reported by Kemler (1978) with kindergarten children. Spiker and Cantor (1982) suggested that the nature of the stimuli may account for the differences in results in the probe studies. The interference occurred with conventional unitary stimulus compounds (e.g., large red square) in a difficult task with two irrelevant dimensions. The probes did not interfere, however, in the studies where the dimensional values were "partitioned," that is, placed in separate spatial locations (e.g., red patch next to square outline). Investigations of the ability of young children to deal effectively with these two types of stimuli are discussed in a later section.

For children in first grade, Cantor and Spiker (1979) found that the introtacts facilitated performance, a finding consistent with results reported by Phillips (1974) for second graders. It may be that the introtact probes encourage these children to use strategies that are available, but not always used.

Cantor and Spiker (1982) also demonstrated that the temporal placement of the probe has profound effects on performance. They noted that Kemler (1978) had found evidence of outstanding "short-term efficiency" in kindergarten children; that is, they made nearly perfect use of current feedback information in choosing a new hypothesis. She found no evidence, however, of "long-term efficiency," that is, planning across trials toward the solution. Kemler had devised a particularly ingenious story-and-game context for her tasks, and she also used posttrial introtact probes given at the end of each trial with full feedback information in view. In previous studies, pretrial probes were given just prior to the choice response. Cantor and Spiker reasoned that posttrial probes would constrain the children to make full use of the feedback information but would not promote better learning unless the children also learned to shift dimensions. Cantor and Spiker used kindergarten children in a factorial design with pretrial versus posttrial probes as one factor, and with presence versus absence of training in shifting dimensions as a second factor. The results confirmed, on the one hand, that the posttrial probes markedly facilitate *short-term* efficiency for both types of pretraining. They showed, on the other hand, that posttrial probes only improve *long-term* efficiency when dimensional fixation is minimized through training in shifting dimensions.

Some of the best evidence for long-term planning across trials was obtained in a developmental study with children in kindergarten through third grade in which Cantor and Spiker (1984) used toy animals as stimuli instead of the conventional color-form compounds. The child's task was to figure out which animal was "special." Eight animals were presented on each trial in groups of four. The child tried to choose the set of four containing the special animal and was given appropriate feedback information. The animals were regrouped from trial to trial, so that all animals except for the special animal appeared in both correct and incorrect sets. The task is analogous to a four-dimensional simultaneous problem, except that the animals were not paired into relevant and irrelevant dimensions. Posttrial probes were used, and learning-to-learn pretraining was given to all children. Although age differences were found, performance was excellent at all age levels. In spite of the relative complexity of the task, 79% of the kindergarten children learned, and 39% made no strategic errors. Short-term efficiency was excellent at all age levels, and there was clear evidence of long-term planning across trials even at the kindergarten level.

Processing of Multidimensional Stimuli

The ability of young children to analyze multidimensional stimuli has received considerable attention from developmental psychologists during the past decade (e.g., Kemler, 1983; Kemler & Smith, 1978; Shepp, 1983). The pervasiveness of dimensional fixation in simultaneous tasks led Spiker and Cantor to conduct a series of studies aimed at clarifying the nature of the difficulty that young children experience in tasks with multidimensional stimuli. For this purpose, two types of stimuli were used: the conventional unitary compounds (e.g., large blue circle) and partitioned stimuli in which the dimensional cues are presented in separate spatial locations (e.g., large arrow, irregular-shaped blue patch, and outline of a circle). The ability of young children to encode, recode, and reason with these two types of stimuli was investigated.

Cantor and Spiker (1980) began by comparing the ability of kindergarten and second-grade children to identify and remember the two types of stimuli in match-to-sample and delayed match-to-sample tasks, respectively. Half the children received prior training in labeling the values of the three dimensions used. Children at both age levels identified and remembered the unitary stimuli better than the partitioned stimuli. Name training improved performance in the identification task for both ages and both types of stimuli, but facilitated memory only for partitioned stimuli in kindergarten children. The results suggested that unitary stimuli are perceived in a more integral unanalyzed fashion and are probably encoded visually. Memory for partitioned stimuli, on the other hand, appears to require verbal encoding, which is less likely to occur in kindergarten children unless they receive special training.

Spiker and Cantor (1980) obtained further support for these hypotheses, again using kindergarten and second-grade children. The identification and memory tasks from the previous study were used on half the trials. On the remaining trials, the child was asked to recode the dimensional values prior to the identification or memory task. For example, if the display stimulus was a small red square, the recoded stimulus would be a large blue circle. Half the children were given extensive pretraining in dimensional labeling and recoding. Spiker and Cantor reasoned that if children do in fact perceive unitary stimuli in unanalyzed visual form, then a recoding task that requires dimensional analysis should be more difficult for unitary stimuli than for partitioned stimuli.

The results confirmed that unitary stimuli are easier to remember than partitioned stimuli but are harder to recode. Moreover, the pretraining facilitated performance in recoding, particularly in kindergarten children, who found the recoding tasks very difficult. Spiker and Cantor concluded that young children deal very effectively with unitary stimuli when dimensional analysis is not required (as in recognition memory) but have difficulty in analyzing such stimuli into dimensional components (as in the recoding tasks). Furthermore, kindergarten children are far less likely than are second graders to use dimensional labels appropriately, even with partitioned stimuli, although they profit considerably from special training in labeling and analyzing dimensions. These results are consistent with the finding of a particularly high incidence of dimensional fixation in discrimination tasks with unitary stimuli. Moreover, they are consistent with other literature demonstrating deficiencies in labeling strategies in young children (e.g., Flavell, Beach, & Chinsky, 1966; Kendler, 1972).

As a further test of the hypothesis that the dimensional structure of unitary stimuli is less accessible than that of partitioned stimuli for young children, Spiker and Cantor (1983b) measured the time required to label the dimensional values of both types of stimuli. Children in kindergarten through second grade were presented with four instances of either partitioned or unitary stimuli on each trial and were asked to name the dimensional values as rapidly as possible (e.g., large blue circle, small red square, etc.). As expected, the children took longer to label the unitary stimuli and made more naming errors in doing so. The differences in response times between partitioned and unitary stimuli decreased with age. The kindergarten and first-grade children had considerable difficulty in naming the unitary stimuli, and many did so very haltingly.

Another facet of the processing of multidimensional stimuli was investigated in a series of three studies by Spiker, Cantor, and Klouda (1985), using one-trial reasoning tasks. In a relatively simple version of the task, the child might be shown a card with red and square on it, either in unitary or partitioned form, and told that the experimenter was thinking about one of those things (red or square). The experimenter then presented a second stimulus (e.g., red and triangle), saying either that "The thing I am thinking about *is* on this card," (solution: red) or else that "The thing I am thinking about *is not* on this card" (solution: square). The child's task was to figure out which thing the experimenter was thinking about.

Children in kindergarten and first grade were given a series of reasoning tasks of increasing complexity, which could all be solved in one trial but contained more irrelevant dimensional information. For example, the child might be shown a card with a red triangle and a red square on it and told that the thing the experimenter was thinking about was not on a card with a red square and a blue square (solution: triangle). Remarkably, children at both age levels showed nearly errorless performance for both types of stimuli and for all levels of complexity, provided they were given feedback information and preliminary experience with very simple problems. In these tasks, young children clearly do not have difficulty in analyzing dimensional compounds and in disregarding irrelevant dimensional features of the stimuli. Perhaps performance here is less dependent on dimensional labeling than is the case in the recoding tasks that are so difficult for children of these ages.

A VIEW TOWARD THE FUTURE

Throughout his career, Spiker has provided valuable insights into the role of theory in psychology (e.g., Spiker, 1956a, 1960a, 1977b). In his own research, he consistently directed his efforts toward the ultimate scientific goal of constructing theories to predict and explain behavior. As we have seen, his discrimination learning theory is remarkably successful in making accurate quantitative predictions of children's performance under many conditions in a wide variety of learning and transfer tasks. Although his research during the past decade has not involved the direct testing of theoretical predictions, the work was nevertheless theoretically motivated. He views the studies on hypothesis testing and the processing of multidimensional stimuli as necessary fact gathering in preparation for theoretical advances. In a summary of the research on hypothesis testing (Spiker & Cantor, 1983a), he outlined some implications of the recent findings for future theoretical development. He pointed out that cognitive hypothesis-testing theories, as well as incremental associative theories, will require modification in order to provide adequate explanations of problem solving in children and adults. The associative theories, which have been highly successful in predicting learning in younger children, do not adequately handle the emerging hypothesis-testing skills that are now evident as early as 5 years of age. The cognitive theories, which have been very successful in predicting the performance of practiced adults, do not take into account the less-than-perfect processing that characterizes children's problem solving and probably also that of unpracticed adults. Thus, Spiker points to the need for building theories to explain the *acquisition* of strategies at all age levels. The theoretical schema proposed by Spiker and Cantor (1979a) is a first step in the construction of a theory that will successfully encompass the developmental transition to the use of strategies in problem-solving tasks.

CONCLUDING REMARKS

When Lew Lipsitt first asked if I would be willing to help edit a festschrift for Charlie, I agreed enthusiastically, for it is an honor he most richly deserves. His pioneering role in establishing the field of experimental child psychology, his outstanding leadership of the Institute of Child Behavior and Development, his unsurpassed teaching, his scholarly productivity, and his profound influence on students are all well known. My purpose here is not to elaborate further on these points, but rather to express my thanks to Charlie for the many benefits I have derived from our association of 25 years.

I have been particularly fortunate in having the opportunity to learn from Charlie both inside and outside the classroom, to serve as a faculty member under his leadership in one of the finest academic units in existence, and to collaborate with him in the laboratory. In his role as administrator, Charlie provided his faculty with whatever we needed for our teaching and research, and he saw to it that we had the time to do both. Charlie also served as an outstanding role model for young professors. We learned by his example that a good professor is both a teacher and a scholar, and is one who cooperates rather than competes with his colleagues. No one I have known is more willing to share his time and expertise with those around him. His love of teaching, coupled with his own unquenchable thirst for new knowledge, provides his students and colleagues with an unending opportunity to learn along with him, and to be a part of the intellectual excitement that surrounds him. My scholarly collaboration with Charlie has been equally rewarding. I have learned how to construct theory and how to get children to learn things no one ever knew they could learn. Above all, I have learned from Charlie that a sense of humor about everything and everybody, including oneself, makes it all possible. I consider it a rare privilege indeed to be Charlie Spiker's research collaborator and faculty colleague.

REFERENCES

Amsel, A. (1958). The role of frustrative nonreward in noncontinuous reward situations. *Psychological Bulletin, 55,* 102–119.

Amsel, A. (1962). Frustrative nonreward in partial reinforcement and discrimination learning: Some recent history and a theoretical extension. *Psychological Review, 69,* 306–328.

Bigelow, A. E. (1970). *Effects of verbal training on transfer problems of discrimination learning.* Unpublished master's thesis, University of Iowa, Iowa City.

Birch, D., & Vandenberg, V. (1955). The necessary conditions for cue-position patterning. *Journal of Experimental Psychology, 50,* 391–396.

Birge, J. S. (1941). *The role of verbal responses in transfer.* Unpublished doctoral dissertation, Yale University, New Haven, CT.

Bower, G. H., & Trabasso, T. (1964). Concept identification. In R. C. Atkinson (Ed.), *Studies in mathematical psychology.* Stanford, CA: Stanford University Press.

Campione, J. C., & Brown, A. L. (1974). The effects of contextual changes and degree of component mastery on transfer of training. In H. W. Reese (Ed.), *Advances in child development and behavior* (Vol. 9, pp. 69–114). New York: Academic Press.

Cantor, G. N. (1955). Effects of three types of pretraining on discrimination learning in preschool children. *Journal of Experimental Psychology, 49,* 339–342.

Cantor, G. N., & Spiker, C. C. (1954). Effects of nonreinforced trials on discrimination learning in preschool children. *Journal of Experimental Psychology, 47,* 256–258.

Cantor, J. H. (1965). Transfer of stimulus pretraining in motor paired-associate and discrimination learning tasks. In L. P. Lipsitt & C. C. Spiker (Eds.), *Advances in child development and behavior* (Vol. 2). New York: Academic Press.

Cantor, J. H., & Spiker, C. C. (1976). The effects of labeling dimensional values on setting differences in shift performance of kindergarten children. *Memory and Cognition, 4,* 446–452.

Cantor, J. H., & Spiker, C. C. (1977). Dimensional fixation with introtacts in kindergarten children. *Bulletin of the Psychonomic Society, 10,* 169–171.

Cantor, J. H., & Spiker, C. C. (1978). The problem-solving strategies of kindergarten and first-grade children during discrimination learning. *Journal of Experimental Child Psychology, 26,* 341–358.

Cantor, J. H., & Spiker, C. C. (1979). The effects of introtacts on hypothesis testing in kindergarten and first-grade children. *Child Development, 50,* 1110–1120.

Cantor, J. H., & Spiker, C. C. (1980). Factors affecting children's recognition memory for multidimensional stimuli. *Bulletin of the Psychonomic Society, 16,* 345–348.

Cantor, J. H., & Spiker, C. C. (1982). The effect of the temporal locus of the introtact probe on the hypothesis-testing strategies of kindergarten children. *Journal of Experimental Child Psychology, 34,* 510–525.

Cantor, J. H., & Spiker, C. C. (1984). Evidence for long-term planning in children's hypothesis testing. *Bulletin of the Psychonomic Society, 22,* 493–496.

Esposito, N. J. (1975). Review of discrimination shift learning in young children. *Psychological Bulletin, 82,* 432–455.

Flavell, J. H., Beach, D. R., & Chinsky, J. M. (1966). Spontaneous verbal rehearsal in a memory task as a function of age. *Child Development, 37,* 283–299.

Gagne, R. M., & Baker, K. E. (1950). Stimulus predifferentiation as a factor in transfer of training. *Journal of Experimental Psychology, 40,* 439–451.

Gholson, B., & Beilin, H. A. (1979). A developmental model of human learning. In H. W. Reese & L. P. Lipsitt (Eds.), *Advances in child development and behavior* (Vol. 13). New York: Academic Press.

Gholson, B., Levine, M., & Phillips, S. (1972). Hypotheses, strategies, and stereotypes in discrimination learning. *Journal of Experimental Child Psychology, 13,* 423–446.

Gibson, J. J. (1950). *The perception of the visual world.* Boston: Houghton Mifflin.

Gibson, J. J., & Gibson, E. J. (1955). Perceptual learning: Differentiation or enrichment? *Psychological Review, 62,* 32–41.

Guldmann, H. (1972). *The effects of dimensional verbalization upon children's performance on reversal and extradimensional shift discrimination problems.* Unpublished doctoral dissertation, University of Iowa, Iowa City.

Haner, C. F., & Brown, P. A. (1955). Clarification of the instigation to action concept in the frustration–aggression hypothesis. *Journal of Abnormal Social Psychology, 51,* 204–206.

Holton, R. B. (1956). *Variables affecting the change in instrumental response magnitude after reward cessation.* Unpublished doctoral dissertation, University of Iowa, Iowa City.

Holton, R. B. (1961). Amplitude of instrumental response following cessation of reward. *Child Development, 32,* 107–116.

Hoyt, J. M. (1960). *Effect of similarity of reversal cues on learning of successive stimulus reversals in children.* Unpublished master's thesis, University of Iowa, Iowa City.

Hoyt, J. M. (1962). *Conditional discrimination and serial reversal learning in children.* Unpublished doctoral dissertation, University of Iowa, Iowa City.

Hull, C. L. (1930). Knowledge and purpose as habit mechanisms. *Psychological Review, 37,* 511–525.

Hull, C. L. (1943). *Principles of behavior.* New York: Appleton–Century–Crofts.

Hull, C. L. (1952). *A behavior system.* New Haven: Yale University Press.

Karpf, D., & Levine, M. (1971). Blank-trial probes and introtracts in human discrimination learning. *Journal of Experimental Psychology, 90,* 51–55.

Kemler, D. G. (1978). Patterns of hypothesis testing in children's discriminative learning: A study of the development of problem-solving strategies. *Developmental Psychology, 14,* 653–673.

Kemler, D. G. (1983). Holistic and analytic modes in perceptual and cognitive development. T. J. Tighe & B. E. Shepp (Eds.), *Interactional analyses: Perception, cognition, and development.* Hillsdale, NJ: Lawrence Erlbaum Associates.

Kemler, D. G., & Smith, L. B. (1978). Is there a developmental trend from integrality to separability in perception? *Journal of Experimental Child Psychology, 26,* 498–507.

Kendler, H. H., & Kendler, T. S. (1962). Vertical and horizontal processes in problem solving. *Psychological Review, 69,* 1–16.

Kendler, H. H., & Kendler, T. S. (1968). Mediation and conceptual behavior. In J. T. Spence (Ed.), *The psychology of learning and motivation* (Vol. 2). New York: Academic Press.

Kendler, T. S. (1972). An ontogeny of mediational deficiency. *Child Development, 43,* 1–17.

Kendler, T. S. (1979). The development of discrimination learning: A levels of-functioning explanation. In H. W. Reese & L. P. Lipsitt (Eds.), *Advances in child development and behavior* (Vol. 13). New York: Academic Press.

Kurtz, K. H. (1955). Discrimination of complex stimuli: The relationship of training and test stimuli in transfer of discrimination. *Journal of Experimental Psychology, 50,* 283–292.

Levine, M. (1963). Mediating processes in humans at the outset of discrimination learning. *Psychological Review, 70,* 254–276.

Lubker, B. J. (1962). *The effect of training on cue-position patterning in discrimination learning.* Unpublished doctoral dissertation, University of Iowa, Iowa City.

Lubker, B. J. (1967). Irrelevant stimulus dimensions and children's performance on simultaneous discrimination problems. *Child Development, 38,* 119–125.

Lubker, B. J. (1969a). Setting similarity and successive discrimination learning by children. *Journal of Experimental Child Psychology, 7,* 188–194.

Lubker, B. J. (1969b). The role of between- and within-setting irrelevant dimensions in children's simultaneous discrimination learning. *Child Development, 40,* 957–964.

Lundback, E. (1971). *The effects of dimensional naming upon children's performance in a modified optional shift problem.* Unpublished master's thesis, University of Iowa, Iowa City.

McCandless, B. R., & Spiker, C. C. (1955). Experimental research in child psychology. *Child Development, 27,* 75–80.

Mednick, S. A., & Lehtinen, L. E. (1957). Stimulus generalization as a function of age in children. *Journal of Experimental Psychology, 53,* 180–183.

Miller, N. E. (1948). Theory and experiment relating psychoanalytic displacement to stimulus-response generalization. *Journal of Abnormal Social Psychology, 43,* 155–178.

Norcross, K. J., (1958). Effects on discrimination performance of similarity of previously acquired stimulus names. *Journal of Experimental Psychology, 56,* 305–309.

Norcross, K. J., & Spiker, C. C. (1957). The effects of type of stimulus pretraining on discrimination performance in preschool children. *Child Development, 28,* 79–84.

Norcross, K. J., & Spiker, C. C. (1958). Effects of mediated associations on transfer in paired-associate learning. *Journal of Experimental Psychology, 55,* 129–134.

Phillips, S. (1974). *Introtacts in children's discrimination learning.* Unpublished doctoral dissertation, State University of New York at Stony Brook.

Price, L. E., & Spiker, C. C. (1967). Effect of similarity of irrelevant stimuli on performance in discrimination learning problems. *Journal of Experimental Child Psychology, 5,* 324–331.

Reese, H. W. (1961). Level of stimulus pretraining and paired-associate learning. *Child Development, 32,* 89–93.

Restle, F. (1962). The selection of strategies in cue learning. *Psychological Review, 69,* 329–343.

Ryan, T. J., & Watson, P. (1968). Frustrative nonreward theory applied to children's behavior. *Psychological Bulletin, 69,* 111-125.

Shepard, W. O. (1953). *Mediated generalization with high interstimulus similarity.* Unpublished master's thesis, University of Iowa, Iowa City.

Shepp, B. E. (1983). The analyzability of multidimensional objects: Some constraints on perceived structure, and attention. In T. Tighe & B. E. Shepp (Eds.), *Interactional analyses: Perception, cognition, and development.* Hillsdale, NJ: Lawrence Erlbaum Associates.

Shepp, B. E., & Turrisi, F. D. (1966). Learning and transfer of mediating responses in discrimination learning. In N. R. Ellis (Ed.), *International review of research in mental retardation* (Vol. 2, pp. 86-120). New York: Academic Press.

Spence, K. W. (1936). The nature of discrimination learning in animals. *Psychological Review, 43,* 427-449.

Spence, K. W. (1937). The differential response in animals to stimuli varying within a single dimension. *Psychological Review, 44,* 430-444.

Spence, K. W. (1952). The nature of the response in discrimination learning. *Psychological Review, 59,* 89-93.

Spiker, C. C. (1956a). Experiments with children on the hypotheses of acquired distinctiveness and equivalence of cues. *Child Development, 27,* 253-263.

Spiker, C. C. (1956b). Effects of stimulus similarity on discrimination learning. *Journal of Experimental Psychology, 51,* 393-395.

Spiker, C. C. (1956c). The effects of number of reinforcements on the strength of a generalized instrumental response. *Child Development, 27,* 37-44.

Spiker, C. C. (1956d). The stimulus generalization gradient as a function of the intensity of stimulus lights. *Child Development, 27,* 85-98.

Spiker, C. C. (1956e). Stimulus pretraining and subsequent performance in the delayed reaction experiment. *Journal of Experimental Psychology, 52,* 107-111.

Spiker, C. C. (1959). Performance on a difficult discrimination following pretraining with distinctive stimuli. *Child Development, 30,* 513-521.

Spiker, C. C. (1960a). Research methods in children's learning. In P. H. Mussen (Ed.), *Handbook of research methods in child development* (pp. 374-420). New York: Wiley.

Spiker, C. C. (1960b). Associative transfer in verbal paired-associated learning. *Child Development, 31,* 73-87.

Spiker, C. C. (1963a). Verbal factors in the discrimination learning of children. In J. C. Wright & J. Kagan (Eds.), *Basic cognitive processes in children* (Monographs of the SRCD, Vol. 28, No. 2, pp. 53-71).

Spiker, C. C. (1963b). The hypothesis of stimulus interaction and an explanation of stimulus compounding. In L. P. Lipsitt & C. C. Spiker (Eds.), *Advances in child development and behavior* (Vol. 1, pp. 233-264). New York: Academic Press.

Spiker, C. C. (1970). An extension of Hull-Spence discrimination learning theory. *Psychological Review, 77,* 496-515.

Spiker, C. C. (1971). Application of Hull-Spence theory to the discrimination learning of children. In H. W. Reese (Ed.), *Advances in child development and behavior* (Vol. 6, pp. 99-152). New York: Academic Press.

Spiker, C. C. (1973). *The contemporary scope of Spence's 1936-37 discrimination learning theory.* Paper read at Conference on Discrimination Learning Models, Rockefeller University, New York City.

Spiker, C. C. (1977a). The estimation of parameters from systems of nonlinear questions. *Journal Supplement Abstract Service, 7,* 64 (28 pages).

Spiker, C. C. (1977b). Behaviorism, cognitive psychology, and the active organism. In H. Datan

& H. W. Reese (Eds.), *Life-span developmental psychology: Dialectical perspectives on experimental research.* New York: Academic Press.

Spiker, C. C., & Cantor, J. H. (1973). Applications of Hull-Spence theory to the transfer of discrimination learning in children. In H. W. Reese (Ed.), *Advances in child development and behavior* (Vol. 8, pp. 223–288). New York: Academic Press.

Spiker, C. C., & Cantor, J. H. (1977). Introtacts as predictors of discrimination performance in kindergarten children. *Journal of Experimental Child Psychology, 23,* 520–538.

Spiker, C. C., & Cantor, J. H. (1979a). The Kendler levels-of-functioning theory: Comments and an alternative schema. In H. W. Reese & L. P. Lipsitt (Eds.), *Advances in child development and behavior* (Vol. 13, pp. 119–135). New York: Academic Press.

Spiker, C. C., & Cantor, J. H. (1979b). Factors affecting hypothesis testing in kindergarten children. *Journal of Experimental Child Psychology, 28,* 230–248.

Spiker, C. C., & Cantor, J. H. (1980) The effects of stimulus type, training, and chronological age on children's identification and recoding of multidimensional stimuli. *Journal of Experimental Child Psychology, 30,* 144–158.

Spiker, C. C., & Cantor, J. H. (1982). Cognitive strategies in the discrimination learning of young children. In D. K. Routh (Ed.), *Learning, speech and the complex effects of punishment.* New York: Plenum.

Spiker, C. C., & Cantor, J. H. (1983a). Components in the hypothesis-testing strategies of young children. In T. Tighe & B. E. Shepp (Eds.), *Interactional analyses: Perception, cognition, and development.* Hillsdale, NJ; Lawrence Erlbaum Associates.

Spiker, C. C., & Cantor, J. H. (1983b). The dimensional analysis by children of multidimensional stimuli. *Bulletin for the Psychonomic Society, 21,* 449–452.

Spiker, C. C., Cantor, J. H., & Klouda, G. V. (1985). The effect of pretraining and feedback on the reasoning of young children. *Journal of Experimental Child Psychology, 39,* 381–395.

Spiker, C. C., Croll, W. L., & Miller, A. A. (1972). The effects of verbal pretraining on the multidimensional generalization behavior of children. *Journal of Experimental Child Psychology, 13,* 558–572.

Spiker, C. C., & Holton, R. B. (1958). Associative interference in motor paired-associate learning as a function of amount of first-task practice. *Journal of Experimental Psychology, 56,* 123–132.

Spiker, C. C., & Lubker, B. J. (1964). Experimental tests of the hypothesis of stimulus interaction. *Journal of Experimental Child Psychology, 1,* 256–268.

Spiker, C. C., & Lubker, B. J. (1965). The relative difficulty for children of the successive and simultaneous discrimination problems. *Child Development, 36,* 1091–1101.

Spiker, C. C., & McCandless, B. R. (1954). The concept of intelligence and the philosophy of science. *Psychological Review, 61,* 255–266.

Spiker, C. C., & Norcross, K. J. (1962). Effects of previously acquired stimulus names on discrimination performance. *Child Development, 33,* 859–864.

Spiker, C. C., & White, S. H. (1959). Differential conditioning by children as a function of effort required in the task. *Child Development, 30,* 1–7.

Tempone, V. J. (1965). Stimulus generalization as a function of mental age. *Child Development, 36,* 229–236.

Tighe, L. S., & Tighe, T. J. (1966). Discrimination learning: Two views in historical perspective. *Psychological Bulletin, 66,* 353–370.

Tighe, T. J., & Tighe, L. S. (1972). Stimulus control in children's learning. In A. D. Pick (Ed.), *Minnesota symposium on child development* (Vol. 6, pp. 128–157). Minneapolis: University of Minnesota.

White, S. H. (1958). Generalization of an instrumental response with variation in two attributes of the CS. *Journal of Experimental Psychology, 56,* 339–343.

White, B. N., & Spiker, C. C. (1960). The effect of stimulus similarity on amount of cue-position patterning in discrimination learning problems. *Journal of Experimental Psychology, 59,* 131–136.

White, S. H., & Spiker, C. C. (1960). The effect of a variable conditioned stimulus upon the generalization of an instrumental response. *Child Development, 31,* 313–319.

White, S. H., Spiker, C. C., & Holton, R. B. (1960). Associative transfer as shown by response speeds in motor paired-associate learning. *Child Development, 31,* 609–616.

Zeaman, D., & House, B. J. (1963). The role of attention in retardate discrimination learning. In N. R. Ellis (Ed.), *Handbook of mental deficiency.* New York: McGraw-Hill.

Zeaman, D., & House, B. J. (1974). Interpretations of developmental trends in discriminative transfer effects. In A. D. Pick (Ed.), *Minnesota symposia on child development* (Vol. 8). Minneapolis: University of Minnesota Press.

4

Toward Understanding
the Hedonic Nature
of Infancy

Lewis P. Lipsitt
Department of Psychology
and
Child Study Center
Brown University

PROLOGUE

General agreement exists today among infant development scholars, or so it seems to me, that the typical human neonate emerges into the extrauterine world with all systems functioning, with a capacity for self-regulating its rudimentary body systems, and even with a modicum of learning ability. This is particularly likely if the life and intrauterine milieu of the fetus involves no physical stigmata, and when the birth occurs under conditions of no special risk. When I began studying the development and behavior of infants almost 30 years ago, fresh out of my University of Iowa training, such assertions as these could not be made with much confidence.

Human lore keeps insisting that there is nothing new under the sun. Ritual denigrations of the child psychologist's talents, moreover, often press the point that Grandmother knew best. The fact is, however, that we have a much better understanding today than we did a quarter of a century ago about the nature of infancy. Our knowledge today of the precursors of a secure and satisfying infancy, on the one hand, and of the ways in which infant behavior and development can become destabilized, on the other, far exceeds the common sense even of today's grandmothers, let alone those of yore. We now have an empirical data base of much greater scope for our factual assertions about the significance of events in early life, and about the sensory, learning, and cognitive capacities of infants (Lipsitt & Werner, 1981; Werner & Lipsitt, 1981). This is critical for an understanding of the ways in which normal children come to assimilate information from the environment, and an appreciation of how they cope with life stresses

(Lipsitt, 1983). It is important also for comprehending that high-risk children can in fact avoid the adverse developmental outcomes that their early vulnerability might have predicted (Garmezy & Rutter, 1983). We had little of this 25 years ago.

How did we get so smart so fast? I would conjecture that a gradual but positively accelerating accretion of knowledge has taken place over the past quarter-century about the ways in which infants and children assimilate information from their surroundings, organize this information, and retain and utilize it in further encounters with environmental events. This scientific knowledge has helped to reveal the sensory, learning, and memorial capacities of infants in a way that these had not been appreciated previously. One must acknowledge also, as an aside, that the field of child development has been somewhat better comprehended by the public and the media over the past two decades, even if this has not been reflected in funding opportunities for relevant research. For reasons that perhaps will be better understood by future historians, but are probably related to the worldly successes of the biological, chemical, and physical sciences, people have come to demand more of the developmental scientist. Rising to the expectation, developmental scientists have in turn had more to say about the practical implications of their behavioral research during this period. This has promoted the tendency, perhaps already inherent in normal parenting, for families to capitalize on the newly publicized sensory capacities and curiosities of very young children and to try pushing their children's cognitive resources to their intellectual frontiers. Parents sometimes describe their intentions in words just like these!

We have a clearer view today of the ways in which infant behavior and development can be explored. Child developmentalists are now more keenly aware, more self-conscious, than ever before as to how their investigative methods are inextricably interwoven with the "facts." Looked at one way, Johnny may be seen as "securely attached," while looked at somewhat differently (for example, with a different focus of observation or using an alternate operational definition), Johnny may be seen as quite detached. Neither observation is necessarily incorrect or unsupportable.

Like it or not and circumstantial as this may appear, our rather poor reputation in predicting outcomes from early experiences or developmental assessments must be attributed at least in part to the shifting sands on which so many developmental constructs are built. Developmental psychologists have perhaps lived too comfortably with concepts like the "invulnerable child," that wonder of human nature who from our understanding of the importance of early adversity should be a poorly adjusted individual, but turns out to be either unaffected by the stresses of early childhood or actually tempered by them—"vulnerable but invincible" (Werner & Smith, 1982). As a descriptive assertion about certain facts of development, the notion has the same sloe-eyed beauty as Freud's concept of "reaction formation," which allows us to sneak apologies into our explanatory network for the developmental surprise, itself a euphemism for our failure to predict and understand. As it turns out, the very young infant is hardly ever as surprising as older children. This may be, of course, because they do not have as much of a history to violate. Regardless, the neonate gives us an interesting and scientifically fruitful position from which to observe the origins of life trajectories.

An Approach to the Study of Infant Behavior

Newborns behave in rather interesting ways that we might not notice easily without importing a systematic empirical approach into the nursery. Their surprisingly orderly behavior has important implications for understanding the nature of infancy and makes especially good sense, moreover, when regarded in the light of both Darwinian and modern behavior theory (Rovee-Collier & Lipsitt, 1982).

I will report here on some ways in which newborns alter one aspect of their instrumental behavior, sucking, dependent on the incentive value of the fluid they receive contingent upon that behavior. This self-regulatory, psychomotor activity seems to enhance the pleasures of sensation. In turn, the hedonic sensations underlying the behavior are apparently correlated with the so-called reinforcing value of the contingent stimulation and thus provide the "satisfying states of affairs" that Thorndike (1911) argued are required for learning to occur. I want to make the suggestion that a variety of reinforcing conditions or incentives, like the sweet taste, are essentially collapsible in that they have common quantitative effects upon behavioral outcomes. A situation thus exists to permit theoretical organization of certain complexities of neonatal behavior, a step that is aided by appropriating conceptualizations of traditional behavior theory relating to incentive-motivational processes (e.g., Spence, 1956).

Infant Studies at Brown University

Immediately upon leaving the doctoral training program in child psychology at the University of Iowa, I took a position as Instructor of Psychology at Brown University. Harold Schlosberg, Chairman of the Department of Psychology at Brown, had explained to me, prior to my acceptance of the position, that the department had decided to expand its rigorous experimental psychology graduate training program to include experimental child psychology. The metamorphosis of the department was prompted by and would capitalize upon the advent of a large-scale research program in which Brown University would become one of 12 research centers across the country to collect longitudinal data from birth to 7 years of age on about 50,000 children in all. This so-called National Collaborative Perinatal Project would have as its mandated objectives the study of the causes of cerebral palsy, mental retardation, and other neurological disorders. One obligation I would have, in return for partial support of my academic salary from this project, would be to help in the organization of the psychological features of this study as it got underway at Brown. At the same time, it was hoped that through the new community affiliations that this "biomedical out-reach" program would bring to Brown, particularly with a cooperative maternity hospital, the Department of Psychology could develop laboratory resources to enable the department to undertake a serious effort in the training of child psychology researchers. There was no requirement that I specialize in infancy. Indeed I had had little training in infant behavior and development per se at Iowa. What I did have was an excellent background in research methods with children, owing in large part to my studies with Charles Spiker. I thought, perhaps riding too high on youth and naivete, that this made me quite adept at (or at least adaptable to) a variety of research situations. Harold Schlosberg had great distinction in the field of experimental psychology, and he was a renowned authority on conditioning processes. He had also had prior experience in the study of fetal behavior of cats, and had done research on the long-term effects of infantile frustration in rats. He believed in the importance of *development*. I told Harold of my desire to establish a sensory assessment and infant learning laboratory, especially to study newborns. He was more than pleased, and helped me greatly during the formative stages of my infant research program. The Iowa-Brown axis of my life was thus established, and I continued to benefit from all I had learned from Charlie Spiker. I think I still do.

Savoring the Sweet Taste

Over the next decade, much of the work of my laboratory at Women and Infants Hospital of Rhode Island, and also my research with older infants that was carried out in Brown's follow-up testing unit established for the National Collaborative Perinatal Project, was devoted to exploring the classical conditioning and operant learning capacities of children in the first year of life (Lipsitt, 1963, 1966; Lipsitt, Pederson, & DeLucia, 1966). By the end of that decade it was apparent, at least to my satisfaction, that normal, full-term infants are expert learners when the procedures implemented capitalize upon the organismic design of the child for survival, and maximize pleasant sensations (and, of course, avoidance of annoyance). This work has been thoroughly reviewed in Rovee-Collier and Lipsitt (1982). It is not my intent to dwell on it here except to indicate that my burgeoning fascination with the importance of hedonic factors in early childhood, which is still with me, took shape as I realized that appetitional and aversive behaviors are the stuff of which early human learning processes are made. Moreover, these approach and avoidance behavior systems are mediated by (1) pleasure, or simple satisfactions in their less extreme form, and (2) pain or, less extremely, irritation.

My transition to the study of incentive motivational aspects of early learning processes was facilitated by research that Trygg Engen and I, and our students, were then carrying out on the sense of smell in newborns (Engen & Lipsitt, 1965; Engen, Lipsitt, & Kaye, 1963). The panorama of infants' facial expressions, seen also by Steiner (1979), and particularly when observed in association with heart rate and respiratory changes, had a marked effect upon my appreciation of the hedonic "precocity" of babies. Soon we mounted a fairly systematic series of studies of taste responsivity in infants, which continues to this day. It is on an aspect of this work, which I believe one day will return us full circle to the closer study of the hedonic substrate underlying infantile learning processes, that I elaborate in my remaining space.

The human newborn is acutely responsive to minimal alterations in the chemical constituency of fluids on the tongue. Modern polygraphic and myographic recording of tongue movements and various parameters of sucking behavior now enables documentation of the fine discriminations that infants can make. We can now document subtle sucking changes that occur when the infant controls its own fluid intake. In real-life breastfeeding, an infant may suck slowly or quickly, may take more or fewer rest periods between sucking bursts, may invest less or more sucks per burst, all resulting in varying numbers of sucks over a several-minute interval. Such self-regulatory behavior can be studied in the laboratory under conditions in which the fluid the baby receives, suck by suck, is sweet, sweeter, or not sweet at all. The fluid can be arranged to be delivered in small drops or large.

We have used a sucking apparatus and a set of fluid wells with associated pumps, especially devised in our laboratory for the purpose, to record the infant's sucking behavior under conditions in which the presentation of the fluid is made contingent upon sucking behavior. The machinery is preset so that a suck of a particular minimal amplitude is required to trigger the pump to deliver a drop of fluid that is preset to be of a specific volume (e.g., .02 ml versus .04 ml) and, by preselecting which pump will be activated by sucking within a given period, of a given sweetness (e.g., 5% sucrose versus 15% sucrose). Because quite small drops of fluid are involved— though ample to trigger differential patterns of sucking behavior for different sweetnesses—the sucking behavior and taste discrimination of babies can be studied over a fairly long period of time without appreciably affecting ingestion. Under the aforementioned conditions, a newborn may suck for as long as a half hour without receiving as much as an ounce of fluid.

Newborns suck, and pattern their bursts and pauses, differently depending on whether fluid is delivered or not. Sucking on a blank nipple characteristically entails short bursts (for example, 6–8 sucks) of rapid sucking separated by relatively long pauses, for example, 15 seconds. If .02 ml drops of plain distilled water are now made to flow into the nipple, and to the infant's mouth contingent upon the same sucking behavior, the infant slows down its sucking within bursts, begins to invest more sucks per burst (e.g., 12–15), and now takes shorter and fewer rest periods between bursts. Moreover, if the baby is now allowed to receive 5% sucrose contingent upon its criterional sucking behavior, the bursts become still longer, the sucking rate within bursts becomes slower still, and the baby commences to take still fewer and shorter pauses. The pattern continues as we move the child to drops of the same size, but now of a 15% sucrose solution. Interestingly, with increasing incentive value of the fluid, defined in terms of the increasing concentrations of sucrose, the infant actually ends up sucking more times per minute even while sucking at slower rates within bursts. This is accomplished by taking shorter and fewer rests.

Interesting too is the fact that with increasing concentrations of the sweet fluid, at least up to a point (at about 15% sucrose), the continuously monitored heart rate, computer-read at the end of a testing session for each incentive condition separately and burst-by-burst within incentive conditions, reveals that the heart rate climbs progressively to higher levels. This set of effects was noted in one of our earliest studies of the phenomena (Lipsitt, 1974; Lipsitt, Reilly, Butcher, & Greenwood, 1976), has been routinely repeated since then, and occurs regardless of the order in which the incentive conditions are administered.

The enhanced heart rate phenomenon occurs whether we average rates throughout a recording period including the pauses, or utilize the beats just within sucking bursts. Moreover, it makes no difference if we control for burst length by utilizing, say, the first ten sucks of each burst only. The newborn's heart rate responds quickly to the changed sweetness of the fluid and, as it were, quickly seeks the rate appropriate for that incentive condition. The sucking rate within bursts becomes altered within just two or three sucks (about two sec). The whole process happens fast but visibly on the raw polygraph record as it peels from the machine. Visitors to the laboratory have often remarked that they realized from the research reports that the phenomenon is a striking one, but that they thought it must require much averaging of responses to document; they did not appreciate that it is easily seen in individual subjects. Newborn babies are indeed remarkably sensitive to certain kinds of stimulation from their environment. What has just been described, it should be noted, is most pronounced in essentially normal full-term babies, and the effects are in fact compromised in babies who are born at risk (Cowett, Lipsitt, Vohr, & Oh, 1978). It perhaps should not be so surprising to us that oral stimulation relating to nutrition and survival would be a successful candidate for special biological selection.

The data from these studies substantiate our supposition that a hedonic or "savoring process" is operative in the earliest days or even minutes of life. But the story is not finished. We have dealt only with one facet of the reinforcement value, or incentive efficacy, of the fluid. The pumps through which the infants self-administer the fluids in our laboratory setting are so constructed as to permit variations in the size of the drops that the babies can receive contingent upon criterion responses. Charles Crook therefore asked next whether the magnitude of the incentive fluid per suck would have any effect upon the patterns of sucking behavior seen (Crook, 1976, 1977; Crook & Lipsitt, 1976). He was able to document essential collapsibility of the sweetness and magnitude of the drop as joint determinants of the incentive value. Specifically, Crook found that with increasing size of the drops received contingent upon their criterion responses, newborns slow down their sucking behavior within bursts, take shorter and fewer rest periods between bursts, invest higher average numbers of sucks per burst, suck more times per minute, and have higher heart rates within bursts. The response parameters thus were shown by Crook to move consistently in the same directions for increasing magnitudes of the drops with sweetness held constant, as for increasing sweetness of the drops when magnitude of the drop is held constant.

It appears reasonable to conclude at this time that infants respond to qualities of the nutrients delivered contingent upon their own behavior, such that their behavior patterns are symbiotic with those of their caretakers, jointly optimizing the pleasures of sensation and enhancing ingestion of fluids that are more rather than less nutritious. The heart rate enhancement effect, like the "pleasant faces" that often accompany intake of sweet substances, may be regarded hypothetically as an aspect of the organic signaling system, conveying that the feeding process is proceeding well. That this interpretation does not strain credulity is suggested by the fact that frowns, tongue thrusts, and regurgitation of fluid characteristically convey to the caretaker that the feeding is *not* going well, and that some adjustment in the process is required. Common observation suggests that such adjustments, in those situations, usually do occur in normal mother-infant dyadic relations.

One further facet of the incentive reinforcement phenomenon in newborns relates to the differential efficacy of varying schedules of reinforcement (Bosack, 1973, based upon his doctoral dissertation, 1967). Of great interest is the fact that the so-called schedules of reinforcement (Skinner, 1938) work in about the same way on the baby's self-regulated sucking behavior as both the sweetness and magnitude of reinforcement, previously described. In one of the first manipulations of incentive motivational variables in my laboratory, Bosack varied the schedules of reinforcement for which the newborns sucked. Two experiments were conducted to compare sucking behavior under nutritive and non-nutritive (no-fluid) sucking conditions, using several fixed-ratio schedules of reinforcement. The findings were some of the first we had of the effects just described.

Bosack found, without benefit of the on-line computational procedures we use today, that babies while engaging in nutritive sucking (for .10 cc drops of 5% dextrose and distilled water solution) produced higher overall sucking rates but lower within-burst rates than when sucking for no fluid. Burst lengths were longer during nutritive than during no-fluid sucking, and fewer bursts occurred overall during nutritive sucking because the bursts were longer. For present purposes, however, the most important effect was that density of reinforcement when manipulated in terms of schedule produced effects consonant with those seen for sweetness and magnitude of reinforcement. For example, in one of his studies involving 50 newborns, 10 subjects received a drop of fluid for every three sucks, 10 every five, 10 every seven, 10 every nine, and 10 never. The subjects' sucking responses during these varying reinforcement schedule periods were compared with their behavior during a period of comparable length (5 min) immediately preceding. The results revealed an increasing rapidity of response within bursts from fixed ratio three (FR3) to FR5 to FR7 to FR9, and on to no-fluid, or no sweet-taste reinforcement at all. Thus, the thinner the reinforcement schedule, the more rapidly did the babies suck within bursts. The denser reinforcement schedules had effects like "sweeter" and "large-drop" reinforcement conditions in the aforementioned studies.

The other side of the hedonic coin, that representing aversive responses to ordinarily annoying stimuli, has been studied in this as well as other laboratories. Crook (1977) utilized the sensitivity of sucking parameters such as length of sucking burst to study the neonate's response to mildly aversive as well as pleasant stimuli. In order to study infants' responses to negatively hedonic substances, he modified our usual procedure of allowing the baby to suck and thereby self-regulate the amount of fluid received (an operant process). Instead, Crook administered three drops of either sweet or salty fluid one drop at a time, and recorded the length of the immediately subsequent sucking burst in response to these targeted stimulus conditions (e.g., a .05 Molar salt solution) in comparison with response to a neutral (control) stimulus such as the same magnitude drop of plain distilled water.

Our laboratory demonstrated in this way that while increasing concentrations of the sweet fluid yielded *longer* sucking bursts than to the distilled water administered on alternating control trials, increasing concentrations of salt produced *shorter* bursts relative to the plain water. Thus newborn infants can be seen as responding hedonically in both directions, which is to say that newborns both increase and decrease their ingestion-relevant behaviors depending upon the savory quality of the stimulus on the tongue. Crook's technique, like the one involving self-regulated intake of fluids, holds much promise for the careful study of the psychophysics of taste in infancy. Such psychophysical studies are important in and of themselves, but must also be regarded as a prerequisite for the eventual close comparison of the efficacy, in standard learning situations, of differentially reinforcing appetitive events.

In our most recent applications of this technique, it has been possible to characterize newborns in terms of their individual differences in "avidity." By adopting a standard procedure for assessing avidity, it is possible to obtain a characterization of each infant in terms of his or her "hedonic slopes" on several parameters of sucking and for the heart rate measure. This is accomplished by first allowing the baby to suck for 2 minutes, receiving no fluid at all, then for 2 minutes receiving .02 ml drops of plain fluid for each criterion suck, then 2 minutes of 5% sucrose, then the same for 15% sucrose, followed again by 2 minutes of no fluid. (Whether we average the first and last [no fluid] periods or analyze only the first four periods, leaving off the final no-fluid period, the results are essentially the same.) The four incentive conditions form the base for the hedonic slopes. For example, an infant may suck 15 times in 2 minutes for no fluid, 25 times for water, 40 times for 5% sucrose, and 65 times for 15% sucrose. By the method of least squares, a slope may be fit to the points, and this slope then characterizes the infant for that parameter and these incentives at this time.

We look forward to these quantitative characterizations of newborns enabling the study of the possibly enduring effects of early behavioral dispositions (like levels of neonatal avidity), and of the interactive effects of these early characterizations with later experiences to jointly determine ultimate developmental outcomes. People like us working in infant laboratories feel that we are at the very beginning of this process, and that it is a very exciting time in the history of the child development field in which to be living. Recently we have made a modest finding, for example, that those children with the steepest hedonic slopes as newborns are more likely than their less avid peers to be securely attached to their mothers at one year of age, utilizing the Ainsworth Strange Situation assessment technique (Lipsitt, Pierce, Weinreich, & Cheng, in preparation). We have the idea and lots of confidence that ultimately the mysteries of infant behavior and development will yield to inventive exploration, experimental analysis, and thoughtful design. Ultimately, knowledge of infants' capacities for the appreciation of the pleasures and annoyances of sensation should provide much-needed insight into the mechanisms and processes by which stimuli, particularly those known (at least since Thorndike) as creating a "pleasant state of affairs" and delivered contingent upon the behavior of the learning organism, become so powerfully important in determining subsequent behavior.

The Infant Learner

Much of early human behavior, like that of other mammals, is endogenously generated. These unconditioned responses, gifts of the species, are prewired to specific stimulus features of the environment and have in all likelihood evolved in connection with the promotion of survival—of the species and of persons. Thus, touches near the corner of the mouth elicit rooting reflexes in the newborn. Similarly, fluid at the back of the tongue produces mandatory swallowing behavior. Many of the stimuli that impel specific behaviors go well beyond simple stimulus-response relations. A given stimulus may propel the organism into a pattern of behavior much larger in scope than the initiating stimulus-response connection. One response leads to another until the entire series of behaviors, like a row of dominoes, plays itself out. The complex oral activity of the newborn whose lips are lightly stimulated serves as a model. The lips open, the head turns toward the stimulus and bears down on any protruding object, the lips create a pressure seal around that object, sucking behavior occurs, and any fluid generated is moved by tongue action to the rear of the buccal cavity where swallowing is stimulated. Similarly, pressure on the soles of the newborn's feet instigates not just withdrawal of the stimulated limb, but an alternating pattern of stepping responses subcortically mediated by a constellation of (presumably) mandated stimulus-response connections.

Some aversive reactions have the same quality suggestive of an underlying, compelling congenital structure. For example, the occurrence of respiratory occlusion, or even the mere threat of smothering, will generate in intact newborns a series of behaviors likened by ethologists to the fixed-action behavioral patterns of lower animals. The baby shakes its head from side to side, and then pulls its head backwards, seemingly in a well orchestrated effort to become free of the offending object that threatens the intake of air. If neither of these maneuvers has the effect of freeing the respiratory passages for breathing, the hands and arms, if not restrained, rise to the gradually vasodilating face. The infant comes to look increasingly angry, hand swiping occurs in front of the face, and eventually the baby bursts forth with a cry that appears to be the fail-safe culmination of a critical objection to the potentially life-threatening environment.

These are the types of environmental challenges that are the most likely to produce rapid and lasting learning. Flight from offensive stimulation, and the assurance through effective appetitional maneuvers guaranteeing sustenance, go to the heart of survival. It can be noted, in this connection, that such life situations, both of an approach and of an avoidant nature, typically carry with them a hedonic "overload." Emotional reactivity usually runs high in respiratory-threat situations and, indeed, in voracious eating episodes. It may be suggested, therefore, that we are not likely to succeed in understanding well the psychobiological significance of these infantile behavior patterns without dealing *concurrently* with their reflexive or habitual aspects, on one hand, and their affective components, on the other. In this view, the cognitive and emotional structures can hardly be effectively separated. Each seems to derive its impetus at least in part from the other. Hedonic concomitants may provide the incentive motivation required to perpetuate vital congenital behavior patterns of infants, assuring that these fixed action patterns will indeed "play themselves out" to the point of removing the risks to survival. In this way the pleasures of sensation may be seen as accomplices, helping to assure the occurrence of prosurvival behaviors. Multiple dimensions of the incentive-granting environment, moreover, seem to share the mission, or "overdetermine" the consequence, helping humans as a matter of organic economy to survive and, in the process, to enjoy themselves.

ACKNOWLEDGMENTS

The newborn research on which this contribution is based was supported from time to time by the W. T. Grant Foundation, the March of Dimes Birth Defects Foundation, the Harris Foundation, the MacArthur Foundation, the United States Public Health Service, and Brown University. I am indebted to my long-time research associate in this work, Bernice M. Reilly, R.N., and to Women and Infants Hospital of Rhode Island where these studies were carried out. Helen Maddock Haeseler, Administrative Assistant for the Child Study Center, and my secretary, has been of inestimable assistance over a 25-year period.

REFERENCES

Bosack, T. N. (1973). Effects of fluid delivery on the sucking response of the human newborn. *Journal of Experimental Child Psychology, 15,* 77–85. (Based on doctoral dissertation, Brown University, Univ. Microfilms [Ann Arbor, MI], 1967, No. 68-1441.)

Crook, C. K. (1976). Neonatal sucking: Effects of quantity of the response-contingent fluid upon sucking rhythm and heart rate. *Journal of Experimental Child Psychology, 21,* 539–548.

Crook, C. K. (1977). Taste and the temporal organization of neonatal sucking. In J. M. Weiffenbach (Ed.), *Taste and Development: The Genesis of Sweet Preference.* DHEW Publication No. (NIH) 77-1068, U.S. Dept. of HEW, NIH, pp. 146–160.

Crook, C. K. & Lipsitt, L. P. (1976). Neonatal nutritive sucking: Effects of taste stimulation upon sucking rhythm and heart rate. *Child Development, 47*, 518–522.

Cowett, R. M., Lipsitt, L. P., Vohr, B. and Oh, W. (1978). Aberrations in sucking behaviour in the low birth weight infant. *Developmental Medicine and Child Neurology, 20*, 701–709.

Engen, T. & Lipsitt, L. P. (1965). Decrement and recovery of responses to olfactory stimuli in the human neonate. *Journal of Comparative and Physiological Psychology, 59*, 312–316.

Engen, T., Lipsitt, L. P. & Kaye, H. (1963). Olfactory responses and adaptation in the human neonate. *Journal of Comparative and Physiological Psychology, 56*, 73–77.

Garmezy, N. & Rutter, M. (Eds.) (1983). *Stress, Coping, and Development in Children.* New York: McGraw Hill.

Kobre, K. R. & Lipsitt, L. P. (1972). A negative contrast effect in newborns. *Journal of Experimental Child Psychology, 14*, 81–91.

Lipsitt, L. P. (1963). Learning in the first year of life. In L. P. Lipsitt & C. C. Spiker (Eds.), *Advances in Child Development and Behavior,* Vol. 1, New York: Academic Press.

Lipsitt, L. P. (1966). Learning processes of human newborns. *Merrill-Palmer Quarterly, 12*, 45–71.

Lipsitt, L. P. (1974). The synchrony of respiration, heartrate and sucking behavior in the newborn. In *Mead Johnson Symposium on Perinatal and Developmental Medicine: Biological and Clinical Aspects of Brain Development. 6*, 67–72.

Lipsitt, L. P. (1977). Taste in human neonates: Its effects on sucking and heart rate. In J. M. Weiffenbach (Ed.), *Taste and Development: The Genesis of Sweet Preference.* DHEW Publication No. (NIH) 77-1068, US Dept of HEW, NIH.

Lipsitt, L. P. (1983). Stress in infancy: Toward understanding the origins of coping behavior. In N. Garmezy & M. Rutter (Eds.), *Stress, coping, and development in children.* New York: McGraw-Hill.

Lipsitt, L. P. & Werner, J. S. (1981). The infancy of learning processes. In E. S. Gollin (Ed.), *Developmental plasticity.* New York: Academic Press.

Lipsitt, L. P., Pederson, L. J. & DeLucia, C. A. (1966). Conjugate reinforcement of operant responding in infants. *Psychonomic Science, 4*, 67–68.

Lipsitt, L. P., Pierce, S., Weinreich, G., & Cheng, G. Continuity from neonatal avidity assessments to 12-month measures of attachment. In preparation.

Lipsitt, L. P., Reilly, B. M., Butcher, M. J., and Greenwood, M. M. (1976). The stability and inter-relationships of newborn sucking and heart rate. *Developmental Psychobiology, 9*, 305–310.

Meltzoff, A. N. & Moore, M. K. (1977). Imitation of facial and manual gestures by human neonates. *Science, 198*, 75–78.

Meltzoff, A. N. & Moore, M. K. (1983). Newborn infants imitate adult facial gestures. *Child Development, 54*, 702–709.

Pfaffmann, C. (1960). The pleasures of sensation. *Psychological Review, 67*, 253–268.

Rovee-Collier, C. & Lipsitt, L. P. (1982). Learning, adaptation, and memory in the newborn. In P. Stratton (Ed.), *Psychobiology of the human newborn.* Chichester, England: Wiley.

Skinner, B. F. (1938). *The behavior of organisms: an experimental analysis.* New York: Appleton-Century-Crofts.

Spence, K. W. (1956). *Behavior theory and conditioning.* New Haven: Yale University Press.

Steiner, J. E. (1979). Human facial expressions in response to taste and smell stimulation. In H. W. Reese & L. P. Lipsitt (Eds.), *Advances in Child Development and Behavior,* Vol. 13, New York: Academic Press.

Thorndike, E. L. (1911). *Animal intelligence.* New York: Macmillan.

Werner, E. E. & Smith, R. S. (1982). *Vulnerable but invincible: A longitudinal study of resilient children and youth.* New York: McGraw-Hill.

Werner, J. S. & Lipsitt, L. P. (1981). The infancy of human sensory processes. In E. S. Gollin (Ed.), *Developmental plasticity.* New York: Academic Press.

5 Metaphor: A Portal for Viewing the Child's Mind

David S. Palermo
The Pennsylvania State University

The focus of this chapter is upon the usefulness of metaphor in language as a substantive problem for exploring theoretical concerns about the child's developing mind. Before discussing the issues per se, however, I would like to place those issues in a historical context, for the ideas to follow have developed over a long period of time. In fact, the foundation for these ideas surely was established in the courses I took as a graduate student with Charlie Spiker. Whereas he may have no sympathy with the particular theory presented, one thing he instills in all of his students is the importance of theory to the scientific endeavor. Theory, he taught, serves to specify the interesting questions, organize the research to be done, and give meaning to the data observed. Charlie, and the students who have taken his courses, will recognize the threads of his teaching woven in the fabric of what follows regardless of whether they agree or disagree with the tenets proposed.

I have been interested in language acquisition since I was a graduate student in the Iowa Child Welfare Research Station at the University of Iowa back in the early 1950s. In those days when the experimental child psychology movement was just getting off the ground under the leadership of Boyd McCandless, Al Castaneda, and Charlie Spiker, it was not exactly heretical to raise questions about language and its acquisition, but such questions led to shoulder shrugs, methodological discussions, and suggestions that it was too soon to approach such complicated issues when we were not clear on the variables influencing the acquisition of much simpler forms of behavior. Serial and paired-associate learning were as close as researchers got to language in those days, and the equipment used for that research was not easily adapted to children. Because these obstacles appeared to be insurmountable at the time, I did my dissertation on a different topic!

A few years later, in collaboration with James J. Jenkins, I began to approach the problem of language through the medium of word associations. Our research eventually led us to formulate a theoretical scheme to account for the processes of language acquisition (Jenkins & Palermo, 1964). The mediation model we proposed, created within the paradigmatic view of Behaviorism, was presented in 1961 at a conference attended by, among others, Chomsky (Bellugi & Brown, 1964). The fallout of the intense confrontation between some of us, mostly psychologists, and Chomsky and his colleagues, who were operating within a different paradigmatic world view (cf. Kuhn, 1970), led at least some of us to go home and find out what the new paradigm was all about. As a result, Jenkins and I both changed our paradigmatic views. In the ensuing years I have focused my efforts on understanding how the child comes to understand and produce meaningful linguistic utterances. Initially, my research was conceived within the frame-work of feature theory (e.g., Katz, 1972). In those days, the acquisition of meaning was conceptualized as the accretion of features as opposed to the acquisition of wholistic concepts. It was assumed that the child discovered the meanings of words by gradually acquiring the hierarchically related set of features, or primitive meaning elements, which were required to know the complete meaning. Failure of the child to distinguish the meanings of two words such as "more" and "less," for example, was attributable to the failure of the child to have acquired the single additional feature indicating that "less" refers to the negative pole of extent to which "more" does not refer (H. Clark, 1970).

Feature theory, as well as the various revisions of that theory (e.g., E. Clark, 1974), has stimulated a great deal of research, but the theory has never struck an intuitive chord with me. In support of my intuitive discomfort, there has now accumulated a significant body of research that fails to yield data in line with predictions from the theory (cf. Richards, 1979). The most convincing evidence for me that the feature theory failed to meet the empirical test was a study Holland and I conducted (Holland & Palermo, 1975) in which we devised a very complicated and graded series of steps that we thought would teach preschool age children the meaning of the word "less." As it turned out, the training required only that we tell each child that given two amounts of clay, for example, the big one had more and the little one less. With that information, there was no question we could ask the children about less that was problematic for them. In short, the children knew the concept and only needed to know the word used to express that concept.

Given that the child has many concepts and only needs to learn the words to express the known concepts, the feature theory seems superfluous.

Demonstrations that the same word appears to be understood in some contexts but not in others (cf. Kuczaj & Maratsos, 1975) adds to the inadequacies of feature theory. Moreover, it is clear that a list of features without some principled organization of those features does not provide the meaning of any word or the concept for which it stands (cf. Armstrong, Gleitman, & Gleitman, 1983; Palermo, 1978a). For example, a list of the parts of which a car is composed does not provide the meaning for the word car. Consider also the logical argument that in order to know from what to abstract the features, one must already know the whole that feature theory was designed to explain, and interest in feature theory as an account of the developmental process must evaporate (cf. Nelson, 1974). Although most persons now agree that feature theory cannot provide a satisfactory account of the processes of semantic development, criticism of the theory should not be misconstrued. Analyses of wholes into features or parts is clearly something of which the child's mind is capable, although equally clearly the child does not create the whole from the parts or features.

If the wholistic concept comes first, as I am suggesting, then we are dealing with an abstraction at the concept level rather than at the feature level. Instead of asking questions about what features comprise the meaning of a word and how they are acquired, we need to ask questions about what objects, events, and relations in the world are subsumed under particular concepts and how the child acquires those concepts and the names for them. Furthermore, we need to be concerned with the observation that all particular objects or events subsumed under a concept are not equally representative of that concept (Rosch, 1975). Thus, a child with the concept "bird," for example, will be able to classify and subsequently learn the names for robin and emu. The child is likely, however, to learn the name for robin earlier and more quickly than the name for emu because the robin is a better or more prototypic exemplar of the concept "bird" than is emu. The emphasis upon abstract conceptualization of meaning and its relation to the acquisition of meaning as well as my version of prototype theory was at the heart of earlier versions of the theory I am proposing here (e.g., Palermo, 1978a,b). The rest of this chapter continues the formulation of the theoretical position that has been evolving since those earlier versions.

The story begins with an interest I have developed in metaphor. That interest arose initially for me because metaphor is a particularly troublesome semantic form for feature theory to handle. But as one begins to get into the literature, it becomes clear that the problem is much broader than any attack on feature theory. Metaphor is an enigma that has received the attention of philosophers from Aristotle (cf. Cooper, 1932), to Cassirer (1946), and Black (1962); literary figures from Coleridge (Barfield, 1970) to Robert Frost (Cox & Lathem, 1949); linguists from Jakobson (1960) to

Lakoff (Lakoff & Johnson, 1980); and psychologists from Kurt Goldstein (1946) to Robert Sternberg (1977) to name but a very few of those over the centuries and in a variety of disciplines and theoretical camps who have become entangled in this fascinating form of linguistic expression for creative concepts. Thus, I was led to try to understand this form for conveying meaning, the implications it has for constructing a psychological theory of meaning, the manner in which meaning is acquired by the child and the relation of meaning to knowledge. The discussion that follows touches on each of these issues.

THE NATURE OF METAPHOR

Although there are a variety of syntactic forms for a metaphor, the prototypical metaphor takes the form "X is a Y"; e.g., "My love is a fever," "My soul is an enchanted boat," and "The ostrich is a giraffe-bird." The first is attributed to Shakespeare, the second to Shelley, and the third to a 2 or 3-year-old Russian child (Chukovsky, 1968). The first term of the metaphor, usually referred to as the tenor, is stated to be equivalent to or a member of the category specified by the second term, usually referred to as the vehicle after Richards (1936). The two diverse conceptual categories specified by tenor and vehicle interact and, thereby, give rise to a new meaning through an unstated ground or relation. It is, of course, the unstated ground integrating the two terms that is the riddle of metaphor. The issue concerns the manner in which one person can create an original or unique relationship between two disparate concepts and, without stating the relationship explicitly, communicate that relationship or meaning to another person. There is no surface structure hint in a metaphor as to the underlying meaning that is conveyed by bringing together the two domains joined to form the metaphoric meaning.

One of the interesting things about metaphor in this context is that most metaphors are clearly and obviously false, at least on any so-called literal interpretation of the sentence. There is no literal sense in which love is a fever or soul is a boat, enchanted or otherwise. Notice, however, that sentences such as "My zebra is a horse" or "Porpoises are fish" are not taken as metaphors but merely as false statements. One considers a person who utters such statements to have made an error, not to have created a metaphor. Thus, metaphors are often literally false, but they are not interpreted as false. A metaphor, however, need not be false and may be both literally true and metaphorically meaningful as in "He is the heavy one in the group," referring to the overweight intellectual in the group.

Metaphor is intriguing, therefore, for at least two reasons. First, it is often a false statement interpreted, as a rule, without attention to or awareness of the falsity. Second, there is nothing in the statement to suggest the ground that is the key to the meaning.

If we consider these matters from a developmental perspective, the mystery increases. In light of the characteristics of metaphor already considered, it would be our first guess that it would take a rather intellectually advanced child to comprehend or produce a metaphor. In fact, one of the earliest studies by Asch and Nerlove (1960) provided data that led them to the conclusion that children do not really understand metaphor until they are 11 or 12 years old. Those results fit very nicely with the age at which children are presumed to enter the formal operational stage within a Piagetian theoretical framework. Everything seemed to make sense until a resurgence of interest and research on children's comprehension and production of metaphor that began about 15 years after the Asch and Nerlove study. That research suggested that preschool children produce a large number of spontaneous metaphors (Billow, 1981; Chukovsky, 1968), and more recent research indicates that preschool children also comprehend metaphors presented to them (Broderick, 1983; Vosniadou, Ortony, Reynolds, & Wilson, 1984). In addition, Wagner, Winner, Cicchetti, and Gardner (1981) published a paper providing data that they interpret as demonstrating metaphorical responding in infants before language is available. The infants matched, for example, a rising auditory stimulus with a visually presented arrow pointing upward and a descending auditory stimulus with a downward pointing arrow.

These developmental data are not easily reconciled with the rather abstract conception we have of the poetic metaphor. It does not seem to me, however, that there is any basic difference between a child's observation that she is "barefoot all over," that the husband of a grasshopper is a "daddy hopper," or that a mint candy creates a draft in the mouth, and Shelley's "my soul is an enchanted boat" or Keats' "love is a dressed up doll." The latter are about more abstract topics, perhaps, but the nature of the expressions is the same. Furthermore, as Leondar (1975) has pointed out, the very teaching of word meanings to young children is often by metaphor. To use her example, suppose a child knows the category daddy and the category doggie. The child never confuses the two, but one day the child's parent says that the child's doggie is a daddy. As Leondar (1975) points out, "Like any vigorous metaphor, the assertion will appear to be arrant nonsense . . . The metaphor, then, lures [the child] to seek the points of connection between fathers and dogs in his effort to make sense of apparent nonsense . . . in the ordinary deployment of the language system . . . metaphor can serve as the agent of discovery" (p. 278-279). In short, the data suggest a reconceptualization of metaphor or of children that takes into account that young children do produce creative metaphors as well as comprehend at least some of those created by others. We need a framework that can bring these observations together under a single theoretical umbrella.

In reflecting upon this matter I have focused on two key aspects of the problem. The first has to do with the ambiguity of metaphor, and the second relates to the changing ability of the child to create and comprehend metaphors of increasing degrees of abstractness or complexity.

AMBIGUITY OF MEANING

The phenomenon of ambiguity, it seems to me, is of particular importance to psychology, and yet it has been generally ignored in most theoretical efforts of our colleagues, although some have proposed the theoretical apparatus to deal with the problem. It seems obvious that any metaphor is an ambiguous statement. There are multiple meanings that one may give to a metaphor. In fact, some literary analysts spend a lifetime trying to puzzle out the metaphoric meanings of an author.

Ambiguity of meaning is, of course, not limited to metaphor. We find ambiguity of meaning in perception as, for example, in the Nekker cube, the Ames rooms, the vase-face pictures, and a variety of other perceptual phenomena. Clinical psychologists use ambiguity as a tool of the trade in projective tests. Psycholinguists talk about the ambiguity of sentences such as "They fed her dog biscuits." Industrial psychologists focus on how the same events are interpreted in different ways by labor and management. Cross-cultural psychologists study differences in interpretation by different societies. And, of course, developmental psychologists spend most of their time trying to figure out why children interpret the world of events differently than adults, as well as the developmental processes that bring the child to the adult meanings.

These are, perhaps, the most obvious cases of ambiguity, but I would like to argue that ambiguity of meaning is everywhere. Whereas we often note some of these examples of ambiguity as curiosities that are interesting in their own right, we seldom try to show how they may be related. I argue here that ambiguity is not merely an unusual curiosity but, rather, ambiguity is a pervasive phenomenon. It is the rule, not the exception, and we must account for it in our theories. It seems to me that there is a common theme or key to understanding each of the instances of ambiguity, and that theme is *meaning*. In every instance, we are trying to account for the meaning people, or animals for that matter, give to the environmental events impinging on their sensorium. If you don't assign a meaning, you don't know how to behave with respect to those environmental events.

If we accept the proposition that the world of objects, events, and relations is indefinitely ambiguous with respect to meaning, there are several questions that arise immediately for any theory of meaning. Why do we seldom notice the ambiguity that is present? What are the constraints that limit the number of meanings that are applied to various objects, events, and relations? What leads to changes in meanings that are applied to the same objects, events, and relations? Any theory of meaning will have to deal with at least this set of questions.

I begin with the constraints on meaning, for that leads most directly to the other issues. Behavioristically oriented psychologists have looked for the constraints on meaning solely in the stimulus. The problem for behaviorists, of which everyone is well aware at this stage, is that they assumed that they could account for all meaning solely in terms of the stimuli impinging on the sensorium. In rejecting the behaviorist's position, however, we cannot ignore the stimulus altogether. The clue as to the importance of the stimuli and the resolution of this issue comes, I think, from Gibson (e.g., 1977). He argues that the environment has structure that consists, for example, of surfaces and layouts that provide affordances. The structure is assumed by Gibson to be real. The structure exists, however, in concert with the animal in the sense that a particular animal can take the structure into account only if it can perceive the structure. Meaning, on the other hand, is not in the structure but in the interpretation of the structure. The interpretation or meaning of the structure is not real and out there in the physical world, nor is it in the sensory system; rather it is constructed by the mind of the individual. To use Gibson's (1977) words, "an affordance consists of physical properties taken with reference to a certain animal . . . [it] is not like a value . . . nor is it like a meaning which is almost always supposed to depend upon the observer" (p. 69). Thus, the person, or knower, does not derive meaning from the world of objects and events, for there is no meaning out there in the stimuli to be picked up or received; rather, there is a knowable structure to which meanings may be given. The meaning that may be constructed is, of course, constrained by the actual structure in-so-far as it is delivered by the senses. There are, therefore, two types of constraints on meaning related to the stimuli: constraints imposed by the actual structure of the environment and constraints imposed by the sensory capacities of the knower. For most animals, the constraints are limited to the sensory capacities but, in the case of humans, we have extended our senses such that we can know more of the structure with a microscope, for example, than without it. Such extensions have allowed the construction of new meanings previously constrained, in this example, by lack of the sensory capacity for microscopic structure.

The issue of meaning, however, leads to questions for which answers are not manifest in stimuli and responses. Consideration of meaning requires us to deal with what has come to be called deep structure as opposed to surface structure. The idea of deep structure, as we all know, was introduced most recently to psychologists by Chomsky (1957) in connection with language. Deep structure refers to the underlying mental structure and associated processes from which the surface, or observable, manifestations of behavior are derived. Chomsky and Piaget, despite their other disagreements (Piattelli-Palmarini, 1980), agree that the study of the abstract deep structure, not the concrete observable surface structure, should be the focus of our science. Some cognitive theorists and some developmental theorists have accepted that presupposition and have attempted to develop theories about mind and not about behavior. This concern with mind or deep structure requires theories of how the mind creates and assigns meanings to stimuli, rather than how the mind obtains meaning from stimuli. In contrast to the traditional view, which assumes that meaning is out there in the environment to be picked up or learned, the assumption made by these cognitive and developmental theorists is that meaning is constructed by the person and attributed to the environment out there. Meaning is in the head of the organism and our task is to establish the processes by which it is created.

Looked at from this perspective, we can recognize that the world is meaningless as such. It has no inherent meaning to be discovered and only gains meaning insofar as the organism creates meanings for it. The world is, therefore, by definition ambiguous with respect to meaning. We are faced with the theoretical task of accounting for how the organism, be it human or otherwise, resolves the ambiguity or creates a meaning from the indefinitely large number of possible meanings that could be created. In addition, we need to account for why an organism fails to notice the ambiguity of the world or any particular stimulus in it.

A frequent answer to these questions about ambiguity is the argument that ambiguity is resolved for us by the context. We fail to note that a picture, a sentence, or any other stimulus is ambiguous because it occurs in a context that points to or determines a particular meaning among several possible meanings. Researchers who take this position typically try to demonstrate the different meanings that an event may have in different contexts. Having demonstrated that one context leads to one meaning of an ambiguous sentence or picture, for example, and that a different context leads to another meaning, they argue that the context disambiguates the ambiguous stimulus. Thus, a theory that takes into account the context will have the power to account for the meaning of any particular stimulus. Alas, this approach will not do. Aside from maintaining the presupposition, already rejected, that the meaning is out there formed by the stimulus, it fails to recognize that this approach leads naturally to an infinite regress. Because the context itself is an ambiguous stimulus, it must be disambiguated by its context and so on. One must, by definition, know the whole in order to understand the meaning of any part. There is no way, in principle, that something that is itself ambiguous can disambiguate another ambiguity.

Given this state of affairs, the meanings of stimuli must be related at some more abstract level that takes into account the whole as well as the parts. Because stimuli can have multiple meanings, and because the person who interprets those stimuli usually is aware of only one meaning, it seems clear that the disambiguation must come from the person attending to and giving meaning to the stimulus. In other words, the person must have some sort of abstract conceptual framework that gives the person a basis for making a judgment about the meaning of individual stimulus events in the environment. In short, each person must have, what I have called elsewhere (Palermo, 1982, 1983), a theory of the world, a theory that allows the person to interpret the world of stimuli.

AMBIGUITY AND A THEORY OF THE WORLD

A theory of the world, as I have described it, is a conceptual structure that is used to interpret events, objects and relations. It is no different, in principle, from a scientific theory that is constructed to interpret events, objects, and relations within a limited domain. Scientific theories are constructed in an attempt to make explicit the set of basic assumptions and deductively connected laws about the world. In what follows, I assume that the individual also constructs a theory of the world with an implicit set of basic assumptions from which lawful relationships are deduced. The challenge to psychologists is to make explicit the assumptions, deductive and inductive rules, and classificatory schemes used by the individual person to construct a theory of the world. We use our theory to make sense of our senses; to determine the particular meanings to be placed upon our empirical experiences that could have an indeterminate number of possible meanings. Thus, the world of stimuli with its particular structural characteristics is presented to us and our understanding of it, and our predictions about it are created through the conceptual framework I have labeled a theory of the world.

Assumptions of the Theory of a Theory of the World

If we accept the hypothesis that individuals interpret the events in their environment within the framework of their theory of the world, there are a number of assumptions related to and implications that follow from that position. The first basic assumption is that the world can be rendered coherent, regular, and predictable. We, as individuals, presuppose that the world is dependable and can be understood in a meaningful way, although we may not feel that we do understand all of it all of the time. We assume that, in principle, it is understandable despite our lack of knowledge or understanding at the moment. Thus, we assume a meaningful world and we construct the best account of it that we can. Various expectancy theories make this same type of assumption as does Grice (1975) in discussing conversational implicatures.

It is clear, however, that the meanings attributed to objects and events are constructed within a framework that cannot always be correct. Thus, a second assumption is that we interpret the environment in terms of the way it ought to be, according to our theory, and not necessarily as it is. Each of us makes certain assumptions about the world, and we predicate other aspects of our theory on those assumptions. We make decisions, judgments, form attitudes and beliefs, and act according to our theories of how we expect the world to be. Generally our theories are not contradicted and, therefore, we are in a position to assume a confirmation of our conception of how the world is and how it operates. On other occasions, however, we find that our theory is not confirmed. We are surprised by events we had not anticipated. A third assumption is that such failures to confirm our theory lead to consideration of additional variables and/or revision of the theory. There is, therefore, an implicit recognition that our theories (like all theories) are fallible and therefore need to be modified as we continue to use them.

Before moving to the obvious developmental implications of this theory, three additional points should be taken into consideration, although they are not elaborated here. First, we are not necessarily aware of our theories of the world. They are a part of our tacit knowledge system. Thus, we cannot articulate the rules we follow in, for example, riding a bicycle, creating a sentence, making a decision, or rendering a judgment. The systematic characteristics of our behaviors in these areas is taken as evidence of such rules, although some question has been raised about how rules could be applied with respect to judgments and values (Martin, 1982). Second, the theories we hold are not necessarily logically consistent across domains. It is, after all, a theory of the world, and even our renaissance scholars have not been able to take into account all of science, for example, in one theory. Because we cannot know all the background knowledge required for a consistently rational theory of the world, individuals develop schemata, or subtheories, over limited domains that may not be consistent with schemata in other domains. The overall theory of the world of an individual may either provide rules that allow for inconsistencies of schemata in different domains, or the schemata will be changed when inconsistencies among schemata become apparent to the person. Third, theories of the world are not limited to humans. Presumably, all animals have theories of the world that guide their behaviors. The relative importance of biology, learning, and culture upon the theories of different species will, of course, vary widely.

As an aside, it should be noted that the two points about conscious awareness and logical consistency distinguish the theories of individuals from theories in science. The latter are efforts (not always successful) to make accounts of particular domains both conscious, and therefore explicit, and logically consistent, at least within a scientific domain.

DEVELOPMENT OF AN INDIVIDUAL'S THEORY

Returning now to a consideration of the matters of fallibility and of modification in our theories, we are led to issues related to the origin and development of an individual's theory. It is assumed that each individual animal must have a theory of the world from at least the time of birth. The initial theory may be little more complicated than the one postulated by Lewin (1946), but it seems likely that the newborn child must have a natural implicit system of rules for classifying and responding to his or her world. Otherwise the world of the infant would be the blooming, buzzing confusion suggested by James. Furthermore, the infant's behavior with respect to the world would be in a similar random state. Neither of these conditions appears to be characteristic of the infant.

One of the most important results that has come from the upsurge of research on infants during the past 25 years is the increasing realization of the previously unsuspected cognitive capacities with which the infant enters the world. We have now become aware that the human infant can and does categorize the world of physically different objects into classes that are treated as if they were the same. For example, Molfese has demonstrated that newborn infants give differential cortical responses to language and nonlanguage acoustic signals (Molfese, Freeman, & Palermo, 1975) and to phonetic and nonphonetic speech stimuli (Molfese & Molfese, 1980). Not only are there cortical response differences, but there are now numerous replications in a variety of contexts of the study by Eimas, Siqueland, Jusczyk, and Vigorito (1971) demonstrating phonemic speech perception. These studies provide clear evidence of natural auditory classificatory capabilities in very young infants.

In the area of visual classification, the work of Day and his colleagues (Day & McKenzie, 1973; Schwartz & Day, 1979) has provided us with evidence that very young infants exhibit shape constancy and the ability to use relational information to recognize shape. As they suggest, infants have an innate ability to perceive shape. In the present context, these data support the classificatory cognitive capabilities of the infant. A cube, regardless of its orientation, is classified as the same cube and as different from other objects. Bornstein (1976) has demonstrated categorical perception of hue as well in infants.

In fact, a review of the literature indicates that there is accumulating data to suggest that there are very sophisticated perceptual categorization or classification abilities available to the infant from the time of birth (Acredolo & Hake, 1982). Thus, the infant from the very beginning is capable of differentiating many of the structural characteristics of the world. The meaning of those structural differences, at least as interpreted by adults, will come later. For example, the infant can differentiate /mama/ from /papa/ at a month of age but the meanings of those terms will not be acquired until several months later.

Some of the most exciting infant research I know of, however, has been reported by Leslie Cohen and his collaborators (e.g., Cohen & Younger, 1983). Their efforts have moved beyond what might be identified as perceptual research into an area in which the distinction between the classification of the structural aspects of the world and classification on the basis of meaning becomes less clear. They have used the habituation technique to study what might be called the ecologically more valid category of stuffed animal. They presented three groups of 7-month-old infants with either a picture of a single stuffed animal repeatedly for 10 trials, or 10 different stuffed animals over 10 trials, or 10 different toy objects over 10 trials. On the 11th trial all infants were presented with either a picture of a rattle not previously seen by any group or a new stuffed animal. The results revealed habituation by the group given repeated presentations of the same picture of a stuffed animal over the 10 trials, but dishabituation to a new stuffed animal and to the rattle. The group given the changing stuffed animals showed continued habituation through the 11th stuffed animal trial but dishabituated to the rattle. Finally, there was failure to exhibit habituation by the group presented different toys on each trial including both test stimuli. The results have been interpreted by Cohen to indicate that the infants were responding categorically. Seven-month-old infants formed a category of toy stuffed animals on the basis of being shown pictures of 10 different toy stuffed animals. Note that these data make it clear that the child remembers the pictures over the series of trials, forms an abstract class based upon the set of pictures, and the class, in turn, allows the infant to differentiate between toy stuffed animals and other objects such as a rattle. This experiment has been replicated several times, including once at Penn State (Garber, 1982), with other groups of infants and with other materials.

Subsequent work has demonstrated that by 10 months of age, infants can abstract a prototypical representation based upon experiencing exemplars of the category. In this case (Strauss, 1981), infants were presented with faces constructed from a police Identikit that allowed five variations in eye separation, nose width, nose length, and head length. After familiarization with 14 examples of faces, infants demonstrated less interest in a novel test face constructed from the middle values on all the dimensions than in a novel face constructed from other values. In short, they had formed an abstract class for which the middle values were the most familiar or prototypic.

Most recently Cohen has extended this work to classes or categories that are ill defined, i.e., categories that have overlapping attributes with other categories. In this case, he has created two classes of animals varying on four binary dimensions: Body size (large-0 or small-1), neck length (long-0 or short-1), leg length (long-0 or short-1), and number of legs (two-0 or four-1). One class consisted of four animals with three out of four of the binary stimulus dimensions taking a value of zero and the other dimension a value of one (e.g., an animal with a large body, long neck, long legs, and four legs or a small body, long neck, long legs and two legs). The other class consisted of four animals with three out of four of the binary stimulus dimensions with a value of one and the other dimension with a value of zero (e.g., an animal with a large body, short neck, short legs, and four legs or a small body, long neck, short legs and four legs). The difference between the two classes is that three of the four dimensions with binary choices always came from one set of values for one class, and three of the four binary choices always came from the other set of values for the other class. Each value of every dimension appeared at least once in exemplars of both classes. Ten-month-old infants were taught to turn their heads to one side for one class and to the other side for the second class.

The infants had no difficulty learning the head-turning responses to the two different ill-defined classes. Furthermore, they were 95% correct in responding to new, previously unseen, transfer stimuli consisting of animals with four of four appropriate values on the binary dimensions.

Exploring the issue further, Cohen reports an experiment in which he used animal stimuli composed of five dimensions with three values on each dimension. In this case, the procedure was to correlate some of the attributes of the stimuli, whereas allowing others to vary in an unsystematic or uncorrelated manner. Thus, the three dimensions of body, tail, and feet were correlated such that if the animal had a giraffe body, then it also had a feathered tail and webbed feet. The ears and number of legs, on the other hand, varied unsystematically. If the animal had a cow's body it also had a fluffy tail and club feet; again the ears and number of legs varied unsystematically. The infants were shown four habituation animals twice for 20 seconds each, and then they were tested for their looking time to three different stimuli: A previously unseen correlated stimulus, a previously unseen uncorrelated stimulus, and a stimulus that was entirely novel. The results indicated that 10-month-old infants dishabituated to the uncorrelated and the novel stimuli, but not the unseen correlated stimulus. In short, the 10-month-old infants do not respond in terms of attributes in isolation but, like Schwartz and Day's subjects, they respond in terms of relationships among attributes.

Schwartz and Day's infants were 2-to-4 months of age, whereas Cohen's infants were 10 months of age. Cohen and his collaborators have, however, used 4 and 7-month-old infants in their research, and they report a developmental trend in performance on their tasks. Four-month-olds appear to respond in terms of independent attributes; 7-month-olds are able to respond in terms of correlated attributes or patterns for simple stimuli, but they fail with more complicated stimuli; and 10-month-olds always respond in terms of patterns or relations among attributes. The Schwartz and Day results clearly reflect pattern responding with simple geometric forms, and I have no doubt that 10-month olds would not be able to respond to some more complicated patterns. In short, I think we can conclude that responding in terms of patterns or relations among attributes of stimuli is a natural response characteristic of the human. As Cohen and Younger (1983) put it "the processes 10-month-old infants use to generate categories seem quite similar to those used by older children and adults" (p. 216). Although Cohen and Younger are cautious in limiting their conclusion to 10-month-old infants, there seems to be enough other data in the literature on a variety of tasks to eliminate the age restriction and argue that humans, regardless of age, form categories in the same way.

This sample of previously unsuspected knowledge about the infant's perceptual and conceptual capacities suggests that the infant, as the adult, has a set of rules establishing abstract concepts and organizing those concepts in relations that allow the interpretation of concrete events and appropriate responses to those events within the framework of the infant's theory of the world. The theory is a grammar of the world and the infant's relations to the world. The infant, thus, enters the world predisposed or constrained to order it in particular ways. Presumably those constraints are characteristically human and established by the biological structure of the species. The recent research with infants is beginning to expose the nature of the theories with which humans begin.

We know, however, that the initial natural or biologically based theory of the infant changes as the child develops. In addition to further biological changes that occur with maturation, we know that the child's interactions with the environment influence conceptual development. Thus, the child's natural predispositions or initial theory is modified by specific environmental experiences. When, for example, a response of the child fails to yield an expected outcome according to the child's theory, a revision in the theory is required to bring the theory in accord with that experience. This process of theory development is a continuous one throughout an individual's lifetime.

Because the empirical experiences of different individuals vary, one might expect that across persons there would be widely different theories of the world. Clearly that is not the case. The very fact that we can communicate with each other makes it obvious that our theories of the world have many commonalities. The commonalities within a species are assumed to be based at one level upon the commonalities that exist in the biological structures of the organisms involved. In the same sense that dogs can communicate with dogs, chimps with chimps, and birds with birds, people can communicate with people because each member of a species has a biological commonality that forms, in part, the basis for the theory of the world held by the species member. The genetic characteristics of humans that are passed from one generation to the next and set in motion for the individual at the time of conception establish the sensory equipment, central nervous system, and other biological characteristics that underly the common structure we will impose upon our world. That common biological structure establishes, in part, the manner in which we will be predisposed to classify and to relate, given any empirical experience. Thus, the biological structure constrains the theory we develop. The natural conceptual base has, of course, evolved over time as the evolution of humans has taken place.

At a second, and not entirely independent level, the commonalities in our theories of the world are made possible by the commonalities in the culture in which societal members are immersed. Common child-rearing practices, religions, belief systems, and values influence the theories individuals within the culture develop. The cultural commonalities, too, have evolved over time as the evolution of various societies has taken place. The cultural characteristics of a society are also passed from one generation to the next and establish, among other things, particular languages and the rules and practices of conduct and custom that govern the conceptualization of interactions among humans in societal groups.

Thus, biological and cultural commonalities act to constrain our theories of the world and provide a common base that results in similar theories across different people. Whereas commonalities in theories across people is clear, it is also obvious that theories of individuals do differ. Variation in theories among people are inevitable because of individual differences in biological structure, cultural community, and specific individual experiences. Thus, variation comes about because the same experiences have different meanings for persons with different biological structure as, for example, in children of different ages; variation occurs because the same experiences have different meanings for persons reared in different cultures; and variation results from differences in specific individual experiences over a lifetime.

Thus, the biological, cultural, and experiential variables mold individual theories, establishing commonalities through the inherent similarities of each set of variables across individuals and, at the same time, establishing differences through the variation in each set of variables between individuals. Because these sets of variables influence us from the beginning of life, we all have a theory of the world from the very beginning. That conceptual framework allows us to understand the particulars of the world. It is a system of rules for making judgments about what is and what ought to be, what goes together in classes or categories, and the bases for distinctions and relations. The empirical experiences are organized and given meaning in terms of the concepts and relations of the cognitive system. The cognitive system has been referred to here as a theory of the world. The theory of each individual makes it possible for the individual to create a meaning for the empirical experience and, thus, avoid the inherent ambiguity of that experience.

The theoretical framework here proposed is not unique. The Kantian influence is obvious, and variations on this theme have been proposed by others (e.g., Weimer, 1977). Within developmental psychology, the position presented here is similar in many ways to the theoretical framework proposed, for example, by Lewin (e.g., Lewin, 1946) to account for a child's intellectual and social development, and by Piaget to account for the development of intelligence (e.g., Piaget, 1971). Both of these theorists tried to conceptualize the manner in which the individual constructs an account of the world that, in turn, determines the behavioral characteristics congruent with that conceptual construction. Whereas these two theorists did not start from the issue of ambiguity, their theories can account for ambiguity. Piaget argued that what changes in the intellectual development of the child is structure. He took the position that the process of adaptation is a constant but, as a function of interaction with the environment, structure changes. Each stage of development is associated with a different structure so that the same environmental events have different meanings because of the different structures to which they are assimilated in the adaptation process. Lewin (1935), on the other hand, argued that the life space increases in complexity or differentiation as a function of what he called social facts, content, or knowledge. Putting it in Lewin's words, "From the greater differentiation, the greater wealth of inner levels, there must thus result for the given person a greater richness of ways of conceiving and observing" (p. 233).

KNOWLEDGE AND THE THEORY

Earlier I indicated that there were two key aspects of the problem of metaphor on which I wished to focus: the ambiguity of metaphor and the developmental issue. In thinking about the second aspect of metaphor, namely the changing ability of the child to create and comprehend metaphors of increasing degrees of abstractness or complexity, I have moved away from Piaget and toward Lewin. It seems to me that there is an accumulating body of evidence to suggest that Piaget may have been in error in his conception of structural change. What I argue here is that structure is also a constant and what changes is knowledge about content. If there is structure in Piaget's sense, and I am not sure there is, structure remains constant as well as the processes applied to each experience to assimilate them to our theory and accommodate our theory to those experiences throughout our lifetime. What changes is our knowledge about, or to use Lewin's term, differentiation of the objects, events and relations that we encounter in the world of our experience. The process of change in knowledge may be clarified in terms of the example I gave earlier of using a microscope. We can know a great deal about objects without a microscope, but the microscope allows us additional knowledge about those objects. Regardless of whether we view the object with the naked eye or through the microscope, however, we conceptualize the structure of what we see using the same categorical and relational principles. As we interact more with our environment and, thereby, acquire more knowledge about it, with or without a microscope, we are able to see and, therefore, give meaning to more of it. Knowledge changes while process, and/or structure if you wish, remains the same.

A different example may make the point even more clearly as well as expand what I have in mind here. The mind imposes the categories of phonemes, words, and sentences upon the stream of sound known as speech. In order to divide the speech stream into the meaningful categories of word and sentence, however, one must know the language. Thus, meaningful categorization presupposes knowledge of the domain and the dimensions that may be used to divide the domain. The initial knowledge of the structural "contours" must be innate in order to get the whole process started. The meaning of those differentiated categories, however, must be acquired through the processes related to knowledge acquisition.

Arguing that knowledge changes, rather than structure, suggests that learning is the basic mechanism of cognitive change. In fact, that is what I wish to argue, but I am not attempting to resurrect the learning theories of the behavioristic paradigm. The latter theories focused primarily upon surface structures and rote learning. Whereas there is little question that we all learn some things by rote, i.e., remember without meaning, and it is important to understand the factors that influence rote learning, I am not talking about that type of learning. I am referring to the acquisition of understanding as opposed to the acquisition of a response. The difference is, perhaps, best exemplified with something like the multiplication tables. Rote memory will allow a child to remember that 5 times 3 is 15. The perfect recall of the correct answer, however, gives no indication of whether the child understands that 5 times 3 is 15 because if you add three fives you will obtain 15, if you subtract two fives from 15 you will be left with the third five, if you divide 15 by 5 you will get 3, and so on. It is the latter understanding of the multiplication operation applied to the number set that would allow the child to check on rote memory when he or she is not sure of the memorized answer. I refer to that understanding or knowledge as the learning of importance. In order to understand multiplication in this sense, one must understand the deep structure of the number system, and that presupposes some knowledge of how to count and something about the nature of the operations of addition, subtraction, and division. It is in this sense that I refer to changes in knowledge about content as the process that allows for cognitive development. Each increase in knowledge rests upon a foundation of prior knowledge that is a prerequisite. Thus, for example, one does not try to teach multiplication before the foundation of, for example, counting and addition have been established. Once the prerequisites have been set in place, the child has achieved a stage at which multiplication may be acquired. In this sense, the accumulation of knowledge is a stage or step function. Those who have been involved in programmed learning understand the sequencing idea well, although, for the most part, the focus of programmers has often been upon rote learning and/or pragmatically determined sequencing, as opposed to an analysis of the deep structure of the knowledge being taught. Until we understand what it means to understand multiplication, such programs, although they often do succeed, will be hit or miss affairs with no theoretical basis for creating new ones.

If an analogy between scientific theory and theory of the world is considered again, the arguments about knowledge being made here relate to the accumulation of facts in the realm of scientific theory. Our theory of the world is a theory within which the events of the world and our relation to them are construed. In the course of our lives we accumulate more and more facts relative to that theory via our tests and experiments exploring aspects of the world. The theory expands to account for new objects, events, and relations as those tests and experiments continue. In scientific theories we usually refer to these activities as increasing the factual basis of the theory and extending the theory to new domains. In the case of our theory of the world, I am calling it increasing the knowledge base of the theory. In both cases, we are accounting in greater and greater detail for more and more substance but always giving it meaning within the framework of the abstract theory we use to conceptualize the structure we perceive.

In summary, the argument being made here is that the newborn infant is biologically predisposed, as a function of being a member of the species homo sapiens, to organize his or her conceptualization of the world in particular ways. In other terms, the child has a theory of the world from the very beginning. Recent research suggests that the initial theory may be much more comprehensive than, say, Kurt Lewin (1946) envisioned when he discussed his concept of the infant's life space. In any case, as the infant interacts with the environment, the theory becomes fleshed out, modified, and differentiated with respect to the environmental objects, events, and relations the infant encounters. The theory is the child's basis for understanding the events of the world, for giving meaning to the world and the specific objects, events, and relations in it. Initially all the knowledge is acquired by direct experience, knowledge by acquaintance, to use Russell's term. As a representational system is acquired, the child may acquire knowledge by description. In either case, the child's theory of how the world is and ought to be is expanded. The expansion occurs as a function of the dual adaptation processes suggested by Piaget: assimilation to the theory of the moment and accommodation of the theory to that assimilated. The constraints on the processes and the processes themselves never change, for they are established by the biological characteristics of the species. Only the content or knowledge to which the theory may apply, not the manner in which the theory is constructed, change.

Why, you may ask, do I take such a position? Why do I change my theory of the world? In connection with the arguments regarding ambiguity, I have already presented some of the research that seems convincing to me—research with infants. But, in addition to those data and the logical arguments presented, there is considerably more evidence that seems to fit the picture. The work of Langer (1980), for example, demonstrates empirically the precursors of logical and mathematical operations in the behaviors of 6–12-month-old infants. Langer interprets his observations of infant constructions to show extensive and intensive equivalence, iterative ordering, reversible relations as well as combinativity, relational, and conditional operations. These data suggest that the cognitive processes for logic and mathematics are available to the infant long before the representational system and various other cognitive developments usually associated with them have been acquired. As Langer also shows, there are clear developmental steps in the building of these protological operations in anticipation of their further development with the acquisition of the representational system. In short, the infant has the processes but not the knowledge base of the adult to which the processes may be applied.

Cohen, (Cohen & Younger, 1983) as I indicated earlier, comments that "the processes . . . infants use to generate categories seem quite similar to those used by older children and adults . . . the mechanism they use to form categories is quite sophisticated . . . they are . . . capable of using multiple attributes to form categories and even of taking the correlation among these attributes into account" (p. 216). I reiterate that Day's work with Schwartz and McKenzie may be interpreted to show the same processes at work in younger infants as those studied by Cohen.

There are a number of other researchers working on other problems who have come to similar conclusions. In the area of language, for example, Hardy and Braine (1981) conclude after several studies of the case system of 4 and 5-year-old children that:

> the adults' case system is remarkably similar to the children's . . . the definition of the case roles, and the way in which they are organized, probably remain unchanged . . . What changes during development after five years . . . is the knowledge that these roles can at times be reassigned to the syntactic categories of sentence subject, object, and prepositional phrase . . . Thus, while we learn more about exceptions during development, and the basic system may become amplified and refined, it is probably not fundamentally reorganized. (pp. 220–221)

Macnamara (1982), in his book concerned with how children are able to learn the names for things, comes to the conclusion that he "knows of no evidence that the minds of children and adults differ structurally" (p. 236). He goes on to state that in the course of reviewing the evidence, "we have seen considerable evidence that even to learn names for things, a modest part of what the very young child learns even in language, they [children and adults] must be structurally equivalent" (p. 236). Macnamara came to these conclusions because a child who learns names for things must know how to comprehend three-place predicates of referring, many-place predicates relating to truth, and the relation between referring predicates and truth-judging predicates as well as a powerful propositional logic, among other things. Note that Langer's work suggests that the logic Macnamara indicates is required is available to the child learning language.

In the area of conceptual development, Keil (1979, 1981) has argued and presented data to support the contention that there are constraints on the learnability of natural classes and relations among classes. These constraints on class formation are both universal and invariant throughout development. To put it in Keil's terms: "Although a child's knowledge in a particular domain may be less differentiated than an adult's, it is systematically related to the latter, for structures at all ages share many formal properties... What knowledge children do have conforms to the same formal constraints as adult knowledge, but it is less elaborated" (p. 202).

In the area of memory there are similar arguments being made. Chi (1978), for example, on the basis of research on memory for the places of chess pieces on a board, argues that the knowledge base of the individual determines the memory performance. She demonstrated that 10-year-old chess experts could remember chess piece placement much better than adult chess novices. The adults, on the other hand, showed better recall of 10 digits. More recently, Kail and Nippold (1984) have reported a developmental study of retrieval from semantic memory. The results indicated that the older the subjects, the greater the total number of items retrieved, but the form of the retrieval curve over time was the same for all ages, the number of clusters of items was constant across ages, and at all ages the prototypic category members were recalled first followed by typical and atypical members. They argue that the amount of knowledge the child has changes with age, but the processes used to retrieve that knowledge are the same at all ages.

In short, it seems to me that the evidence accumulates to suggest that the infant enters this world biologically predisposed to process it in particular ways. Thus, the infant is prepared to distinguish figure from ground, red from blue, triangle from square, language from noise, /pa/ from /ba/, and so on. Furthermore, the child is ready to classify new stimuli as similar on the basis of dimensions to which the child is biologically predisposed to attend and abstract. The infant is also prepared to reevaluate these classifications when prior evaluations do not result in expected outcomes. In order to be able to categorize different objects, events, and relations, it is presupposed that the infant has a memory process that allows the construction of the past in-so-far as it is conceived to bear on the present. The child's theory of the world allows for the reconstruction of the past, not necessarily as it was, but as it ought to have been given the current theory. The theory is continually expanding as the child continues to interact with the environment and is forced to modify the theory due to the failures of the theory to fulfill expectations. The failure of the theory to fulfill expectations results from failure to make appropriate discriminations, classifications, or relations with respect to the objects, events, and relations in the world. Learning to make new discriminations, formulate new classifications, or establish new relations allows for new meanings, which is what we ordinarily call increasing our knowledge. Thus, by increasing our knowledge base, we attempt to increase the frequency with which our theory accurately allows us to anticipate the world through correct interpretations of the meaning of the world.

Consider the simplest of examples. A young boy approaches a dog with the theory that dogs are friendly, playful, soft, lovable animals. This particular dog on this particular occasion bites the child. The child is forced to revise his theory of the world on the basis of the incongruity of his theory and his empirical data. Theory revision is inevitable but the nature of the revision is not clear. The boy may revise his theory in such a way as to separate this particular dog on this occasion from the class of friendly, playful, soft, lovable animals; i.e., the child may consider this an isolated instance uncharacteristic of dogs and revise his theory only to the extent of noting an exception to his rule. On the other hand, the boy may revise his theory in such a way as to exclude from the category of friendly, playful, soft, and/or lovable things this particular dog, dogs of this breed, dogs in general, or all animals. Which type of revision will depend upon the child's current theory, the knowledge upon which it is based, and the meaning constructed for this particular event. This example relates to a specific interaction with an external world, but theory revision may result from internally constructed events as well. We can, and often do, think through a series of steps to a goal and recognize that we would be led to an error by one route, which forces us to revise without any overt act or external stimulus involved.

Now you may recall that the title of this presentation implied a discussion of metaphor. One may ask what all this has to do with metaphor as a portal to the child's mind. I try to respond in concluding. Metaphor, as I have suggested, is an ambiguous statement that often takes the form of equating one object or event with another in some unspecified, and often literally false, way. To create or comprehend a metaphor requires, it seems to me, the exposure of one's theory of the world and the knowledge upon which it draws. There is little question that a metaphor such as "Bees are buccaneers of buzz" would not have the same meaning for a child of 5 as for Emily Dickenson who created it. The child, however, may fail to understand the metaphor, not because he or she does not have the cognitive capacity, structure, or cognitive processes to comprehend metaphors, but because the child does not have the knowledge of buccaneers that is the key to comprehending the message about buzzing bees that Dickenson was attempting to convey. This is not to say that the 5-year-old will assign no meaning to the metaphor. The child may interpret the metaphor as some foolish gibberish of an adult, a profound utterance not meant for children, a strange kind of buzzing made by bees, or any of an indefinite number of other possible meanings. What is selected is a function of the child's theory of the world and the knowledge upon which it is based. Only by discovering that theory can we discover the mind of the child.

If we take the position that children, as adults, create a meaning for all experiences presented to them, then the argument often advanced that children may understand literal language early, but only gradually come to understand metaphors, makes no sense. We can rephrase the question in at least two ways so that it does make sense. We could ask, for example, when do children come to understand metaphors as adults do? That question then becomes one that focuses upon the child's acquisition of meaning systems comparable to those of adults. Clearly that is a legitimate developmental question, but it is much broader than the question of metaphor, in particular, or even figurative language, in general. A more manageable question for research purposes would relate to the types of metaphors that can be understood at various developmental levels. The latter question assumes that the process of understanding and producing metaphors is the same for children and adults, i.e., understanding and creating meanings, but the concepts that can be understood and produced as metaphor may differ with the conceptual system of the individual. Thus, "my soul is an enchanted boat" may be understood only by an adult but "my yellow plastic baseball bat is an ear of corn" may be understood by child and adult. Equivalent understanding by child and adult in this and other cases implies that the meaning given to the utterance will be comparable for child and adult.

The importance of metaphor lies in the potential that the study of metaphor processing holds for revealing the nature of the abstract dimensions and rules used in creating meaning for them, i.e., the nature of the child's knowledge and theory of the world. If we think of metaphor as the creation of a new meaning from the merging or interaction of two conventionally unrelated meanings, we can begin to ask questions about the nature of the emergent meanings, the context in which the metaphor is created, the developmental characteristics of the person creating or comprehending the meaning, and, perhaps most important, the characteristics of the abstract dimensions and generative rules used to achieve the meaning. It is an exciting theoretical–empirical challenge.

REFERENCES

Acredolo, L. P., & Hake, J. L. (1982). Infant perception. In B. B. Wolman & G. Stricker (Eds.), *Handbook of developmental psychology.* Englewood Cliffs, NJ: Prentice–Hall.

Armstrong, S. L., Gleitman, L. R., & Gleitman, H. (1983). What some concepts might not be. *Cognition, 13,* 263–308.

Asch, S., & Nerlove, H. (1960). The development of double function terms in children: An exploratory study. In B. Kaplan & S. Wapner (Eds.), *Perspectives in psychological theory.* New York: International Universities Press.

Barfield, D. A. (1970) *What Coleridge thought.* Wesleyan University Press, Middletown, Conn.

Bellugi, U., & Brown, R. W. (Eds.). (1964). *The acquisition of language.* Chicago: University of Chicago Press.

Billow, R. M. (1981). Observing spontaneous metaphor in children. *Journal of Experimental Child Psychology, 31,* 430–445.

Black, M. (1962). *Models and metaphors: Studies in language and philosophy.* Ithaca, NY: Cornell University Press.

Bornstein, M. H. (1976). Infants are trichromats. *Journal of Experimental Child Psychology, 21,* 425–445.

Broderick, V. K. (1983). *The development of metaphor comprehension and the skills of extraction and fusion.* Unpublished master's thesis, The Pennsylvania State University.

Cassirer, E. (1946). *Language and myth.* New York: Harper.

Chi, M. T. H. (1978). Knowledge structures and memory development. In R. Siegler (Ed.), *Children's thinking: What develops?* Hillsdale, NJ: Lawrence Erlbaum Associates.

Chomsky, N. (1957). *Syntactic structures.* The Hague: Mouton.

Chukovsky, K. (1968). *From two to five.* Berkeley, CA: University of California Press.

Clark, E. V. (1974). Some aspects of the conceptual basis for first language acquisition. In R. L. Schiefelbusch & L. L. Lloyd (Eds.), *Language perspectives: Acquisition, retardation and intervention* (pp. 105–128). Baltimore: University Park Press.

Clark, H. H. (1970). The primitive nature of children's relational concepts. In J. R. Hayes (Ed.), *Cognition and the development of language* (pp. 269–278). New York: Wiley.

Cohen, L. B., & Younger, B. A. (1983). Perceptual categorization in the infant. In E. K. Scholnick (Ed.), *New trends in conceptual representation: Changes in Piaget's theory?* (pp. 197–220). Hillsdale, NJ: Lawrence Erlbaum Associates.

Cooper, L. (1932). *The rhetoric of Aristotle.* New York: Appleton–Century–Crofts.

Cox, H., & Lathem, E. C. (Eds.). (1949). *Selected prose of Robert Frost.* New York: Collier Books.

Day, R. H., & McKenzie, B. E. (1973). Perceptual shape constancy in early infancy. *Perception, 2,* 315–320.

Eimas, P., Siqueland, E. R., Jusczyk, P., & Vigorito, J. (1971). Speech perception in infants. *Science, 171,* 303–306.

Garber, B. (1982). *The role of age and prototypicality in infants' categorization of natural stimuli.* Unpublished master's thesis, The Pennsylvania State University.

Gibson, J. J. (1977). The theory of affordances. In R. Shaw & J. D. Bransford (Eds.), *Perceiving, acting and knowing.* Hillsdale, NJ: Lawrence Erlbaum Associates.

Goldstein, K. (1946). Methodological approach to the study of schizophrenic thought disorder. In J. S. Kasanin (Ed.), *Language and thought in schizophrenia.* Berkeley, CA: University of California Press.

Grice, H. P. (1975). Logic and conversation. In P. Cole & J. L. Morgan (Eds.), *Syntax and semantics Vol. 3: Speech acts.* New York: Academic Press.

Hardy, J. A., & Braine, M. D. S. (1981). Categories that bridge between meaning and syntax in five-year-olds. In W. Deutsch (Ed.), *The child's construction of language* (pp. 201–222). New York: Academic Press.

Holland, V. M., & Palermo, D. S. (1975). On learning "less": Language and cognitive development. *Child Development, 46,* 437–443.

Jakobson, R. (1960). Linguistics and poetics. In T. A. Sebeok (Ed.), *Style in language.* Cambridge, MA: MIT Press.

Jenkins, J. J., & Palermo, D. S. (1964). Mediation processes and the acquisition of linguistic structure. In U. Bellugi & R. W. Brown (Eds.), *The acquisition of language. Monograph of the Society for Research in Child Development, 29,* 141–169.

Kail, R., & Nippold, M. A. (1984). Unconstrained retrieval from semantic memory. *Child Development, 55,* 944–951.

Katz, J. J. (1972). *Semantic theory.* New York: Harper & Row.

Keil, F. C. (1979). *Semantic and conceptual development: An ontological perspective.* Cambridge, MA: Harvard University Press.

Keil, F. C. (1981). Constraints on knowledge and cognitive development. *Psychological Review, 88,* 197-227.

Kuczaj, S. A., II, & Maratsos, M. P. (1975). On the acquisition of *front, back,* and *side. Child Development, 46,* 202-210.

Kuhn, T. S. (1970). *The structure of scientific revolutions.* Chicago: University of Chicago Press.

Lakoff, G., & Johnson, M. (1980). *Metaphors we live by.* Chicago: University of Chicago Press.

Langer, J. (1980). *The origins of logic: Six to twelve months.* New York: Academic Press.

Leondar, B. (1975). Metaphor and infant cognition. *Poetics, 4,* 273-287.

Lewin, K. (1935). *Dynamic theory of personality.* New York: McGraw-Hill.

Lewin, K. (1946). Behavior and development as a function of the total situation. In L. Carmichael (Ed.), *Manuel of child psychology.* New York: Wiley.

Macnamara, J. (1982). *Names for things.* Cambridge, MA: MIT Press.

Martin, J. F. (1982). Presentationalism: An essay toward self reflexive psychological theory. In W. B. Weimer & D. S. Palermo (Eds.), *Cognition and the symbolic processes* (Vol. 2). Hillsdale, NJ: Lawrence Erlbaum Associates.

Molfese, D. L., Freeman, R. B., Jr., & Palermo, D. S. (1975). The ontogeny of brain lateralization for speech and nonspeech stimuli. *Brain and Language, 2,* 356-368.

Molfese, D. L., & Molfese, V. J. (1980). Cortical responses of preterm infants to phonetic and nonphonetic speech stimuli. *Developmental Psychology, 16,* 574-581.

Nelson, K. (1974). Concept, word, and sentence: Interrelations in acquisition and development. *Psychological Review, 81,* 267-285.

Palermo, D. S. (1978a). Semantics and language acquisition: Some theoretical considerations. In R. N. Campbell & P. T. Smith (Eds.), *Recent advances in the psychology of language: Formal and experimental approaches* (pp. 45-54). NATO Conference Series, Vol. 4B. New York: Plenum.

Palermo, D. S. (1978b). *Psychology of language.* Glencove, IL: Scott, Foresman.

Palermo, D. S. (1982). Theoretical issues in semantic development. In S. Kuczaj (Ed.), *Language development: Syntax and semantics* (pp. 335-364). Hillsdale, NJ: Lawrence Erlbaum Associates.

Palermo, D. S. (1983). Cognition, concepts, and an employee's theory of the world. In F. J. Landy, S. Zedeck, & J. Cleveland (Eds.), *Performance measurement and theory* (pp. 97-115). Hillsdale, NJ: Lawrence Erlbaum Associates.

Piaget, J. (1971). *Biology and knowledge.* Chicago: University of Chicago Press.

Piattelli-Palmarini, M. (1980). *Theories de language, theories de l'apprentissage.* Cambridge, MA: Harvard University Press.

Richards, I. A. (1936). *The philosophy of rhetoric.* Oxford: Oxford University Press.

Richards, M. M. (1979). Sorting out what's in a word from what's not: Evaluating Clark's semantic features acquisition theory. *Journal of Experimental Child Psychology, 27,* 1-47.

Rosch, E. (1975). Cognitive representations of semantic categories. *Journal of Experimental Psychology: General, 104,* 192-233.

Schwartz, M., & Day, R. H. (1979). Visual shape perception in early infancy. *Monograph of the Society for Research in Child Development, 44,* (Whole No. 182).

Sternberg, R. J. (1977). Component processes in analogical reasoning. *Psychological Review, 84,* 353-378.

Strauss, M. S. Infant memory of protypical information. (1981) Paper presented at the meeting of the Society for Research in Child Development, Boston.

Vosniadou, S., Ortony, A., Reynolds, R. E., & Wilson, P. T. (1984). Sources of difficulty in children's understanding of metaphorical language. *Child Development, 55,* 1588-1606.

Wagner, S., Winner, E., Cicchetti, D., & Gardner, H. (1981). "Metaphorical" mapping in human infants. *Child Development, 52,* 728–731.

Weimer, W. B. (1977). A conceptual framework for cognitive psychology: Motor theories of the mind. In R. Shaw & J. Bransford (Eds.), *Perceiving, acting, and knowing* (pp. 267–311). Hillsdale, NJ: Lawrence Erlbaum Associates.

6

Collecting Data

Sheldon H. White
Harvard University

But if it be asked us, whether some realities do not exist, which are entirely independent of thought; I would in turn ask, what is meant by such an expression and what can be meant by it. What idea can be attached to that of which there is no idea?

C. S. Peirce, "The Logic of 1873"

An acceptable religion will be one that is "alive." And so too a successful philosophy. What the younger Hegel would demand of his own Phenomenology, *therefore, would be not so much clarity or cleverness, not so much the truth of its conclusions or the profundity of its pronouncements, but its sense of vitality, a "bacchanalian revel." The purpose of philosophy is celebration as well as understanding, to express and augment the life of the human spirit, not to analyze and process it.*

Robert C. Solomon, *In the Spirit of Hegel*

This is a paper for a course I took with Charles Spiker 30-odd years ago and which, in my mind, I still take from time to time. As with a number of important courses I took as a student, I'm still working through it. Some courses deal with subtle and complicated problems. You settle the issues as best you can, and then still later, you see new dimensions of the problem and you undo and redo the settlements.

Charles Spiker's course is the "home base" of a perennial issue to me ... in part because of what he dealt with, in part because of his approach as a teacher. Like any graduate student settling down to become a psychologist, I worried about what I was getting into. I confronted questions about psychology's program. "What kind of an enterprise is psychology? What good is it? How can this field staunchly maintain that it is a science when everyone sees there are problems? Why are there all these *kinds* of psychologists? How much of this stuff is real?"

In the middle 1950's, it was conventional for psychologists to explain the field on the basis of the philosophy of science of logical positivism. In the first course I took, Charles Spiker offered an introduction to psychological research simply, carefully, and with a sincerity and intelligence that were unmistakable and appealing. Further on in our graduate work, we studied the history and philosophy of psychology with Gustav Bergmann, a philosopher of science of some distinction, who offered incisive and engaging enlargements of the view of psychology first set forth to me by Spiker. By then I was doing research with Spiker. I had the rare experience of doing research within a sense of a larger plan, with each study being an episode in a continuing, purposeful train of thought.

It was intriguing to do psychological research programmatically. I had come from a "broken home"—Harvard in the late 1940's, with some psychology in the Department of Psychology and some in the Department of Social Relations. Harvard's two psychologies were disconnected; ideas and studies flew around. Each side set forth fragments of justification. Neither could fully explain either itself or the other side.[1] The vision of The State University of Iowa was clear, coherent and (to use a word that Spiker was fond of) "monolithic." Iowa practiced a circumscribed and narrow science, but it *said* it practiced a circumscribed and narrow science. Psychology, Iowa said, was too immature to take on the big questions just yet. Better to start small, in a clear area, and leave the bigger questions until we are scientifically ready for them. There were never behavioristic sermons on human nature out of Iowa in those days. Small was beautiful.

Not all psychologists are bothered by philosophical questions. Most psychologists take the legitimacy of the field for granted—what is, is—or they listen to somebody's story about the field, find that it makes sense, and adopt it without struggling to find problems. There is much to be said for a serene and healthy-minded willingness to take psychology as it comes. I was not able to muster it; neither was Charles Spiker. We both searched for the meaning of psychology in his first course. I have seen a draft of the

---

[1]As this chapter was being completed, Harvard's Department of Psychology and Social Relations voted to become once again a Department of Psychology.

paper he has prepared for this volume. He, too, still takes his course from time to time.

Charles Spiker was a consummate teacher, an integral part of an Iowa graduate education that has remained in my mind and has served as a solid foundation for my work as a psychologist for many years. Many psychologists view the Iowa at which I studied in slightly mythic terms. In the early 1950's, Iowa stood for a pure vision of the possibility of a scientific psychology. Iowa cherished the Hull-Spence learning theory, the philosophy of science of logical positivism, and a program for the development of psychology that envisioned it as, ultimately, something to be encompassed by a behavioristic system of stimulus-response laws and theories. Many psychologists believed in all this in the 1940s and 1950s. Led by Kenneth Spence, Iowa stood out because it propounded the learning theory program zealously and forthrightly and because Iowa research spoke well for the program. The research had quality. Again and again, it threw off intriguing findings and phenomena. Other psychologists followed the findings and in so doing had to deal with the theory.

Some years ago, I became skeptical about the settlement that Iowa taught, and said so (White, 1970). It seemed to me there was more to psychology than the philosophy of science of logical positivism said there was, and more to psychological research than the programmatic behaviorism of the traditional Hull-Spence theory of learning. Having lost my feeling for the older settlement, I had no choice but to begin exploring the possibilities of some other meaning for the field. This I have tried to do in writings exploring the basic processes by which knowledge is gathered and shared in the discipline (White, 1976a, 1977), the historical place and meaning of the discipline of psychology (White, 1976b, 1978, 1983a, 1983b, 1985a, 1985b, in press; Siegel and White, 1982), and psychology's role as a moral science helping people to find meanings and values appropriate for their activities and roles in a modern society (White, 1975, 1978, 1983c, 1985a; Rein and White, 1977, 1981, 1982).

These papers denied the letter of Iowa's program for psychologists, but I believe they affirmed the spirit in which that program was advocated. Meaningful psychological research can only be done programmatically, with some sense of how local activities fit into a larger enterprise, and some intelligent convictions about the value of that enterprise for everyday human affairs.

Many of the shortcomings of the traditional philosophy of science derived from the principle of the "unity of science" and the belief that lessons from the physical sciences could and should be used to instruct psychologists. It seems to me that the best way to begin to understand psychological research is to look at it with open eyes, setting aside the legendry that says it ought to look like something else. We can begin to confront some of the deep questions by watching psychological researchers, particularly at those moments when behaviors are transformed into data.

POINTS OF CROSSING:
HOW ALICE'S ACTIVITIES BECOME DATA

What happens when a person's stream of activity trips off the declaration of a scientific event, and a symbol is recorded to "remember" the event? Since we all know life in experimental situations, we can use an imaginary[2] situation to explore such moments.

Alice and the Five Psychologists

Picture Alice, a nine-year-old in a fourth-grade classroom, active in her schoolwork, occasionally laughing and chatting with friends. The classroom is in an experimental school. There is a large one-way window through which one can view the classroom. Behind that window there are five psychologists, each observing the behavior of our nine-year-old and each making a scientific record. The observations are unobtrusive. Noone has asked Alice to do anything special, and Alice doesn't know the observing psychologists are there.

The five psychologists consist of a behavior modifier, a psychoanalyst, a psychophysiologist, an educational psychologist, and a psycholinguist. They don't know about one another because they sit in separate cubicles behind the one-way mirror.

The behavior modifier is interested in a very slight pattern of stuttering shown by the little girl. So he records incidents of nonfluency in her speech—momentary hesitations or stammers before words—by pressing a button leading to an event recorder each time he detects one. Through

---

[2]The nucleus of this paper was an image of a group of psychologists all studying the same child, unaware of one another, writing diverse parallel descriptions of the child's behavior. I had thought about the possibilities of this situation for some years until the occasion of this volume gave me a chance to write about it. The laws of the human mind are such that it was not until midway in the writing of the paper that I decided that the image was not wholly imaginary. It was probably seeded by a germ of real memory. Some years ago, Lawrence Kohlberg and I were at the University of Chicago, both doing research in the Chicago Laboratory school. Larry had collected some data on obedience to authority and good behavior and, unwittingly working with the same children, I had collected some psychophysiological and reaction-time data bearing on attentional functioning. Paul Grim put together the two sets of data, with Kohlberg and I taking a tolerant but skeptical attitude. In fact, there were interesting relationships between the two sets of observations of the same children (Grim, Kohlberg, and White, 1968)).

previous observations of Alice, he has developed the idea that eye-to-eye contact initiated by others is a stimulus "controlling" her stuttering. So he has a second button and, each time he sees eye-to-eye contact, he presses that button.

The psychoanalyst is interested in any and all forms of verbal or symbolic aggression. He wants to explore his hypothesis that diverse acts of aggression on Alice's part are rooted in a nuclear personality configuration of sibling rivalry. So each time Alice says something or does something that seems to betoken aggression to others, he takes notes recording in words an account of the incident, how it began, who else was involved, and how Alice responded.

The psychophysiologist is interested in diurnal rest-activity cycles, waves of heightened and reduced activity occurring in a cycle that seems to have a periodicity of three to four hours. Like the behavior modifier, he has some buttons and an event recorder. One button is pushed whenever yawns, stretches, or movements interpretable as *self-awakening activity* are detected. He has three other buttons, which he uses according to the following schedule. Every 30 seconds, signalled by a faint little electric buzzer, he must choose one or another to signify whether Alice is: (1) physically moving; (2) quiet, but with eyes focused on something; (3) quiet, with eyes not focused.

The educational psychologist is interested in computing what he calls the "actual teacher-pupil ratio" for each of the 26 children in the classroom. So each time the teacher speaks or makes an action directed towards a specific child he notes which child the teacher directs her attention to. The educational psychologist wants to find out what proportion of the teacher's attention each child in the classroom has. He records the teacher's responses to Alice at the same time that he records her responses to other children.

The psycholinguist is interested in the age when "vice-versa" utterances appear in children's language, believing that vice-versa formulations betoken the Piagetian "reversibility" associated with operational thought. The psycholinguist is observing Alice for a fixed period of time. Every time Alice makes a statement having a vice-versa form, the psycholinguist writes it down. The utterance must embody the form: 'a is in relation m to b; and b is in relation m to a'.

It has taken me some time to stage our little scene. I have been as quick as I can, giving you the programs of five researchers each of whom will someday take from 2 to 10 pages of a journal article to explain to his colleagues what he has done. We have a behavior modifier interested in stuttering, a psychoanalyst interested in aggression, a psychophysiologist interested in wakefulness, an educational psychologist interested in teacher attention, and a psycholinguist interested in "vice-versa" utterances. Now let us play the hypothetical scene for one minute.

Alice stands up from her seat, yawns, stretches, and walks over to a neighbor. (The psychophysiologist presses a button.) She says, "Do you know how to do this page of the worksheet?"

Her neighbor, Sue, glares up at her. (The behavior modifier presses a button.) "You're always asking! Always asking! Don't you ever do your own work?"

Alice: "I showed you *all* my stuff in the reading assignment. *You* asked m-m-*me!*" (The behavior modifier presses a second button.)

Sue: "Yeah, I asked you. I asked you. But I bet you asked me a thousand times to my once!" (The buzzer softly rings. The psychophysiologist chooses a button and presses it.)

Alice, advancing on Sue (The psychoanalyst begins to write): "Look! We're supposed to be uh-uh friends, right? (The behavior modifier presses a button.) The way it goes, one friend helps the other and the other helps her back!" (The psycholinguist begins to write.)

"Now look, it says the man has -uhhh- f-forty bushels of wheat (The behavior modifier presses a button.) and he has to sell them at $2.63 a bushel . . . "

Teacher: "Alice, will you please get back to your seat?" (The educational psychologist makes a checkmark beside Alice's name.) We're going to give all our concentration to the worksheets . . . " (The buzzer sounds again. The psychophysiologist chooses a button and presses it.)

During this one minute of Alice's behavior there were ten scientific events. You can always tell when a scientific event occurs because some psychologist acts to declare and register the event. A scientific event is made by an action of a researcher connected in a rulebound way to the activity of the subject. At the end of the minute each of our five psychologists has written strings of symbols that represent, in some official sense, all that science has seen, knows, and will remember about this time of Alice's life, all that is distilled out of the minute as *data*.

Observations as Translations Into Symbols

The five psychologists have learned much about Alice that is not on their records. They would recognize her if they saw her again. They remember odd things she has said, the way she moved, and fragments of conversation. They may like or dislike her. The memories of Alice's minute vary among the five in nature and detail and, most likely, will quickly fade for all. Attitudes towards Alice will be different among the five—different and hard to adjudicate so as to yield an agreed-upon truth about how everyone feels about Alice.

The lasting observations of the five psychologists are those made according to a consciously declared system. Notice that each observer has a well-specified condition for recording an event. Events lawfully obtained under well-specified conditions are *data*. What do the *data* of the five psychologists tells us about the reality of Alice's life in the minute?

All five psychologists have been "observing Alice's behavior" but each has made a different record. There are five sets of notations, each an enormous simplification. At the end of an hour of such observations our psycholinguist has seven vice-versa utterances written out under Alice's name. One hour of Alice's life and this is what he has to show for it, seven written-out statements. The behavior modifier would summarize his notations: "Eye-contacts followed by stuttering—12; Eye-contacts without stuttering—6; Stuttering without antecedent eye-contacts—15." To do research is to count. The numbers of scientific events are small for some systems of observation: 7 for the educational psychologist, 33 for the behavior modifier. The systems of observation they are using absorb very little information out of Alice's hour. It would be easy to invent systems that absorb very large numbers of events out of that hour. A telemetered electrocardiograph would record about 4000 p-q-r-s-t events during the hour. An eye movement camera might conceivably record as many as 18,000 distinct eye fixations during that time. Yet even rich systems like these would leave enormous amounts of Alice's activities behind.

Strictly speaking, the symbols given in each psychologist's string were made by behaviors of the *experimenter* and are a record of those behaviors. Because the experimenter has bound himself to a system of action, his behavior—selected aspects of it, at selected moments of attention—has been yoked to the child's behavior and reflects selected aspects of it. The scheme of observation, scrupulously followed, rigidly couples an act of the experimenter to an act of the child; a synergy of the two acts is established that one might call a *dyadic automatism* or a *dyadic sensorimotor scheme*. The researcher brings his behavior near to that of the child through his scheme, and then establishes knowledge of the child's behavior out of his own behavior.

Counting Purposes

In one minute, our behavior modifier recorded three acts of stuttering— once when Ellen said "m-m-*me!*", a second time when she said "uh-uh friends", and a third time when she said "-uhhh-f-forty". These are three instances of one thing. What does the 1-2-3 count collect together? The three speeches of Alice were not physically identical. Some might say the three acts of stuttering are "physically similar", but *any* two physical events are physically similar in some way. Why are Alice's three little speeches alike? What the observing psychologist seems to be lumping together are three instances of the same kind of slippage of speech control.

Anyone who "counts behaviors" is counting *purposes* (*motives, intentions, functions, plans, programs, goals, schemes,* or *controls*) as reflected in the subject's activity. This is simply to say that we conventionally address molar behaviors (Hull, 1943, Chapter II), that we are engaged in a functional analysis of behavior (Skinner, 1938), or that Psychology is a "science of the artificial" (Simon, 1969).

We say that we are counting physical events, but observations of speech nonfluencies, eye-to-eye contact, acts of aggression, yawns, stretches, self-awakening activity, physical movement, eyes focussing or not focussing on something, teacher's activity directed towards a child, and sentences embodying a vice-versa logical form, all class together distinctly different physical configurations. What is being counted are indices of Alice's intentions.

The Possibility of Multiple Descriptions

Our five psychologists have selectively absorbed skimpy records of Alice, and they are, with respect to what their data tells them about the minute they have just shared, ships in the night. No man's record looks like the other's. How many different imaginary psychologists could we crowd into that observation room, each one using some different observational system and therefore producing a different record of that minute of Alice's behavior? The number is surely very large. There is no one description of Alice's behavior. Questions of prediction, control, or understanding may well also be description-specific.

The possibility of multiple description does not argue either that Alice's behavior may be described in any way at all, nor that traditional ideals of objective, reliable descriptions of behavior are scientifically meaningless. Each observing psychologist chooses a system coupling his behavior to that of Alice. The consequences of the coupling are, so to speak, in Alice's hands. Her activity "speaks" through the coupling. Two psychologists adopting the same system ought to be coupled to the subject in the same way. They should register the same data, and have interobserver reliability.

Games as Vehicles of Cooperation and Communication

Quite often in work with children, a psychologist describes his research procedure to a child as a "game" though the adult thinks it is a "serious" experiment. In a formal sense, the researcher and the child are playing a game. Selected "moves" of the child are linked by rules to selected "moves" of the experimenter. Activities of either that fall outside the system-of-the-game are irrelevant and immaterial. In unobtrusive observations, the same gamelike linkage couples the activities of the observer and the child.

The communication between the child and each of the five scientists that makes data possible is mediated by the formal game that makes each of their two behaviors directive for the other's. The games of research seem to be of the same family as Wittgenstein's language game. To the psychologist, the game reveals some aspect of the child at the expense of concealing much else. Much information about the child's activity lies out of view, potentially available to other games that might yield other kinds of data. The *person* of the child lies outside the grasp of the game. In his thoughtful presidential address to the American Psychological Association, John Dewey (1900) once defined Psychology as "the ability to turn a living personality into an objective mechanism for the time being." Each of our observing psychologists has complied with Dewey's definition. Has Alice been turned into a machine by the observing psychologist? It is important to recognize that the formal game linking Alice with each psychologist excludes the living personality of the psychologist for the time being no less than that of Alice.

Our five psychologists are out of touch with each other. They have seen different things during Alice's minute. One man cannot confirm or deny another man's account of the minute from his official data . . . though, note, there is an everyday discourse through which they could discuss their sharing of Alice's minute. From a scientific point of view, there is no possibility of falsification between any two men's records. Using a different system of recording, playing a different game with the child, each man sets forth data about Alice having meaning in a different universe of scientific discourse.

Indicative Symbols and Locational Symbols

At the end of an hour in the classroom, the educational psychologist has placed seven checkmarks on his data sheet beside Alice's name. What does this record mean? Obviously, somebody finding this record on a piece of paper on the street—"Alice", followed by seven checkmarks—would have no idea what the checkmarks referred to. He might count the checkmarks and decide this is a record of seven *somethings*.

All symbols, C. S. Peirce argues, have some degree of *ikonicity;* they give a limited picture of their object in advance of interpretation. But, obviously, the educational psychologist's checkmarks do not alone declare what they signify. They are *indicative symbols* pointing to what the experimenter had in mind when he organized the observing game,—that is, to events as defined by the observer's system. Knowing the educational psychologist's system, we can translate the seven checkmarks he has placed beside "Alice" to signify seven acts of attention addressed by the teacher to the child. These are seven acts of somewhat indeterminate physical form; we do not know how alike or different the physical maneuvers of the teacher were. They are timeless and placeless. Nothing about the record tells us whether the seven acts took an hour, a day, or a month.

Some locational symbols on the educational psychologist's data sheet assign the set of indicative symbols to a place in generally understood coordinates of time, place, and person. The data sheet of the educational psychologist has at the top "Stevenson School", "Fourth grade, Rm. 232C", "3 April 1980", "11:00 A.M.". It is by means of locational notations such as these that our five observing psychologists might be expected, perhaps, to someday discover that they were all simultaneously observing Alice's minute.

Choosing What To Look At

Because many descriptions of Alice are possible, the actual description created by a psychologist reflects choice. How does a psychologist choose a system of observation and its associated form of description? Notice that each of the five psychologists observes indicators of a presumptive causative or control structure governing Alice's activity. The several observers position themselves to bring different levels and kinds of control governing Alice's behavior into view. Table 1 briefly indicates the control factors that interest the five observers.

TABLE 6.1
Patterns of Control Addressed
by the Five Psychologists During Alice's Minute

Observer	Control Factor	Alice's Activity
Behavior Modifier	Eye contact initiated by others	Stuttering
Psychoanalyst	Presumptive personal motives created by sibling rivalry	Verbal and physical acts judged aggressive.
Psychophysiologist	Time as a presumptive indicator of physiological rhythms	Judged awakeness; Acts judged as self-awakening.
Educational Psychologist	Teacher activity directed towards Alice	(unspecified)
Psycholinguist	Age as a presumptive indicator of operational thought	Use of a specified conceptual form in language

Alice is a multiadapting, multipurposing organism. "Alice's behavior" is a corporate term, embracing the output of a heterarchical set of physiological, motor, and cognitive control structures. At a simpler level of behavioral complexity, Alice has organizations that produce reflexes, automatisms, and cyclical psychophysiological motor adjustments. Alice can also sustain connected passages of plan-driven behavior that can last for hours or years, activities at a high level of hierarchical complexity. We call all or any of this "Alice's behavior" or "Alice's activity"; but the single term refers to a complex of organized activities that may often be interwoven or going on in parallel with one another. So two psychologists observing Alice's behavior may well address different psychological organizations.

The Psychologists' Purposes

How do the five psychologists choose their different systems of observation? They arrange to see what controls "interesting" patterns of Alice's activity— that is, more or less desired, good or bad patterns of Alice's behavior. Stuttering is something one would like to minimize. Aggression is often a problem for people. Alertness, or the lack of it, is a major factor in many educational and work settings. Teacher attention is a scarce, positive commodity in school classrooms. "Vice-versa" utterances are good things in that they seem to reflect sophistication of thought or language. The five psychologists have each created a system of observation to bring a control factor governing a more or less desired behavior into view.

SCIENTIFIC ACCOUNTS OF ALICE'S ACTIVITIES

Below are a few summary remarks, of what has been said so far about what happens when psychologists collect data.

1. The core of any objective observation of children's behavior is the translation of momentary states of the stream of behavior into data. Using a well-described rule system, rigidly adhered to, indexed states of the child's activity intermittently instigate acts of the observer that create lasting symbols. Assuming that the observer has been faithful, those symbols are interpretable as descriptions of the child's behavior.
2. The symbols do not speak directly about Alice's behavior. The symbols may be interpreted through knowledge of the observer's scheme and, strictly speaking, they refer to the scheme.
3. Small quantities of the child's activity are reflected in any system of observation.

4. Alice's minute can yield many different strings of data, many scientific descriptions, all valid and reliable.

5. Communication between the child and the scientist is both made possible by, and restricted by, formal games.

6. The psychologist who counts behaviors counts indicators of purposes, motives, or control processes.

7. Observing psychologists create indicative symbols, whose meaning can only be interpreted by means of their scheme of observation. They create locational symbols to place their *acts* of symbolization on generally understood loci of person, place, time, and social setting.

8. The many possible descriptions of Alice reflect, in part, the fact that she is a multiply adapting, multipurposing organism, simultaneously engaged in diverse short- and long-term passages of adaptation.

QUANDARIES OF THE 1920S

What kinds of useful descriptions can one offer of the very rich and complex behavior of a little girl like Alice? Present-day psychology has only begun to address that question in a wide-open way. To understand the possibilities and limits of psychological data, we now need to go beyond a formidable array of ideas and methodological settlements of the 1940's and 1950's: the notion that psychology is fundamentally a scientific extension of philosophical epistemology, the doctrine of "naive realism", the conviction that human behavior will describe itself to the unbiased, unbelieving, un-willing observer—that one does not have to take a stand to see, the notion that only hypotheses subject to quick and easy falsification are valid and meaningful in science, and the belief that the only useful information is certain and completely authoritative information.

For a good part of this century, psychologists have accepted all these premises . . . or have uneasily acquiesced to them, or have complained about them without being able to set forth a viable alternative. The premises have been useful and fruitful, to a degree. They have led psychology to link itself with the natural sciences, to adopt their methods and to seek to find social support together with them. Psychology has paid a high price within and without the boundaries of the discipline for limited, somewhat skeptical support amidst the natural sciences.

Psychology's contemporary self-definition represents a solution to some quandaries of the 1920's and 1930's, when to a significant degree psychologists were still struggling to stand free of the philosophy departments and the education schools of American universities. Psychologists aimed to be a free-standing discipline providing authoritative information about mind and behavior, but they faced conceptual and political problems.

Initial attempts to ground a science of psychology on mathematics, measurement, and psychophysics had not been successful. The first experimental psychologists of the late 19th and early 20th centuries had written little "philosophy of science", probably because they understood science to be a simple and straightforward matter. To be scientific was to quantify and measure and find mathematical regularities. So experimental psychologists directed their sensory research towards psychophysical equations, their studies of learning and memory towards hoped-for mathematical laws of learning, and their testing towards "mental measurement." Unhappily, simple and convincing mathematical regularities did not appear in psychological data; how much psychologists' numbers "measured" was problematic, and after a while became a discrete problem for for analysis and discussion. So early American psychological research did not readily bring forth powerful quantitative truths about human behavior. Psychologists of the 1920's and 1930's confronted the problem of finding some other plausible scientific rationale for their discipline.

Psychologists were separating into schools and isms. Tradition now holds that modern psychology sprang from one source, Wundt's brass-instrument laboratory, but there is good evidence that scientific psychology was plural from the beginning.[3] In any case, by the time of the 1920s American psychologists were unmistakably divided into schools, and books were appearing to count and describe the schools (Murchison, 1925, 1930; Woodworth, 1931; Heidbreder, 1933). In Russia, the young Vygotsky noticed psychology's fractionation and he wrote about the "historical crisis" of Psychology (Kozulin, in press). How could one science exist in so many camps?[4]

---

[3]John Dewey's 1887 *Psychology* listed four methods of a scientific psychology: the method of introspection, the experimental method, the comparative method, and the objective method. This plural vision of psychological research probably reflects the heterogeneous psychology taught by his teacher, G. Stanley Hall, in his first graduate seminar at Johns Hopkins (Evans, 1984). William James' 1890 *Principles of Psychology* listed three methods of psychology: introspective observation, the experimental method, and the comparative method. Danziger's (1985) recent survey of the contents of eight major psychological journals between 1879 and 1898 led him to conclude that there were three distinct traditions of early psychological research, which he calls the "Leipzig model", the "Paris model", and the "Clark model" (White, 1985b).

[4]O'Donnell (1979) has recently argued that E. G. Boring tried to submerge psychology's pluralism of the 1920s under a legendary single historical lineage of experimental psychology. Samelson (1980), among others, has argued that Boring had other motives in writing his history. O'Donnell does have a point. During the 1940s and 1950s, after the legend that psychology was born once, in Leipzig in 1879, got well established, psychologists in diverse groups regularly construed themselves as more-or-less-legitimate heirs of Wundt. Experimentalists took the high ground as those most true to the classic questions of the discipline.

Psychologists were divided about whether their discipline could be a natural science. A great cleavage divided the psychologists into, roughly, two clusters. Experimental psychologists said that a scientific psychology had arrived, and that it was time to stop the hairsplitting and the throat-clearing and move on to scientific development. A cluster of hesitant psychologists resisted, saying that psychology was nowhere, that extant empiricism was an empiricism of trivialities, and that it was essential to find some way to handle purpose and motive and intentionality. Psychology was half developed. Psychological research had gotten off the ground where it could address people as natural kinds and where questions, methods, apparatus, and paradigms could be adapted from the natural sciences. Psychologists interested in personality and social psychology stood virtually at the beginning of the beginning, writing think-pieces, prospectuses, and agendae.

Important psychological research was in the hands of other disciplines. Psychologists might wish to own their subject matter, as physicists owned physics and chemists owned chemistry, but they faced the fact that important psychological questions were being addressed by biology, medicine, anthropology, sociology, and so forth, using methods that were outside the scope of Psychology. What was unique to psychology? What was its authority, special place, and mission? What should be the relationship of psychology's work to the work of these other fields?

An Experiment in Scientific Development

Learning theory, operationalism and the philosophy of science, offered a scheme for a scientific psychology in the face of the quandaries of the 1920s and 1930s. The quandaries of the era reflected behaviors of the emerging community of psychologists, behaviors conflicting with the claim that a science of psychology is possible. The remarkable thing about the program was that it was not based upon a careful study of psychologists' behaviors but rather upon a less-than-careful scrutiny of natural scientists' behaviors.

The scheme worked out at that time is familiar today:

• Psychology was a natural science. Although it had failed to establish straightforward measurement and mathematical laws, analysis revealed a somewhat more complex "hypothetico-deductive" arrangement of concepts, laws, and theories that might better serve as a scientific ideal.

• Psychology's pluralism was temporary and unreal. Outlying areas of psychology, like psychoanalysis and social psychology addressed legitimate questions, but gave "premature" answers to them. Studies of learning and conditioning would establish a solid scientific foundation, and new theories built upon the foundation would someday subsume the preliminary formulations of the personality psychologists and the social psychologists.

• There is a unity among all sciences. "Naively" realistic, psychology studies the same world as the natural sciences and stands among them, above biology and below sociology in the reductive chain. One philosophy of science governs all, extracting precepts from the more-developed sciences for the benefit of the less-developed sciences.

The key premise was that the stuff psychology deals with, "behaviors", are events of the physical world. There were arguments about this premise. Human behavior does not seem to occur in cause-and-effect episodes but instead seems to be future-driven, governed by teleonomic organizations of mind and behavior. Could a physicalistic approach contend with purposivism? Many of the hesitant psychologists of the 1920s talked about this question. It was central to the hesitancy. The book that opened the era of learning theory Tolman's (1932) *Purposive Behavior in Animals and Men,* centered its attention on the question as did the book that closed the era, Miller, Galanter, and Pribram's (1960) *Plans and the Structure of Behavior.*

A Science of Purposes

The learning theory program set forth a cooperative normal science acceptable to many intelligent and serious psychologists. The program offered well-rationalized, inexpensive research technologies; genuinely provocative and interesting findings; agendae (the "theories"); a growing body of methodology; and here and there practically useful spinoffs. Obviously, there was much that was positive and valid about the program. What was problematic was the argument that it offered a complete solution to a science of behavior.

What it offered was a science of lower-level purposes. Behaviors are not regular physical phenomena. A smile may be a physical event, but two smiles are not repetitions of an identical physical event. Two smiles are two physical events judged to be the same because they reflect the agency of the same purpose or program of activity. Some philosophers would say that the term "smile", like all the terms of psychology, has *intentional inexistence.* Hull (1943) would call the smile a *molar behavior*—that is, a goal-seeking pattern of activity.

Studying behaviors, the learning psychologists studied purposes, treating them as physical things and using the scientific strategies and tactics of the physical sciences. The physicalistic approach was possible and useful to a degree, but it was inefficient and it generated puzzles and paradoxes. The Gestalt psychologists delighted in finding and exposing the weaknesses, but they gave no serious thought to designing a better research program for psychologists.

Vygotsky, during his brief but brilliant career, wrote about research methods appropriate for the study of intentional human activity. Genetic study is the appropriate science for human behavior, he said. The intentionality within behavior is revealed in "comparative-genetic" or "experimental-genetic" studies in which development is perturbed, disrupted or challenged (Wertsch, 1985). Interestingly, the psychological science of the learning theory era was largely research that Vygotsky would have termed experimental-genetic.

THE NEED FOR A
CONTEMPORARY POLITICS OF PSYCHOLOGY

The traditional philosophy of science is no longer an active force in psychology. Many now question whether it ever described physics adequately but the question has become immaterial for psychologists. Psychology is unlike physics in important ways. One might claim fundamental similarities at a time when psychologists were at the beginning of the beginning, but now there is a wide-spreading diversity of psychological research activities that do not fit the physicalistic model. We need to systematically examine what psychologists do. Psychology has 100 years of its own history, and an examination of that history can give insights into how, when, where, and why people have built Psychology as a collective process of knowledge-gathering.

The distillate of that historical study should be more than a "philosophy of science or a "philosophy of psychology". Writings about fundamental psychological questions may go far back in intellectual history, but the establishment of Psychology as a human enterprise is grounded in the social history and social changes of the late 19th century. Professional psychologists appeared then. It was then that positions and salaries were set aside, that resources for laboratories and journals were given, and that public expectations endorsed the new psychologists and placing demands upon them.

Something more than a dawning public interest in science and/or epistemology is necessary to account for all this. Psychology's prescientific ancestry is to be found in moral philosophy as well as in natural philosophy (Cofer, in press; Evans, 1984; White, 1985b). We need a description of psychology that talks about why some people have wanted to become psychologists and others have wanted to listen to psychologists; why society has given psychologists status, places, and resources; and how the community of psychologists has built the mutual agreements, customs, and practices of a shared empiricism and shared knowledge. To a limited extent, we can create this kind of description for developmental psychology.

EARLY SOCIAL ORIGINS OF DEVELOPMENTAL PSYCHOLOGY

Many of the contemporary research activities of developmental psychology continue lines of research first undertaken by 19th century nonpsychologists interested in children. When G. Stanley Hall moved from Johns Hopkins to Clark University, and from experimental psychology to child study, he turned towards a mixed audience of college presidents, psychologists, educators, kindergarteners, social workers, child savers, physicians, workers with handicapped children, and parents—many parties, all interested in one way or another in the scientific study of children. Hall's first questionnaire study, "The Contents of Children's Minds", extended studies previously done by German schoolteachers. People engaged in child study in advance of the new psychologists and independently of them (Siegel and White, 1982).

What did all these people hope to obtain from the then-brand-new New Psychology represented by President Hall? In a narrower sense, what they probably hoped to obtain was the establishment of sustained and sophisticated research traditions like those represented by our five psychologists engaged in the study of Alice—five students of important facets of Alice's behavior, each a member of a larger community of researchers elaborating a methodology and a body of knowledge, sharing their knowledge with professionals working with Alice in the interests of her speech, her physical and emotional well-being, and her education. The image of science linked to sound social practice has been around since Sir Francis Bacon.

Psychology's lineage is a lineage of belief in governance based on knowledge and reason. It is not primarily an epistemological lineage. Psychology's predecessors were "philosophers" in an older, broader, nonprofessional sense of that term—people we would be likely to call "intellectuals"—who thought about the rational improvement of society and who put forth psychological and epistemological writings as building blocks of their larger social schemes (White, 1978; Cofer, in press).

Why did so many people of the late 19th century turn to President Hall and his hastily improvised child study questionnaires? They wanted a sense of what was universal in child development grounded on the study of the child.

People wanted a sense of the natural course of a child's development, and of the possibilities of modifying that course in a positive or negative direction. Social arrangements were changing. People were intervening in child development in new ways, trying to train handicapped children, or acquiring the power to change the family circumstances of abused and neglected children. How much could one hope to benefit a child with a new environment, or with special training given either early or late?

Advantaged children were going to school more. Democratic ideals held that all should be helped to "fulfill their potential" and to seek as large a place in society as their abilities could obtain for them. Again, some sense of the natural, the optimal, the unchangeable versus the negotiable in child development helped teachers and parents to understand what, in conscience, they could be held responsible for in educating children and readying them for adult careers.

What are the universal characteristics of children? For a long time to come, parents and teachers would have to put up with either evolutionistic fables about Everychild or thin, cautious, and bloodless accounts of the traits of statistical imaginaries such as "the average child" or "the normal child". The living personality of the child, set aside for the time being by psychological researchers, has only here and there begun to peek out at us in the midst of our scientific formulations.

A SCIENCE OF VALUES

During psychology's history, child study/developmental psychology has been called upon to suggest ideals and values, to help assign responsibilities and find ways and means for dealing some aspects of children's development, and to absolve adults of responsibility for some others. How can "value-free" science give values? Developmental psychology continues a philosophical lineage in which "development" or "evolution" or "progress" have been taken to define the arrow of history and the good ends that men should seek to attain (White, 1976b, 1983a). G. Stanley Hall treated child study as the empirical ground for a scientific moral science. People today call upon developmental psychology to declare what is good or bad for children (Rein and White, 1977; White, 1983c, 1986).

Is the scientific study of Alice good for Alice? Our five psychologists gathered about Alice address ostensibly technical questions about factors controlling Alice's speech, her mental health, her relations with others, and her education. Each is a professional and so committed to a distanced, cool, objective address to the little girl. Each has faced an "ethics committee" certifying that their work with Alice meets standards of scientific ethics. Yet each faces in the end personal responsibilities and commitments to Alice that are neither technical nor negotiable. They are as human beings committed to Alice's welfare, obliged to consider her well-being and the minimization of harm to her. The charter that got the one-way mirror built and allows them access to Alice as a person commits them to participation in her socialization and education. Their activities are humane, evaluative, and value-laden. They seek through their research to clarify ends as well as means.

REFERENCES

Cofer, C. (in press). Human nature and social policy. In L. Friedrich-Cofer (Ed.), *Human nature and public policy: Scientific views of women, children, and families.*, New York: Praeger.

Danziger, K. (1985). The origins of the psychological experiment as a social institution. *American Psychologist, 40,* 133-140.

Dewey, J. (1967). *Psychology.* (J. Boydston et al., Eds.) Carbondale and Edwardsville, IL: Southern Illinois University Press. (Original work published 1887).

Dewey, J. (1965). Psychology and social practice. In J. Ratner (Ed.), *John Dewey: Philosophy, psychology, and social practice.* New York: Capricorn. (Original work published 1900).

Evans, R. B. (1984). The origins of American academic psychology. In J. Brozek (Ed.) *Explorations in the history of psychology in the United States.* Lewisburg: Bucknell University Press, pp. 17-60.

Grim, P. F., Kohlberg, L., and White, S. H. (1968). Some relationships between conscience and attentional processes. *Journal of Personality and Social Psychology, 8,* 239-252.

Heidbreder, E. (1933). *Seven psychologies.* New York: Appleton-Century-Crofts.

Hull, C. L. (1943). *Principles of behavior.* New York: Appleton-Century-Crofts.

James, W. (1981). *The principles of psychology.* (F. H. Burkhardt & F. Bowers, Eds.) Cambridge, MA: Harvard University Press. (Original work published 1890).

Kozulin, Preface to Vygotsky, L. S. (in press) *Language and thought.* (2d, revised ed.). Cambridge, MA: M.I.T. Press.

Miller, G. A., Galanter, E., and Pribram, K. H. (1960). *Plans and the structure of behavior.* New York: Holt, Rinehart, and Winston.

Murchison, C. (1926). *Psychologies of 1925: Powell lectures in psychological theory.* Worcester, MA: Clark University Press.

Murchison, C. (1930). *Psychologies of 1930.* Worcester, MA: Clark University Press.

O'Donnell (1979). The crisis of experimentalism in the 1920's: E. G. Boring and his uses of history. *American Psychologist, 34,* 289-295.

Peirce, C. S. (1958). The logic of 1873. In A. W. Burks (Ed.) *Collected papers of Charles Sanders Peirce,* Vol. VII. Cambridge, MA: Belknap Press. (quote, p. 211).

Rein, M., and White, S. H. (1977). Can policy research help policy? *The Public Interest,* No. 49, 119-136.

Rein, M., and White, S. H. (1981). Knowledge for practice. *Social Service Review, 55,* 1-41.

Rein, M., and White, S. H. (1982). Practice worries in the helping professions. *Society, 19,* 67-78.

Samelson, F. (1980). Letter. *American Psychologist, 35,* 467-479.

Siegel, A. W., and White, S. H. (1982). The child study movement: Early growth and development of the symbolized child. *Advances in Child Behavior and Development, 17,* 233-285.

Simon, H. A. (1969). *The sciences of the artificial.* Cambridge, MA: M.I.T. Press.

Skinner, B. F. (1938). *The behavior of organisms.* New York: Appleton-Century-Crofts.

Solomon, R. C. (1983). *In the spirit of Hegel: A study of G. W. F. Hegel's Phenomenology of Spirit*. New York: Oxford University Press. (quote, p. 124)

Tolman, E. C. (1932). *Purposive behavior in animals and men*. New York: Appleton-Century-Crofts.

Wertsch, J. V. (1985). *Vygotsky and the social formation of mind*. Cambridge, MA: Harvard University Press.

White, S. H. (1970). The learning theory tradition and child psychology. In P. H. Mussen (Ed.) *Carmichael's Manual of Child Psychology*, 3d Ed. New York: Wiley.

White, S. H. (1975). Social implications of IQ. *Principal, 54*, 4–14.

White, S. H. (1976a). The active organism in theoretical behaviorism. *Human Development, 19*, 99–107.

White, S. H. (1976b). Developmental psychology and Vico's concept of universal history. *Social Research, 43*, 659–671.

White, S. H. (1977). Social proof structures: The dialectic of method and theory in the work of psychology. In N. Datan & H. W. Reese (Eds.) *Life-span developmental psychology: Dialectical perspectives on experimental research*. New York: Academic Press.

White, S. H. (1978). Psychology in all sorts of places. In R. Kasschau & F. S. Kessel (Eds.) *Psychology and society: In search of symbiosis*. New York: Holt, Rinehart, and Winston.

White, S. H. (1983a). The idea of development in developmental psychology. In R. M. Lerner (Ed.) *Developmental psychology: Historical and philosophical perspectives*. Hillsdale, N.J.: Lawrence Erlbaum Associates, 55–77.

White, S. H. (1983b). Developmental psychology, bewildered and paranoid: A reply to Kaplan. In R. M. Lerner (Ed.) *Developmental psychology: Historical and philosophical perspectives*. Hillsdale, N.J.: Lawrence Erlbaum Associates, 233–239.

White, S. H. (1983c). Psychology as a moral science. In F. S. Kessel & A. W. Siegel (Eds.), *The child and other cultural inventions*. New York: Praeger, 1–25.

White, S. H. (1985a) Risings and fallings of developmental psychology. Paper presented at symposium, "Revisioning Developmental Psychology", Society for Research in Child Development, Toronto, April, 1985.

White, S. H. (1985b). Developmental psychology at the beginning. Presidential Address, Division 7. American Psychological Association Convention, Los Angeles, August. (*Developmental Psychology Newsletter,* Fall, 1985, 27–39).

White, S. H. (in press). Building human nature into social arrangements. In L. Friedrich-Cofer (Ed.), *Human nature and public policy: Scientific views of women, children, and families.,* New York: Praeger.

Woodworth, R. S. (1931). *Contemporary schools of psychology*. New York: The Ronald Press.

7

Behavioral and
Dialectical Psychologies

Hayne W. Reese
West Virginia University

INTRODUCTION

The purpose of this chapter is to compare four kinds of psychology—two behavioral and two dialectical—that are based on different world views. The four psychologies are Watsonian behaviorism, Skinnerian behaviorism, Piaget's genetic epistemology, and the Soviet "theory of activity." The chapter begins with a commentary on the ways a world view influences science in general and psychology in particular. Next, each of the four psychologies is described. For each of the psychologies, three sets of issues are considered: (1) the underlying presuppositions, or world view, (2) the conception of intelligence, and (3) the role of the environment.

Before proceeding to the matter at hand, I would like to trace the development of my interests that led to the writing of this chapter. The groundwork was laid in the emphasis at Iowa, when I was a student there, on the philosophical underpinnings of the stimulus–response approach to learning and to child behavior and development. Only one view was taught, but it was by far the dominant one in psychology at that time—the middle to late 1950s—and fit the mainstream of the field and many of its subsidiaries. I recall an incident that supports this characterization of that era: During a job interview at the University of Buffalo in 1958, I was asked informally what I thought of Jean Piaget, and I answered that his career consisted of 30 years of pilot work. The listeners must have agreed; I got the job (my first postdoctoral one). Piaget used searching interviews, rife with leading questions, to find children's reasons for their judgments about various task outcomes, and he used this information to infer the children's mental capabilities. I considered—rightly from the Iowa viewpoint—that this method could produce some interesting hypotheses that could be tested definitively only through experimental manipulations of variables and observations of actual choice-responses, rather than through ratiocinations about answers to leading questions.

The times were already changing, however, as more and more psychologists interested in cognition and cognitive development became impatient with the perceived slow progress being made with the stimulus–response approach and yearned to study more exciting phenomena than discrimination and verbal learning, for example. They were interested in the kinds of phenomena Spence (1940) referred to as the "higher forms of adjustment such as are mediated by the complex symbolic mechanisms" of humans (footnote 6, p. 288). Following Chomsky's lead, many psychologists began to make pronouncements about the in-principle inability of stimulus–response theories to deal with these complex phenomena.

However, not only was their reasoning dubious, but also the alternatives they offered were scientifically deficient from the Iowa viewpoint. They studied new phenomena and they offered new terms for describing these phenomena; but from the Iowa viewpoint they stopped at description because if their theories (or "models" as theories came to be usually called) were intended to be explanatory, they were circular. Circular explanations may be fun to invent, but they are not falsifiable in any scientifically interesting sense. What is the point of inventing mental contents, or competence, that cannot be tested against data, or performance? The Iowa answer was "None."

At Buffalo in the 1960s I heard presentations by computer simulation people, Piagetians, and other cognitivists, and I later came to realize, largely through discussions with my colleague Willis Overton, that their approaches were *different* rather than *deficient*—they were based on different philosophies, not ignorance of a one true philosophy. In the late 1960s I moved to the Department of Human Development at the University of Kansas, which was then and still is a center for a Skinnerian approach to child behavior and development, and I discovered still another underlying philosophy. From then to the present I have continued the comparative study of theories and have found that most theories that have enough scope and precision to have significant numbers of advocates for significant periods of time can be understood from some one of three philosophies or, better, sets of metatheoretical presuppositions that were identified by Stephen Pepper (1942) as mechanism, organicism, and contextualism (pragmatism).

The Iowa viewpoint is mechanistic; it cannot be legitimately used to evaluate theories that are consistent with either of the other sets of presuppositions, nor can the mechanistic stimulus–response approach be legitimately evaluated from these other viewpoints. One example suffices, I hope, to nail down the point and to end this overly long digression: Krechevsky (e.g., 1938) criticized stimulus–response theorists for failing to use *patterns* of responses as the basic unit of analysis; but he failed to realize that from the mechanistic view such patterns *must* be analyzed as chains of separate responses even though such chains are acknowledged to be functionally unitary (Keller & Schoenfeld, 1950, p. 202; Skinner, 1953, p. 224) and even though actual behavior is acknowledged to be a continuous flux (Spence, 1956, p. 44).

My aim in this chapter is to show that explicating the underlying presuppositions is an effective way to make alternative psychologies comprehensible. Perhaps it is the *only* way.

INFLUENCES OF WORLD VIEWS

World views are also called cosmologies, ontologies, paradigms, presuppositions, world hypotheses, world theories, and weltanschauungen, which means "world views." (In Langenscheidt's German–English dictionary [1970, p. 309], the meaning of *Weltanschauung* is given as "Weltanschauung.") Their influence on scientific psychology is described in the present section. They do not provide alternative approaches to the scientific collection of facts, which as shown later always involves careful observation under known conditions. Rather, they provide alternative approaches to the interpretation or explanation of facts (Overton & Reese, 1973; Pepper, 1942).

Roles of World Views

World views are very general models that provide categorical bases for knowledge about reality. Ideally, but not in practice, a world view is so general that its scope covers *all* reality; that is, it provides an interpretation, or a representation, of every phenomenon. Also ideally, but again not in practice, a world view is so precise that it generates one and only one interpretation of each phenomenon within its scope.

World views have a categorical influence on knowledge systems; that is, any world view contains certain categories, or basic concepts, that cannot be violated in any model or theory derived from (or consistent with) the world view. This categorical influence is important because different world views lead to different conceptions of substance, activity, change, fact, truth, explanation, value, etc. They even influence the understanding of appropriate methods for discovery of facts (Overton & Reese, 1973). Because of these differences, world views—and perforce the knowledge systems they influence—are independent of one another.

A world view provides basic subject-matter concepts and rules for making statements about the subject matter. The subject-matter concepts refer to the nature of substance and change (for example), the nature of the relation between a whole and the parts it comprises, and the nature of causality. The rules refer to methods of research, prescribing an analytic or a synthetic approach, for example, and determining the primacy of facts obtained through observation versus facts obtained through inference or rational argument. The rules also include methods for ascertaining truth and value.

For example, in mechanism such concepts as an immaterial mind, wholes as basic units, true chance, and free will are excluded because they are inconsistent with the mechanistic categories of material reality and in principle decomposability and predictability. Also, a whole in mechanism is completely reducible to the movements of parts, and the parts move because of antecedent forces that contact them (in Cartesian mechanism). Research is therefore analytic, decomposing wholes into their constituting parts, and observed facts about antecedents and consequences are held more tenaciously than rational facts about unobserved mediators. The truth criterion is correspondence of knowledge to reality. Finally, value in the mechanistic view is excluded from the methodological rules (but can be included in the subject matter that is studied).

Rules of concept formation, etc. can be adopted dogmatically, of course; but if they are, they cannot be intellectually compelling. In contrast, rules that are categorical, that is, rules that follow as consequences from a world view, are intellectually compelling. Given a particular world view, no other rules would be reasonable. Thus, a major role of world views is to avoid dogmatism by making the rules principled.

The Nature of Scientific Knowledge

In their translation of Aristotle's *Physics,* Wicksteed and Cornford (1929) remarked, "it has been said of the 'Ancients' at large that 'they said everything, but proved nothing'" (p. xix). Along the same line, my father (who was an attorney) once characterized psychology as the science of proving what everybody already knew, which is reminiscent of George Bernard Shaw's comment (quoted in Payne, 1968), "Pavlov is the biggest fool I know; any policeman could tell you that much about a dog" (p. 16). Without the proving, however, what the Ancients said and what everybody already knew was not *science.* (A further point, not relevant here, is that knowledge in psychology has in fact gone well beyond what the Ancients said and what everybody already knew, as Skinner [1974, p. 232] noted.)

Knowledge without proof is still knowledge, but it is not scientific knowledge. In fact, knowledge *with* proof is not scientific unless the proof meets two criteria. One criterion is methodological and the other is theoretical. Before these criteria are considered, a preliminary point is that I have made a verbal leap from the sense of *proof* intended in the preceding paragraph to another sense. The leap is from the sense of definite confirmation that a purported fact is true or, worded more precisely, definite confirmation that a statement about a purported fact is true, to proof in the sense of a test—a judicious examination of a purported fact.[1]

Rationale for the Two Criteria. In distinguishing between the methodological and theoretical criteria, I am not asserting that the facts yielded by application of the methodological criterion are independent of theory. Scientific facts and theories are inseparable (Kessel, 1969; Kuhn, 1970, p. 7). As Dallenbach (1953) said, a study without a theory is not a scientific experiment, it is only busy work; without a theory, such work has no meaning and cannot contribute to scientific knowledge.

A rationale for this position is provided by Rychlak's (1976) distinction between the *methodological* and *theoretical* paradigms of science. The methodological paradigm deals with facts about independent and dependent variables; the theoretical paradigm deals with cause–effect relations and other interpretations of facts obtained within the methodological paradigm. For example, within the methodological paradigm, certain manipulations might be done and certain observations made; but describing these as causes and effects or even as stimuli and responses involves moving to the theoretical paradigm. The methodological paradigm is used to obtain facts, but these facts are not scientific knowledge until they have been interpreted within the theoretical paradigm. In short, the legal maxim "The fact speaks for itself" (*Res ipsa loquitur*) has no basis in the philosophy of science.

Another approach is to examine the metatheoretical underpinnings of methods and theories. Pap (1953) argued that science does not rest on metatheoretical ("metaphysical") presuppositions. He acknowledged that scientists have presuppositions, but he argued that these presuppositions are not metatheoretical. For example, according to Pap the presupposition "every event has a cause" is merely a psychological habit—"the product of

---

[1]Farrant (1977) argued that the second sense is intended in the proverb "The exception proves the rule." It is also intended in "The proof of the pudding is in the eating." Bocheński (1963) referred to the latter as "Engels' famous dictum" (p. 69), but it is actually an English proverb dating at least to the beginning of the 17th century (Tilley, 1950, p. 558). Bergmann and Spence (1941) used it in reference to empirical constructs: "The proof of the pudding is in the eating and not in any particular operational criterion" (p. 5).

ever repeated experiences of uniformity" (p. 33). However, although relevant experiences may be ever repeated in the physical sciences, they are at least rarer in the behavioral sciences. If the "habit" is generalized from the physical sciences to the behavioral sciences, then the generalization needs a basis. If the basis is a metatheoretical position, the presuppositions are principled and cognitively compelling; but if the presuppositions have no metatheoretical basis, they are held dogmatically and are not compelling (Pepper, 1942).

For example, in the world view Pepper (1942) called contextualism, the presupposition that the world is predictable is rejected. In this world view, chance is categorical, that is, it is a basic fact of the universe and not a reflection of inadequate knowledge about the universe. Therefore, novelty, emergence, and unpredictability are basic facts. In psychology, this presupposition allows the assumption of free will in humans, whose behavior is therefore in principle unpredictable. Spiker (1977) said, with respect to this kind of position, "It is difficult to understand why psychologists would continue their research efforts if they believed that organisms had such potential" (p. 99). Overton (1984) also criticized the contextualistic basis for this conception. However, these objections are not relevant because they reflect, respectively, mechanistic and organic views of the world. Contextualists seem to have no difficulty accepting novelty and at the same time continuing their research efforts.

The Methodological Criterion.   The methodological criterion of knowledge refers to the source of the knowledge. For example, the source of commonsense knowledge is everyday experience, the source of literary knowledge is intuition, and the source of religious knowledge is revelation. The source of scientific knowledge is application of a scientific method. Different methods are employed in different sciences, but all sciences are founded on observables (Spiker & McCandless, 1954) and therefore all scientific methods are founded on observation. Specifically, all scientific methods require careful observation of phenomena under known (i.e., specified) conditions. (Baltes, Reese, & Nesselroade, 1977, p. 28, specified *objective* observation under known conditions, but objectivity is problematical and is an unnecessary restriction. Bechtoldt, 1959, specified careful observation under *standard* conditions, but he was explicitly discussing psychological tests as a subclass of observational methods.)

The Theoretical Criterion.   The theoretical criterion of scientific knowledge is that the interpretation, or explanation, is consistent with an adequate world view (for rationales of this criterion, see Kuhn, 1970, chap. 2; Lakatos, 1978, pp. 47–52; Laudan, 1977, pp. 78–81; Overton & Reese, 1973; Pepper, 1942, chap. 4 and 5; Reese & Overton, 1970). For this criterion, a world view is *adequate* if it has reasonably wide scope and reasonable precision.

To summarize, careful observation of phenomena under known conditions yields facts, or information; but in its fullest sense, knowledge refers to understanding as well as information—knowing why as well as knowing what. Therefore, the information obtained by careful observation under known conditions needs to be interpreted or explained. In short, then, knowledge is scientific if it has the empirical proof given by use of a scientific method and the theoretical proof given by adequate interpretation or explanation.

Three Relatively Adequate World Views

Psychology can be defined as the study and explanation of behavioral change. Any psychology that meets the methodological and theoretical criteria of science is by definition scientific. All psychologies that have deserved serious consideration—including the classical introspectionist psychologies of Wundt and Titchener, Gestalt psychology (but perhaps not Gestalt therapy), and Piagetian psychology as well as the studiedly scientific behavioral and information-processing psychologies—have met the methodological criterion of careful observation under known conditions. The world views that underlie these psychologies have been, almost exclusively, mechanism, organicism, and contextualism. These world views are characterized later in the discussions of the psychologies related to them. Briefly, mechanism reflects Cartesian or, alternatively, Newtonian mechanics; organicism reflects Hegelian idealism, and contextualism reflects further development of American pragmatism. All three of these world views are relatively adequate in scope and precision, and therefore they provide theoretical legitimacy to the psychologies they underlie.

BACKGROUND ON BEHAVIORISM

"Behaviorism" is often discussed as a single approach—almost always by nonbehaviorists. Actually, the term behaviorism is applicable to a variety of approaches; two of these, Watsonian behaviorism and Skinnerian behaviorism, are discussed in the present chapter. By "Watsonian behaviorism" I mean to include the "learning theory" or "S-R" tradition (White, 1970, pp. 657-658), "theoretical behaviorism" (White, 1976), "conditioning theory" (Spiker, 1977), and all the "lineal descendents of Watsonian methodological behaviorism" (Kendler, 1967, p. 336; p. 2 in 1971 reprint)—Clark L. Hull, Kenneth W. Spence, Charles C. Spiker,

House and Zeaman, the Kendlers, etc. By "Skinnerian behaviorism" I mean "the approach variously labeled as the functional analysis of behavior, the experimental analysis of behavior, operant conditioning, or Skinnerian psychology" (Etzel, LeBlanc, & Baer, 1977, pp. xv–xvi)—B. F. Skinner, Fred S. Keller, Sidney W. Bijou, Barbara C. Etzel, Donald M. Baer, etc.

History

Behaviorism was introduced by the American psychologist John B. Watson in 1913. It was an optimistic position in that development was attributed to environmental forces rather than to hereditary potentials. Watson said, in his book *Behaviorism* (1925): "Give me a dozen healthy infants, well-formed, and my own specified world to bring them up in and I'll guarantee to take any one at random and train him to become any type of specialist I might select—doctor, lawyer, artist, merchant-chief and, yes, even beggar-man and thief, regardless of his talents, penchants, tendencies, abilities, vocations, and race of his ancestors" (p. 82).

Some have seen this position as not merely wrong, but inherently evil. I see it as gloriously optimistic, holding out hope for everyone regardless of genetic inheritance, and I consider it unfortunate that Watson turned out to have been overly optimistic.[2] He was not completely wrong, however, because even when disordered development has a biogenetic origin, an optimal environment can produce full development up to the biogenetically determined limit, as pointed out by a modern Skinnerian behaviorist, Donald M. Baer (1970).

This confident, growth-oriented approach was well suited to the American temperament, and behaviorism quickly became the dominant psychology in the United States, as suggested, perhaps, by the election of Watson

---

[2]Watson seems not to have realized the overoptimism of the statement, but contrary to Skinner's (1974) characterization of it as a "careless remark" (p. 221), Watson was completely serious. Watson made the statement in a book that he himself criticized in his autobiography (1936), but he was dissatisfied with the hasty preparation of the book rather than its extreme environmentalism. He repeated the statement in the 1930 revision of the book (p. 104) and paraphrased it in his 1928 book *The Ways of Behaviorism* (Watson, 1928b): "The cry of the behaviorist is, 'Give me the baby and my world to bring it up in and I'll make it crawl and walk; I'll make it climb and use its hands in constructing buildings of stone or wood; I'll make it a thief, a gunman, or a dope fiend. The possibility of shaping in any direction is almost endless'" (pp. 35–36). (As an editor I cannot refrain from observing that "the behaviorist" might have become hoarse because this "cry" continued for another 139 words beyond the 55 quoted here.) Watson still considered this position to be possibly correct when he wrote his autobiographical essay, published in 1936, and therein he clearly viewed it not as a principle but as an hypothesis that was worth testing (Watson, 1936).

to the presidency of the American Psychological Association in 1914.[3] Behaviorism also had some impact in China before the communist revolution, although John Dewey's "functional psychology" was dominant there. To a large extent, the impact of behaviorism in China reflected the efforts of Kuo Zing-yang, who seems to have overlapped with Watson at the University of Chicago (Chin & Chin, 1969). Kuo once said (quoted in Chin & Chin, 1969), in the 1920s, "There are only one and a half true behaviorists in this world; Watson is the half. I am the only true behaviorist" (p. 8). His objection was that Watson gave heredity a role; Kuo gave it none.

Actually, Watson gave heredity only a small role, as indicated by the "dozen infants" statement, the "cry" in footnote 2, and the following statement from another article: The human infant, according to Watson (1928a):

is born a squirming mass without instincts, without patterned behavior. . . . We are environmental products. Now you can make of this product a religious mystic like Mrs. Eddy or a militant fundamentalist like Dr. Stratton. You can make of him a play boy like the Prince of Wales, an austere, unverbalized puritan like Mr. Coolidge, a Shakesperian pugilist like Mr. Tunney, an author like Jack London, or an actor like Mr. Sothern (which God forbid). There is almost no limitation to the ways we can shape him if we only start early enough. (p. 967)

Watsonian behaviorism emphasized theoretical explanation and, through the years, it became more and more concerned about finer and finer theoretical details. For example, one of the best representatives of the movement, Kenneth W. Spence, developed his theory to the point where he could predict the block of trials on which two responses performed by rats would differ maximally in frequency after the responses had been rewarded at different rates (Spence, 1956, pp. 205–215). In spite of this success and others, this type of behaviorism began to decline in popularity among psychologists, especially beginning in the 1960s. At the same time, however, the other kind of behaviorism discussed herein, originated by B. F. Skinner in the 1930s, began to rise in popularity.

---

[3]In accordance with the then policy of the American Psychological Association, the 1914 Nominations Committee nominated only one person for President. The committee that nominated Watson for the 1915 presidency consisted of H. C. Warren (Chair), E. L. Thorndike, and J. R. Angell ("Proceedings," 1914, p. 32). The nomination was accepted at the business meeting of the annual convention in December 1914, and "the secretary was instructed to cast the vote of the Association for Professor John B. Watson as president" ("Proceedings," 1915, p. 47). Incidentally, the members of the nominating committee were elected by ballot, without prior nomination, at the annual conventions in the period from 1912/1913 to 1915; Watson was elected to the first of these committees, along with J. R. Angell and E. L. Thorndike ("Proceedings," 1913, p. 44).

Skinnerian behaviorism is much less theory oriented than the Watsonian type, and much more concerned with practical applications. For example, Watsonian behaviorists identify many causal variables in the environment, but the Skinnerians identify only one—contingent stimulation—which (1) is either a naturally occurring or an artificially imposed change in the environment following the occurrence of selected behaviors and (2) results in a change in the frequency of occurrence of the selected behaviors. The difference in emphasis reflects a difference in underlying world view, as is shown in the next two sections.

Methodological and Metaphysical Behaviorism

As expounded by Watson, behaviorism was both a methodological program and a metaphysical position (Bergmann, 1956). Methodological behaviorism is often said to exclude mental events from the realm of science (e.g., Beilin, 1981, p. 7; Day, 1983; Skinner, 1974, pp. 15, 16). In fact, it does no such thing; the culprit is metaphysical behaviorism (Bergmann, 1956). According to Bergmann (1956), the basic tenet of *metaphysical* behaviorism is that "there are no minds," which is an unnecessary extension from the noncontroversial tenet of *methodological* behaviorism, "there are no interacting minds" (p. 266). The latter tenet is merely an assertion that no one mind has any direct causal connection with any other mind (Ryle, 1949, p. 13).

The basic tenet of methodological behaviorism is that "It must *in principle* be possible to predict future behavior, including verbal behavior, from a sufficiency of information about present (and past) behavioral, physiological, and environmental variables" (Bergmann, 1956, p. 270). Put another way by Spiker (1977), the basic tenet is that: "The primitive, undefined terms of the psychological language need not, and indeed should not, differ from those of the physical and biological sciences. . . . [This] definitional tenet stipulates that all *primitive* terms in psychology that refer to the private (mental) experience of subjects are taboo" (pp. 94–95). Unseen private events abound in Watsonian (methodological) behaviorism, including the "fractional anticipatory goal response" (Spence, 1956, pp. 49–51), "implicit verbal behavior" (Bergmann, 1956), and other inferred variables or "hypothetical constructs" (Bergmann, 1951; MacCorquodale & Meehl, 1948; Rozeboom, 1956; Spiker & McCandless, 1954). The issue here is not whether this approach to mental events is fruitful. Rather, the point is that such events are in fact not ignored in methodological behaviorism.

The basic tenet of metaphysical behaviorism may be accepted by a sporadic few psychologists, but the basic tenet of methodological behaviorism (as defined by Bergmann, not as defined by Beilin, Day, and Skinner) is accepted by all behaviorists.

WATSONIAN BEHAVIORISM

Presuppositions

Modern Watsonian behaviorism is consistent with the world view Pepper (1942) labeled mechanism (Overton & Reese, 1973; Reese & Overton, 1970).

Methodology. Relatively early in the development of Watsonian behaviorism, the operationist philosophy of physics was explicitly adopted to provide the definition of adequate methodology (e.g., Bergmann & Spence, 1941). (The adjective "operationist" may be confusing, because "operationism" and "operationalism" have been used to refer to both the pragmatic theory of truth [Pepper, 1942, p. 268] and the mechanistic theory of truth [Bergmann, 1954; 1957, pp. 56–59]. It is used here in the latter sense.)

Model of the Organism. The mechanistic model is also used in Watsonian behaviorism as the representation of the organism. The mechanistic representation of the organism is the so-called "black-box," "empty organism," or "passive organism" model, although it is more aptly called a "reactive" or "responsive" organism model (Reese, 1976a). According to this model, the organism—like the machine—reacts to imposed forces and is at rest in the absence of imposed forces; forces determine movement, given a particular state of the system.

In behaviorism, stimuli are the analogues of forces. These analogues include internal stimuli as well as external stimuli. Some of the internal stimuli are hypothetical: the response-produced mediating stimulus s_m (e.g., Goss, 1961; Reese, 1962), the stimulus s_g produced by the "fractional anticipatory goal response" r_g (Spence, 1960, p. 96), the stimuli produced by frustration, s_f, and emotion, s_e (Amsel, 1958; Spence, 1956, pp. 49–51, 134–137, 1960, pp. 96–99), and drive stimuli s_D (e.g., Brown, 1961, p. 75; Dollard & Miller, 1950, footnote 6, pp. 30–31; Hull, 1943, p. 71; Spence, 1956, p. 166). Other stimuli, such as the "intraorganic stimuli" mentioned by Spence (1956, p. 41), may be physiological.

Conception of Intelligence

Cognition and Language. Watson's (1930, chap. 10) conception of thought as subvocal speech is well known, I presume, and need not be elaborated here other than to note two points about it. First, the research generated by this conception was inconclusive, but it was inconclusive not because of the nature of the findings but because of a flaw in the rationale. Specifically, the best the research could do would be to demonstrate a correlation between thought and subvocal speech—or between thought and any other observable measure, whether behavioral, physiological, or neural—and correlation does not demonstrate causation. That is, the correlation would not demonstrate that thought is reducible to subvocal speech; the subvocal speech could be reducible to thought (Reese, 1971). Second, the reference to subvocal speech was only part of Watson's conception, in that he hypothesized that thought is attenuated action of many sorts, including, of course, subvocal speech, but also including nonspeech actions (Watson, 1930, chap. 11). For Watson, then, language provides only one aspect of thought.

Intelligence. Ferguson's (1954, 1956) theory of intelligence is consistent with Watsonian behaviorism. It is an excellent example of this kind of theory because it refers only to stimulus–response associations and the variables that affect learning and transfer of these associations. Basically, the theory is that intelligence consists of a collection of behaviors that can be learned, that if learned can transfer to new situations, and that if transferred can facilitate appropriate responding or facilitate new learning. According to the theory, the ultimate level of intelligence attainable is influenced by biological factors, and therefore by heredity, but the specific intellectual behaviors that are acquired depend on the environment, including the physical and the cultural environment. Intellectual behaviors are those that yield effective adaptation to the physical and cultural environments; different ones may be effective in different environments, depending on the nature of the physical environment and the culture. Behaviors that yield effective adaptation are rewarded and learned; other behaviors are either punished or nonrewarded and are not learned.

Much cross-cultural research supports this theory. For example, children in isolated fishing villages in Newfoundland were found to be below the norm on verbal abilities but at the norm on spatial abilities, which apparently were more important than verbal abilities in their culture (Burnett, Beach, & Sullivan, 1963).

Role of Environment

Watson's antihereditarian stance is well illustrated by his "dozen infants" statement. Its being wrong is more to be regretted than its extremeness. In fact, such a view is basic to a democratic society, perhaps explaining why the Skinnerian behaviorist Donald M. Baer could still write in 1970: "It seems to me implicit in modern behavioral technology that there must be quite some number of environmental programs, or sequences, which will bring an organism to any specified developmental outcome . . . ; thus, it suggests that behaviorally, it is rarely too late—or too early—for a good outcome" (p. 244).

SKINNERIAN BEHAVIORISM

Presuppositions

The philosophy underlying Skinnerian behaviorism as a science, that is, the philosophy that defines adequate methodology in this approach, is pragmatism. (Reese & Overton, 1970, asserted that behaviorism is mechanistic, but they should have specified that they were referring to Watsonian behaviorism.) The model of the organism is mechanistic. The bases for these assertions are discussed in the rest of the present subsection.

Pragmatism. Pragmatism is an American philosophy, originally advanced as a method for defining truth and value by Charles S. Peirce (1878/1923), John Dewey (1090), and William James (1907). It later "thickened" into a world-encompassing philosophy, or world view, which Pepper (1942) called *contextualism* (p. 268). The basic metaphor of contextualism is an ongoing act. All ongoing acts have two essential features: They have a "content" and they occur in a context. "Writing" is not an act; but writing something (with something on something in some situation at some time) is an act. "Thinking" is not an act, and "rehearsing" is not an act; but thinking something and rehearsing something are acts. All acts—mental as well as physical—are *concrete* in this sense, and any purported "act" that has no content or context is an abstraction, a product of analysis rather than of observation.

Novelty in the sense of true emergence is a basic concept in contextualism (for the reasons, see Pepper, 1942, chap. 10). Therefore, the criterion for truth is not correspondence or coherence, as in mechanism and organicism, respectively. Rather, the criterion is that nothing is worth considering true, or real, unless it makes a difference in practice (James, 1907, p. 46, Lecture 6); that is, the question "Is it true?" is the same as "Does it work?" because the "true" course to anywhere is whatever course gets you there now. This is the "successful working" theory of truth. Pepper (1942) believed that this theory reflects an overly narrow interpretation of contextualism, but he admitted that his broadened theory ("qualitative confirmation") "comes dangerously near overstepping the categorical limits of contextualism" (p. 270), and that the contextualist relies ultimately on successful working ("direct verification"—p. 278).

Skinnerian Methodology. Skinnerian behaviorists (e.g., Day, 1983; Lamal, 1983) seem to have embraced the simpler version of pragmatism—the dogmatic "method" or truth criterion—rather than the full-fledged world view. For example, the goals of Skinnerian behaviorism are to control and predict behavior. (Watson's behaviorism had the same goals, but unlike

Skinner, Watson, 1913, interpreted these goals as *theoretical*.) Skinner (1974) admitted the possibility of mentalistic explanations in psychology, but he argued that they add nothing to the control and prediction of behavior beyond a purely behavioristic explanation and therefore they should be excluded from the science of psychology (164–166, chap. 13). His argument is clearly pragmatic, and he referred approvingly to "an old principle that nothing is different until it makes a difference" (1974, p. 31), which is the truth criterion in pragmatism.

Model of the Organism.   The model used to represent the organism—mechanism—is different from the model used as the source of methodological rules—pragmatism. This apparent inconsistency in Skinnerian behaviorism is resolved by noting that for Skinnerian behaviorists the mechanistic model of the organism is pragmatically useful and therefore its use is consistent with the pragmatic conception of truth—it works.

In Skinner's two-category model of behavior, a distinction is made between respondent behavior and operant behavior. Respondent behavior is controlled by an antecedent stimulus as a result of genetically determined mechanisms or as a result of a particular history of contiguous presentations of two stimuli. However, current deprivation interacts with the genetic mechanisms and the history of stimulus presentations to determine the behavior. Thus, the antecedent stimulus is analogous to force; the respondent behavior is analogous to movement; and the genetic mechanisms and history of stimulus presentations, together with current deprivation, are analogous to the state of the system. Thus, the respondent category is consistent with the mechanistic model.

The operant category is also consistent with the mechanistic model: The analogue of force is antecedent stimulation; the analogue of movement is operant behavior; and the analogue of the state of the system is the history of contingent stimulation, together with current deprivation. A possible objection to this analysis can be forestalled by noting that the analogues are not the same for the respondent and operant categories, but that the differences make no difference at the presuppositional level. The reason is that the analogue of force, for example, is not conceptualized as a *force* but as an analogue of force. It is assigned certain properties and functions of forces, but not others; and the unassigned properties and functions can be ignored (Overton & Reese, 1973).

Skinner's Position on Mechanism.   Skinner (1974) has argued that his approach is not mechanistic: (1) The "push–pull" stimulus–response model is rejected and replaced by the two-category model in which respondent behavior is mechanical and operant behavior is purposive; (2) the mechanistic reactive-organism model is rejected and replaced by an active-organism model; finally, (3) the tenet of methodological behaviorism that mental phenomena cannot be studied is rejected and replaced by the tenet that they not only can be studied but also should be studied because of their importance for understanding observed behavior, as in self-control of overt behavior. These arguments are faulty.

In the mechanistic model the "push-pull" concept (1) means that forces determine movement, given a particular state of the system. As shown in a previous section, operant as well as respondent behavior is consistent with the mechanistic model.

Furthermore, operant behavior is not really purposive. Operant behavior is said to be controlled by its consequences, and according to Skinner (1974), it is "by its nature . . . directed toward the future: a person acts *in order that something* will happen, and the order is temporal" (p. 55; see also Bijou & Baer, 1978, p. 11). However, if the consequences are truly in the future, these statements imply a teleological purposivism. Skinnerian behaviorists reject teleology, and therefore operant behavior should be said to be controlled by antecedent stimuli as a result of a particular history of contingent presentation of reinforcing and/or punishing stimuli. The "purposivism" of operant behavior is merely a reference to this history (Skinner, 1974, pp. 56–57). To be complete, the statement would need to include definitions of the reinforcing and punishing functions, which in turn would involve statements about deprivation.

Although the operant category of behavior entails an active-organism model (2), it is not an active-organism model that is usefully distinguished from the reactive-organism model. A detailed discussion of the issue is presented elsewhere (Baltes & Reese, 1977) and need not be repeated here. The organism in Skinnerian behaviorism is the "source" of behaviors (Bijou & Baer, 1978, p. 26) or is the "host" of behaviors (Baer, 1976) but is not a "seeker of stimulation" (Bijou & Baer, 1978, p. 29), not a "true originator or initiator of action" (Skinner, 1974, p. 225; see also Skinner, 1957, chap. 12).

Skinner (1974) and others (e.g., Mapel, 1977) have noted correctly that Watson rejected the study of mental phenomena (3), and they have also noted correctly that in this respect Watson was overly doctrinaire. However, they have ignored the distinction between methodological and metaphysical behaviorism, previously discussed, and have ignored the fact that modern Watsonian behaviorists study mental phenomena.

The tenet of methodological behaviorism is not that mental phenomena cannot be studied, but that they cannot be *directly* studied in an *objective* way. Studying them subjectively, for example by the method of introspection, is rejected by Skinnerian as well as Watsonian behaviorists; and studying them indirectly is accepted by both Skinnerians and Watsonians (Reese, 1986). In any case, the study of mental phenomena is considered to have limited usefulness in Skinnerian behaviorism, because mental phenomena are considered not to be causal in this view (e.g., Bijou & Baer, 1978, p. 19). Thus, although self-regulation is possible, it is caused not by mental processes but by a history of contingent stimulation, and it is controlled not by mental processes but by the current stimulus situation (Bijou & Baer, 1978, pp. 114, 116).

Conception of Intelligence

Among Skinnerian behaviorists, Skinner seems to have made the major theoretical contribution to the understanding of intellectual development, for example in his analyses of knowing (1969) and verbal behavior (1957). Piaget (1977) characterized Skinner's analysis of verbal behavior as "a simple empiricist associationism," and as "totally unacceptable," adding that "here Chomsky has done great service by his brilliant and incisive criticisms of Skinner's interpretations" (p. 3). One might doubt that Piaget—and Chomsky—understood Skinner's analysis and the various replies to Chomsky's criticism of it (e.g., MacCorquodale, 1970; Paivio, 1971, pp. 393–431), because in fact it is far from simple and it is not associationistic in the sense Piaget seems to have intended (cf. Piaget, 1952, pp. 362, 409).

Important empirical contributions have come from many Skinnerian researchers, such as the group in the Department of Human Development at the University of Kansas who have studied, for example, the development of language (Guess, Sailor, & Baer, 1974; Risley, 1977; Schumaker & Sherman, 1970) and creativity (Goetz & Baer, 1973; Holman, Goetz, & Baer, 1977).

Intellectual Development.   According to Skinnerian theory, intellectual development consists of the acquisition (i.e., learning) of "subjective terms" (Skinner, 1945), rules of various kinds (Bijou & Baer, 1978; Skinner, 1974), and stimulus and response classes (Bijou & Baer, 1978). These acquisitions yield imitation, abstraction, and all the "cognitive skills" such as decision making and problem solving (but not memory, which refers merely to the durability of learned behavior-environment relations: Bijou & Baer, 1978, p. 127). However, the theory is simple with respect to the cause of cognitive development—conditioning. Some of the acquisitions, particularly in infancy, are assumed to involve respondent conditioning; but most are assumed to involve operant conditioning—shaping, fading, generalization, and discrimination, all involving contingencies of reinforcement and/or punishment.

Intellectual development is primarily, then, a matter of managing reinforcers: Reinforcing and/or punishing stimuli are (1) presented or withdrawn (2) in accordance with a selected schedule, (3) depending on the occurrence of selected behaviors (4) in selected contexts. Theoretically, complex patterns of behavior, such as intellectual behaviors, are chains of simpler behaviors, and the chains are acquired in the same way as the simpler behaviors—through the procedure just outlined. Of course, this outline of the procedure glosses over all the difficulties involved: finding appropriate reinforcing and punishing stimuli, including possible systems of token economies; monitoring the contingency schedule; defining and observing the relevant behaviors; etc. These are technical problems, however, and are not the concern of the present chapter. The point here is that the methods of intervention are known and are relatively easy to use—at least they are easy to use in comparison with the methods required in the other views surveyed.

An example is the modification of creativity. In the classroom, the presentation of programmed materials can increase creativity as measured by standardized "creativity" tests, especially when the materials are presented by an instructor (Reese & Parnes, 1970). Direct experimental evidence has demonstrated that contingency management is effective (Holman et al., 1977). However, as Bijou and Baer (1978) noted, much more research is needed to develop detailed procedures for teaching creativity in specific areas (pp. 123–124).

Other problems that remain are to find ways to maintain temporal stability of modified behaviors and to obtain transsituational generalization. However, these problems are recognized and are being analyzed empirically. The expectation is that they will yield to the same kinds of manipulations that have worked for other behavioral problems (e.g., Holman et al., 1977; Stokes & Baer, 1977).

Role of Language.   Skinner (1945) discussed the acquisition of "subjective terms" and attributed it to differential reinforcement by the "verbal community." The problem of immediate concern here is not how this language develops, but the nature of what it refers to. Skinner mentioned "private" stimuli, "covert" or "incipient" behavior, "internal states," and, collectively, "private events" and "private experiences." Private events occur, but according to Skinner we become aware of them only in the process of acquiring language to refer to them: "The individual becomes aware of what he is doing only after society has reinforced verbal responses with respect to his behavior as the source of discriminative stimuli" (p. 277). Apparently, private events are private *experiences,* or mental phenomena, only after they can be described. Knowing, then, is equivalent to describing (Skinner, 1974, p. 30), and self-knowledge is equivalent to describing aspects of "the world within the skin" (chap. 2, 13; see especially pp. 153, 169). In developing the conception further, however, Skinner did not restrict knowing to verbal behavior. For example, "knowing a city means possessing the behavior of getting about in it" (p. 83); "thought is simply *behavior*—verbal or nonverbal, covert or overt" (Skinner, 1957, p. 449).

In Skinnerian behaviorism, verbal description is a way of knowing; but as in Watsonian behaviorism it is only one way of knowing. Although a *rule* is commonly thought of as verbal, in Skinnerian (and Watsonian) behaviorism it can consist of any behaviors. A rule is a set of particular behaviors that occur in a particular sequence (Bijou & Baer, 1978, p. 120). It can affect other behaviors and can affect the reinforcing/punishing function of stimuli that are contingent on other behaviors (p. 121), thereby providing a way to resist would-be controllers, as Baer (1976) said. However, rules are products of a history of contingent stimulation, and once formed they remain susceptible to the effects of reinforcing/punishing stimuli (Bijou & Baer, 1978, p. 122).

Determinism.   A complete determinism would deny the basic concept of contextualism—novelty. In fact, the only kind of change that is inevitable in contextualism is the emergence of novelty; but in a completely deterministic behaviorism "novel" behavior, "decision making," "problem solving," and "creativity," for example, would not be emergent, not truly novel. In Bijou and Baer's (1978) account (and Skinner's), none of these behaviors is truly novel. For example, shaping does not create novel behaviors; it changes the probabilities of behaviors, not their topographies (p. 60). Neither operant nor respondent conditioning produces new behaviors, although both can produce new combinations of behaviors (pp. 38, 58–60). In "decision making," the behavior that occurs is the one with the most powerful reinforcing stimulus, among several reinforcing stimuli present simultaneously (pp. 102–104); "problem solving" requires a learning history that has developed the required behaviors (pp. 118–119) and organized them into the required sequence (pp. 118–119, 120); and "creativity" is a form of problem solving that yields unusual or original solutions (pp. 123–124).

In Bijou and Baer's account, the "cognitive" processes are completely determined, hence are not causal. Thus, in this respect Bijou and Baer's account is consistent with Skinner's characterization of his own brand of behaviorism as deterministic and requires no assumption of chance or accidental causality.

However, the Skinnerian conception of cognition as noncausal is not *entailed* by Skinner's methodological position (Margolis, 1976). The conception is, rather, an empirical conclusion, especially if rewritten to say that reference to mental phenomena does not significantly improve prediction and control of behavior and therefore any causal efficacy they may have can be ignored.

Role of Environment

According to the mechanistic model, change results primarily from imposed forces. From this view, education consists primarily of filling a mental container; experience impresses ideas on an initially blank slate—John Locke's *tabula rasa*. Thus, in behaviorism—whether Watsonian or Skinnerian—changes in behavior are attributed primarily to changes in the environment, including "the world within the skin" (Skinner, 1974, chap. 2 & 13).

Skinnerian behaviorists emphasize the role of the environment—even genetic endowment is determined by "contingencies of survival" (Skinner, 1974, p. 37). During development, as Skinner noted, the child's age changes and, more importantly, the contingencies of reinforcement change (1974, p. 67). The changes with age in the prevailing contingencies explain, for example, Erikson's eight stages of socialization (Skinner, 1974, p. 160).

The theory provides no explicit explanation of the *sequence* of changes in the prevailing contingencies (Reese, 1976a), but the sequence may sometimes result in part from changes in the available ecological reinforcers. As Bijou and Baer (1978, p. 4) noted, standing frees the infant's hands for grasping and carrying and makes visible and attainable a world 2 feet above the floor. Generalizing, one could attribute the sequence of changes to practical constraints, like those which determine that during development the child will crawl before standing, stand before walking, and walk before running. The required empirical analysis has not yet been done, however.

PIAGET'S GENETIC EPISTEMOLOGY

Piaget's "genetic epistemology" is one of the two major current dialectical psychologies. The other one is the Soviet "theory of activity," discussed later in the present chapter. Another group of dialectical psychologies is called the Third Force, to contrast it with the two major forces in American psychology, said to be behaviorism and psychoanalytic theory. The Third Force includes phenomenological psychology, existential psychology, and dialectical humanism. The Third Force is not discussed further herein, because although it is relatively strong in Europe, it has had less impact in the United States. For discussion of Third Force psychologies, see Lessing (1968), Robinson (1979, chap. 6), and Rychlak (1976).

Presuppositions

Piaget is generally regarded as Kantian, but although he may have used Kantian methods, his theory is more consistent with Hegel's philosophy. For example, according to Cellerier (1972), "Piaget's grand design may be characterized as the reconstruction of the Kantian *a priori* categories of knowledge—as developmental necessities" (p. 117). Doing so, however, "refuted the Kantian hypothesis" (p. 117). With the developmental necessities, Piaget's theory is Hegelian rather than Kantian.

Piagetian psychology is consistent with Hegelian dialectical idealism, which in turn is consistent with the world view Pepper (1942) labeled organicism. This world view and its implications have been described in detail elsewhere (e.g., Overton & Reese, 1973; Reese & Overton, 1970) and are discussed only briefly here. The three basic laws of dialectical idealism refer to the unity and struggle of opposites, the transformation of quantitative change into qualitative change, and the negation of negation.

Unity and Struggle of Opposites.   In the law of the unity and struggle of opposites, or law of contradiction, the word "struggle" has too militant an implication; "interaction" would be a better word (cf. Razran, 1978, p. 96). An example of the law in Piaget's theory is the relation between assimilation and accommodation, which can be characterized as referring, respectively, to interpreting or understanding experiences and discovering in experiences new meanings that enrich understanding. These processes are contradictory because in assimilation the person transforms the environment (mentally) and in accommodation the environment transforms the person (again, mentally). The processes are also unitary, however, in that adaptation requires both. Assimilation without accommodation would be unchecked speculation or fantasy, and accommodation without assimilation would be mindless imitation. Adaptation, according to Piaget (1963), is "an equilibrium between assimilation and accommodation, which amounts to the same as an equilibrium of interaction between subject and object" (p. 8). In the terms of the law of contradiction, adaptation reflects the unity of the opposites, assimilation and accommodation.

Transformation of Change.   The law of transformation of change states that quantitative change, which occurs gradually, becomes qualitative change, which occurs suddenly and which leads to further gradual quantitative change. A frequently cited example of this law is the effect of a reduction in the temperature of a liquid substance, a quantitative change that at some point produces a qualitative change to the solid state. In Piaget's theory, skill and knowledge increase within a cognitive stage as a result of assimilation and accommodation. However, assimilation and accommodation are incomplete when the environment is appropriately challenging, and therefore the child experiences discrepancies between the information available in the environment and his or her adaptation to it. These within-stage changes are quantitative, in the sense that the structure of schemes and schemata (which are the mental contents in Piaget's theory) is not affected.

Nevertheless, the changes eventually permit the child to realize sufficient discrepancy to activate the "equilibration" process, by which the structure of schemes and schemata is reorganized—a qualitative change.

Negation of Negation.   The law of the negation of negation is sometimes stated as the relation among thesis, antithesis, and synthesis. According to this law, a thesis creates its own antithesis, and the contradiction between them is resolved by a synthesis in which the thesis is better understood. The antithesis negates the thesis, and the synthesis negates the antithesis, negating the negation. The thesis is incorporated into the synthesis, but at a higher level of understanding. Consequently, by this law development is progressive and cannot be regressive.

In dialectical idealism, the law of the negation of negation is a teleological principle, in which the final synthesis is an End such as Absolute Truth. In Piaget's theory, equilibration reflects the law of the negation of negation: As a result of equilibration, "higher stages displace (or rather reintegrate) the structures found at lower stages" (Kohlberg, 1968, p. 1021); that is, each stage incorporates the lower structures but integrates them in a new, higher way. The sequence of the stages is determined teleologically: It is the only way to get to the end point, the stage of "formal operations."

Model of the Organism.   Behavioral change in Piaget's view reflects changes in the individual's thought. The environment provides *information,* but acts of transformation or translation by the individual are required to produce intellectual *knowledge.* In contrast to the machine model of the organism in behaviorism, the model here is biological, or organic. However, the use of an organic model does not make a theory based on dialectical idealism biological or physiological, because the organic model is a *model,* a *representation* or *metaphor,* and not a description. In the literal sense of the organic model in biology, nutrients are ingested and metabolized to provide the energy for activity and the substrate for organic growth. In the metaphorical sense of the model in psychology, nutrients become experiences; ingestion and metabolism become sensation and perception, or sensation and assimilation/accommodation; and activity and growth refer to psychological processes as well as physical processes.

In the biological domain, the organism is composed of individual cells, but their functioning is conditional upon their place within the organism as a whole. Some biological functions are not assignable in any meaningful way to individual cells but rather must be attributed to tissues or organs—groups of cells functioning together in reciprocal interaction. Such an interaction may be understandable only as the functioning of an ensemble, not as a combination of functions of parts.

Teleology.   The organic model in dialectical idealism is teleological: Growth proceeds along a particular course because the mature state cannot be reached in any other way. For example, the development of an insect proceeds through the stages of the ovum, the larva, and the pupa, in that order, because the adult stage (the imago) cannot be reached in any other way. Analogously, in psychology the direction taken by intellectual development is explained, in this view, by reference to the end state, the mature intelligence of the adult.

The teleology of dialectical idealism is one of its major strengths; it enables theories to explain the direction of development. At the same time, however, teleology is one of the major drawbacks of dialectical idealism: Because of the general disfavor of teleological explanation in science, scientists with other presuppositions generally disfavor these theories.

Conception of Intelligence

In the organic model, the environment has no effect unless the organism ingests and metabolizes it. Metaphorically, the environment is passive, and development of the individual results from the individual's own activities. This principle is reflected in Piaget's distinction between information and understanding.

Information and Understanding.   *Information,* according to Piaget, is a product; it is usually presented verbally; it can be learned but later forgotten; as learned, it is a copy of the material presented (but it may be an inaccurate copy); and the acquisition of information does not produce understanding. *Understanding* is a process; it is nonverbal; it develops and is not forgotten; it constructs reality (but may construct it "inaccurately"); and the acquisition of understanding permits the generation of information. In the Piagetian view, the goal of education is to promote understanding, or intellectual knowledge, rather than to instill mere information.

Piaget was interested in the structure of intelligence, not the contents of memory. He (1970) criticized standard types of school examinations as "harmful" and "artificial," requiring "a kind of memory that has no relation, generally speaking, to that which is employed consciously in life, since it is, in fact, no more than a deliberate and ephemeral accumulation" (p. 108). He suggested that "The only genuine examination, given that emotional disturbances could be eliminated, would be one in which the candidate is free to use his books, notes, etc., and accomplishes a certain amount of work that is merely a continuation of what he has been doing in class: in other words, simply a part of his ordinary schoolwork" (p. 108).

Information can be taught by direct instruction, but according to Piaget— and much earlier St. Thomas Aquinas (*Summa Theologica,* Pt. 1, Question

84, Art. 6)—intellectual knowledge can only be encouraged, it cannot be taught (Piaget, 1970). Aquinas accepted the *tabula rasa* conception of intellect but argued that experience, or sense knowledge, is only the material cause— "the matter of the cause"—of intellectual knowledge; acts of transformation or translation of sense knowledge are required to produce intellectual knowledge. For Aquinas, then, as later for Piaget (and earlier for St. Augustine, *De Diversis Quaestionibus,* Quaestio IX), experience provides the substrate that discovery transforms into knowledge. Intellectual knowledge comes directly from activity of the person, not from activity of the environment.

Role of Language.   In Piaget's theory, "thinking is a self-regulatory activity that begins before language and goes far beyond language" (Furth & Wachs, 1974, p. 19). Although thinking can certainly be influenced by language (Piaget, 1963, 1973), the development of language depends on cognitive development rather than cognitive development depending on language development. Thought, for Piaget, consists of coordinated *schemes,* which are "internalized" actions. ("Internalized" is in quotation marks to indicate that the action is controlled by the actor but may be overt or covert. For example, schemes can be overt physical actions such as pushing or covert mental actions such as classifying.) Language may promote or facilitate the internalization, but it cannot *cause* the internalization (Piaget, 1973, p. 119), which results instead from assimilation and accommodation.

Speech is not necessarily an accurate reflection of thought, in Piaget's theory. In fact, Piaget (1963) said: "[Speech] is not an adequate medium of expression for the young child's thought; he is not satisfied with speaking, he must needs 'play out' what he thinks and symbolize his ideas by means of gestures or objects, and represent things by imitation, drawing and construction" (p. 159).

Role of Environment

In Piaget's theory, cognition is causal. As stated in Furth and Wachs (1974), the "development of intelligence is but the gradual creation of new mechanisms of thinking. It is creation because it is not the discovery or the copy of anything that is physically present. Classes and probability cannot be found in the physical world. They are concepts constructed creatively by human intelligence" (pp. 25–26). This description clearly reveals the idealistic nature of Piaget's theory.

The fundamental causes of development are "intrinsic." Thinking is a self-regulatory activity, and its development is determined by equilibration, an intrinsic process that causes reorganization of the cognitive structure. The environment is not a cause of change, only a condition of change.

Piaget distinguished between *learning* and *development* (Furth & Wachs,

1974). Learning refers to the acquisition of information and specific skills; its determinant is reinforcement, which is an environmental, "extrinsic" determinant; and its products, as noted above, are subject to forgetting. Development, in contrast, refers to the acquisition of understanding, or intelligence, which consists of structurally organized mental actions; the determinant of development is equilibration; and the product of development, once acquired, is not subject to forgetting. Intelligence is a necessary instrument for learning; that is, according to Kohlberg (1968), "the effects of training are determined by the child's cognitive categories rather than the reverse. . . . A program of reinforcement, then, cannot change the child's causal structures" (p. 1023).

Cognitive development would be optimized, in Piaget's view, by presenting materials that prompt the discovery or modification of "schemes." The goal would be to allow the child to consolidate the schemes and their structure, then to experience sufficient cognitive discrepancy to activate equilibration, thus leading to cognitive development.

Cognitive development would not be achieved by, for example, teaching a child to say in a conservation task, "Both are the same because nothing was added and nothing was taken away." Rather, the object should be to prompt the child to discover transitivity, and so forth, and to realize that conservation is a logical necessity and not merely an empirical law.

In this connection, Riegel and Meacham (1978) noted that in the past, family home life provided children direct action experiences of the kinds Piaget said are essential for intellectual development, and the role of the schools was to supplement these experiences with vicarious experiences through reading and hearing the teacher's presentations. Riegel and Meacham added: "More recently, however, television has led to great increases in the child's vicarious experiences, and with productive activities no longer found in most families there are fewer possibilities for direct action by the child . . . , a change that alters some of the essential conditions for development" (p. 43).

To summarize, in the Piagetian approach, one way to change behavior is by direct training, but the obtained change is likely to be impermanent and will not necessarily be the desired change. A better approach is to change behavior by changing the mental actions that control it, but "changing the mental actions" is a matter of promoting, prompting, and encouraging, rather than training.

One final point is that although the environment is conceptualized as a material condition of intellectual development, it has this role only with respect to *normal* development of the *structure* of intelligence. The environment can also function as an efficient cause, in Aristotle's sense (e.g., *Physics,* Bk. 2, chap. 3–7 [194b 16–198b 9]), as when specialized education affects the specific content of intelligence (Piaget, 1972) and when severe malnutrition or brain injury disrupts the normal course of development.

THE SOVIET "THEORY OF ACTIVITY"

The "theory of activity" was originated by Vygotsky and elaborated by his followers, especially Leontyev but also Davydov, Luria, Zaporozhets, Zinchenko, and others (Davydov, 1977; Leontyev, 1945/1981b; Wertsch, 1979, 1981). The theory was explicitly developed as "a concretization of Marxist-Leninist methodology in psychology" (Davydov, 1981, p. 4), and was based on "the Marxist category of activity" (Wertsch, 1981, p. 8), which was summarized in Marx's (1845/1976) *Theses on Feuerbach* (Leontyev, 1972/1974). The aspect of Marxist-Leninist methodology of interest here is dialectical materialism.

Dialectical Materialism

Dialectical materialism is derived from Karl Marx's philosophy, but it is different from historical materialism, which is Marx's analysis of societal development as proceeding through the stages of class struggle, proletarian revolution, dictatorship by the proletariat, and eventually a classless, marketless society. Historical materialism is the source of communist activism. Dialectical materialism is a more general philosophy, or model, in which progress is attributed to the resolution of contradictions.

According to Soviet and Chinese philosophers, dialectical and historical materialism can be separated only analytically, because these materialisms are actually unitary (reflecting the dialectical principle of the unity and interaction of opposites). One consequence of the unity is that Soviet scientists are also activists, at least officially, and are supposed to do their scientific work to promote communist objectives (Payne, 1968, p. 2). Such a position would obviously be unacceptable in the United States; but in spite of the purported unity, the two materialisms can be separated. For example, the French existentialist Jean-Paul Sartre rejected dialectical materialism and retained historical materialism (Lessing, 1968). (In this respect, incidentally, Sartre leaned more toward Hegel than toward Marx, because in spite of Marx's denial of teleology, the stages of societal development in historical materialism have an inevitability that has such a strong implication of teleology that even the Soviet philosophers have trouble with it [see Planty-Bonjour, 1967, pp. 1-2, 129-141].)

The Soviet "theory of activity" can be understood without referring to historical materialism—dialectical materialism is sufficient. Furthermore, the root metaphor of contextualism is clearly evident in dialectical materialism (and the Soviet theory of activity), and therefore dialectical materialism can be understood as a kind of contextualism. In the root metaphor of contextualism, actions are goal-directed, but attainment of a goal may be blocked by competing or interfering actions. When an action is blocked, alternative actions are tried until the goal is attained or is inferred to be unattainable. In the latter case, an alternative goal is set and actions are initiated to attain it. Progress is therefore inevitable because attainable goals are eventually set and attained. However, the progress is explained by antecedent causes rather than by teleology, contrary to dialectical idealism.

Presuppositions

Laws of Change.   Mao Zedong (1965b) said:

> Discover the truth through practice, and again through practice verify and develop the truth. Start from perceptual knowledge and actively develop it into rational knowledge [i.e., conceptual, or theoretical knowledge]; then start from rational knowledge and actively guide revolutionary practice to change both the subjective and objective world. Practice, knowledge, again practice, and again knowledge. This form repeats itself in endless cycles, and with each cycle the content of practice and knowledge rises to a higher level. Such is the whole of the dialectical-materialist theory of knowledge, and such is the dialectical-materialist theory of the unity of knowing and doing. (p. 308)

Mao's statement succinctly expresses most of the laws of change in dialectical materialism. (1) Contradiction is basic (practice versus rational knowledge); but (2) it is resolved by the law of the unity and interaction of opposites (e.g., practice is transformed into rational knowledge); (3) knowledge is negated by practice, but the negation is negated by being incorporated into a higher level of knowledge; (4) the negation of negation is an endless process.

The negation of negation is an endless process because the concept of Absolute Truth is rejected (Mao, 1965b, pp. 304–306). Although Mao (1965b) referred to "the endless flow of absolute truth" (p. 307), he meant the endless flow—the "universality and absoluteness"—of internal contradiction (1965a, p. 345). The process of negation of negation must be endless, because "Marxist philosophy holds that the most important problem does not lie in understanding the laws of the objective world and thus being able to explain it, but in applying the knowledge of these laws actively to change the world" (Mao, 1965b, p. 304). The result must be changes in the nature of contradictions, among which some "are characterized by open antagonism, others are not" (Mao, 1965a, p. 344). (The emphasis on changing the world is consistent with Marx's 11th thesis on Feuerbach [1845/1976]: "The philosophers have only *interpreted* the world in various ways; the point, however, is to *change* it" [p. 8]. The thesis is principled rather than dogmatic—much of Sánchez Vázquez's [1977] book amounts to a rationale for the theses.)

Contradiction—the unity and interaction of opposites—is the fundamental cause of change (Razran, 1978; see also Wozniak, 1975, and the above quotations from Mao Zedong). An example from the domain of memory development is the contradiction between voluntary and involuntary memory, which is also called, by theorists reflecting a variety of world views, effortful versus automatic memory, intentional versus incidental memory, memory as goal versus memory as means, and premeditated versus automatic memory (Reese, 1979).

The law of the transformation of quantitative change into qualitative change, and vice versa, is not obvious in the quotations just given, but it is well exemplified in the Soviet theory of cognitive development (Leontyev, 1945/1981b). An example is the effect of repetition. An action that is deliberately repeated is under conscious control (otherwise, it could not be *deliberately* repeated), and repetition increases the efficiency of the action—a quantitative change. With sufficient repetition, the action can be performed without conscious control—a qualitative change. A child can walk without consciously controlling balance but could not do so as an infant; a skilled driver can drive a car without consciously controlling the steering wheel but could not do so when learning to drive.

The law of the negation of negation is not teleological in dialectical materialism and progress is not an inevitable result of the process per se. Progress occurs, however, because of the nature of contradiction; that is, progress results from the working of the laws. (Nevertheless, the way the laws work out can change and therefore progress is not inevitable.) Marx postulated the classless, marketless state as the end point of historical sociopolitical development, but the preceding quotations from Mao Zedong indicate that such an end point—and its analogue in the domain of cognitive development—does not function as a telos in dialectical materialism. An example of the law in the memory domain is again the effect of repetition. Repetition negates the need for conscious control of an action, but the negation is negated in that the now automatic action becomes subordinated to a more complex deliberate action (Reese, 1976b). As Razran (1978) noted, in Soviet psychology conscious events have a leading role, and unconscious events are subordinate to them (p. 93).

Model of the Organism. Contradiction is internal in dialectical materialism, that is, it resides within an object, a phenomenon, or a relation. Usual examples include the contradiction between positive and negative ions, within an object; the contradiction between the old and the new, within a phenomenon; and the contradictions between the just and the unjust, borrower and lender, and thief and victim, within various kinds of relations (Meacham, 1977; Planty-Bonjour, 1967, p. 114). In each case, the contradiction is between elements within a whole, or unity. For example, the relation between a borrower and a lender is a unity called a business transaction, and the relation between a thief and a victim is a unity called a robbery. The research problem is to analyze the unity into its contradictory or opposing parts, then to discover how they are unitized or reconciled to form the whole.

The relation between the person and the environment is also a unity, in which both the person and the environment are active participants. This conception avoids the extreme environmentalism of behaviorism and the extreme mentalism of dialectical idealism. According to dialectical materialism, behavioral change reflects a reciprocal interaction between the person and the environment. The actions of persons change the environment, and the changed environment changes the persons' actions.

An example is provided by analysis of the conditioned reflex. Behaviorists interpret the conditioned reflex as a response of the organism to a stimulus (Riegel, 1973), but the Soviet theorist Sergei L. Rubinshteyn interpreted it as follows: The action of a stimulus brings about a change in the organism's behavior, and the change in behavior might be said to reflect or mirror the action of the stimulus. However, the characteristics of the organism act like a prism refracting the stimulus, and therefore the change in behavior depends as much on the nature of the organism—refraction—as on the nature of the stimulus—reflection (Payne, 1968, p. 103). (The concepts of refraction and reflection are materialist analogues of Piaget's idealist concepts of assimilation and accommodation, respectively.)

In general terms, the effect of an external cause is mediated through the inner characteristics of the object acted upon. As Payne (1968) noted, "The effect of the agent is modified, refracted by the inner characteristics of the thing on which it acts so that the end effect is to be explained by the combined action of the agent and the thing acted upon" (p. 105). According to Rubinshteyn (quoted in Payne, 1968), the relation is such that, first, "every phenomenon 'represents' or reflects the objects that interact with it by registering in itself the results of their activity; and, second any activity of one phenomenon on another is refracted by the internal properties of the phenomenon on which the activity is exerted" (p. 115).

The phenomena and objects referred to can be concrete objects or can be actions, which are also conceptualized as concrete (Payne, 1968). The history of interactions that is registered can be cultural history. An example is found in research by Luria (1976) on the effects of modernization in Uzbekistan and Kirghizia in 1931–1932, comparing groups that still reflected the traditional peasant culture and groups in various stages of transition. The research revealed differences among the groups in every psychological domain that was examined—perception, generalization, deduction, reasoning, imagination, and self-awareness—clearly revealing the reflection of culture in the way the individual refracts the world.

Conception of Intelligence

Like everything else in dialectical materialism, psychology in the Soviet Union is characterized by contradiction, specifically between the "physiologism" of the science of "higher nervous activity" and the "cognitionism" of the psychology of cognitive development. The contradiction seems to be resolved by conceptualizing the physiologism without reductionism, and the cognitionism without mentalism—that is, the cognitionism is conceptualized as consistent with materialistic environmentalism (Razran, 1978, p. 115). As Rubinshteyn said (quoted from Razran, 1978), "we sense and perceive not sensations and perceptions but things and phenomena in the material world" (p. 92).

Basic Characteristics.   Engels said, "Free will is nothing but the ability to make a cognitive decision" (quoted from Razran, 1978, e.g., p. 105). However, according to Razran, "the Soviet thesis is that decision is in essence not a *choice* of alternatives but a *bound* selection of *right* action, where 'bound' and 'right' follow past and present cognitions and not just reinforcements" (p. 105). Although this view would sound identical to Skinner's without the claimed difference between cognitions and reinforcements, this claimed difference is crucial because it reflects the Soviet distinction between refraction and reflection, which are dialectical opposites. In psychology, refraction means that the effect of the external world is determined by the form and content of thought, and reflection means that the form and content of thought are determined by the external world (Wozniak, 1975, pp. 39–40). Thus, the "cognitionism" as well as the "physiologism" of the Soviet view distinguish it from Skinner's view (see Razran, 1978, pp. 117–118).

The "practice-knowledge-practice" sequence leads to an emphasis on applying knowledge—problem solving, "doing"—that led Mao to attack standard methods of examination as vigorously as Piaget had done (Mao Zedong, cited in Parker, 1977). "Doing" is also important, in the Soviet view, because of the role of repetition in automating actions, including not only physical actions but also mental ones.

The Soviet view attributes causal efficacy to cognition, but avoids mentalism by tying it to materialism. Thinking is doing, in this view, but the "doing" is not necessarily overt behaving. The individual interprets situations, sets goals, formulates actions to achieve the goals, and carries out the actions in a coordinated way, all with conscious control. The actions themselves, whether overt or covert, are deliberate, but they may have components that are carried out and coordinated without conscious control. For example, shopping for groceries is a deliberate action that may include the "automatic" acts of walking, pushing a cart, scanning the shelves, remembering the items to be purchased and the items already in the cart, and so forth. Each of the unconscious acts in this example is itself a complex act that includes simpler acts that are performed and coordinated unconsciously. Kvale (1977) has described the dialectical materialist position in regard to memory as follows:

> In a dialectical conception of remembering as a relationship there are no memory traces, no things or copies stored in an inner bank. Rather, a person's behavioral repertoire and possibilities have been altered by his past experiences. . . . The person has been changed through his experience so that he may re-produce, re-construct, re-cognize more or less vivid and accurate earlier experiences. (p. 177)

This position sounds very similar to Skinner's: "Skinner does not acknowledge any representation or conscious content in the mind or brain; we have an organism behaving. . . . Knowing, to a [Skinnerian] behaviorist, is behaving" (Krapfl, 1977, pp. 307–308). In spite of the similarity, however, a major difference is that in Skinner's theory the analysis stops at the behaving, while in the dialectical theory the conscious experience—the "issue of how the world appears to the remembering subject" (Kvale, 1977, p. 172)—is taken seriously.

Role of Language.   Language is not the only mode of cognition, in the Soviet view, but it is by far the most efficient and effective. The development of language, according to Vygotsky (1978), generates the "mediating function," which is the most powerful way of self-control. Cole and Scribner (1978) have emphasized, however, that Vygotsky's conception of mediation is different from the behavioristic conception. For Vygotsky, mediation is an action, of course, but it is a *higher* behavior or *higher* psychological function, depending upon whether it is a physical action as in the use of tools, or a mental action as in the use of symbols. In both cases it is the means of transforming the world in order to transform the self (Vygotsky, 1978, pp. 54–55).

Language is involved in mediation, or at least in the highest forms of mediation, according to Vygotsky (1978): "The most significant moment in the course of intellectual development . . . occurs when speech and practical activity, two previously completely independent lines of development, converge" (p. 24, italics deleted). "Children solve practical tasks with the help of their speech, as well as their eyes and hands" (p. 26, italics deleted). During development, speech acquires a planning function in addition to its descriptive function: It becomes a means for *refraction* and not merely a product of *reflection* (p. 28).

Role of Environment

The environment is a cause of change in dialectical materialism, rather than only a condition of change. Intellectual development does not result from the growth of understanding, but rather the growth of understanding results from situations presented by the environment, including especially the social environment. This is not merely a copy theory of knowledge, however, because the person not only reflects the environment but also refracts it. The way the person refracts the environment depends on the person's history of interactions with the environment, and in large part this history is determined by the agents of the society in which the person is developing. Changing the society changes intellectual development, and changing intellectual development changes society, as Luria implied had happened in the regions he studied and as Mao Zedong expected to result from the Cultural Revolution of 1966–69 in China.

Short of such sweeping changes in society, which obviously were difficult to implement even in the Soviet Union and China, modification of cognitive development can still be achieved by management of the methods and content of classroom instruction. The development of language is especially important as a means of developing self-control and planfulness ("mediation"), and although cognitive development in early stages requires that the child physically perform actions, in later stages actions can be performed mentally. Hence, purely verbal instruction can be effective (as it also can be in Piagetian theory).

Instruction will be most effective when it is presented in a context that the child can interpret appropriately; that is, the situation should be consistent with the child's "leading activity." For example, the leading activity of a young child is playing (Leontyev, 1944/1981a); hence, the learning situation should be presented as play rather than academic instruction. Thus, in the Soviet view the effective modification of intelligence requires not only careful manipulation of materials (as in Piaget's system) but also careful manipulation of the context in which they are presented.

In any case, intellectual development is not spontaneous, contrary to Piaget's theory. The following statement by Yendovitskaya, Zinchenko, and Ruzskaya (1971) illustrates this point with respect to perceptual development:

> The development of the child's perception does not occur spontaneously, but
> is guided by practice and training. In this process the child acquires mastery

of socio-sensory experience and becomes adapted to the sensory culture created by mankind. Adults form in the child the means of familiarization with the surrounding environment; they acquaint him with the systems of musical tones, speech phonemes, geometric forms, etc., developed by humanity and also teach him how to identify them with the help of language. As a result, the child masters a known system of general sensory standards, which he later applies to his perceptual activity, especially in analyzing reality and reflecting it in synthetic, sensory images. (p. 56)

This quotation, from a chapter by three Soviet developmental psychologists, illustrates four points about the Soviet theory of psychological development, and dialectical materialism. First, even though internal contradiction is the cause of development, development is not *spontaneous* because external conditions are needed to "activate" the internal cause. Second, the external conditions reflect to a very large extent the culture in which the individual is developing. Third, language is given a major role in psychological development, for principled reasons that are too complex to be elaborated in this chapter (for discussion, see Vygotsky, 1962, 1978; Zivin, 1979). Finally, the quotation is typical of much of the Soviet writing about psychological development in that it seems to imply a one-way influence, from the culture to the developing individual, instead of the promised reciprocal interaction. Actually, however, the reciprocal interaction is implied: As the child develops, his or her interpretation (refraction) of the culture changes and the influence (reflection) of the culture therefore also changes.

The environment is of paramount importance in the Soviet view, because even though it is refracted by the individual, and not merely copied, the way it is refracted depends on the individual's knowledge, which depends on the past practice–knowledge–practice sequence (Mao, 1965b). The environment is not merely physical, however; rather, it includes other persons, a particular society, and a particular sociopolitical history. As Luria (1976) concluded:

Sociohistorical shifts not only introduce new content into the mental world of human beings; they also create new forms of activity and new structures of cognitive functioning. They advance human consciousness to new levels. . . . The basic categories of human mental life can be understood as products of social history—they are subject to change when the basic forms of social practice are altered and thus are social in nature. (pp. 163–164)

CONCLUDING REMARKS

The four psychologies analyzed here have different presuppositions, which lead to different conceptions of intelligence and different conceptions of how it develops and how its development can be modified.

The approach in which successful modification is easiest to demonstrate, in the sense of having clear and objective criteria of change, is the Skinnerian behavioral approach. The success of its modification techniques has been demonstrated repeatedly, even for such "abstract" behaviors as creativity. Nevertheless, for those who do not adopt this approach, these demonstrations of success are inconclusive; that is, even though the technology must be acknowledged to be successful in many applications, its success does not demonstrate the adequacy of the theoretical interpretations. That it works is a fact; but why it works is another matter, and it is this question that Watsonian behaviorists and dialectical psychologists consider to be unanswered—in fact, not even asked—in Skinnerian behaviorism. Watsonian behaviorists ask for deduction of the facts from a theory. Dialectical psychologists, whether adopting the idealistic or materialistic version, adopt a different "workability" criterion from that of Skinnerian behaviorism. For them, the issue is not only how to maximize the prediction and control of behavior, which they see as important with respect to description and optimization, but also how to explain why this technology works—a question of understanding of a different sort from that asked by Skinnerian behaviorists. In conclusion, Skinnerian behaviorists start with the assumption that reinforcement works; Watsonian behaviorists and dialectical psychologists want to understand why it works. Whether this level of understanding has any implications for practice is relevant for Skinnerian behaviorists and dialectical materialist psychologists, but not for Watsonian behaviorists and dialectical idealist psychologists.

AUTHOR NOTE

Parts of this chapter were presented in "Cognitive Development: Three Irreconcilable Views" at the IX Simposio Internacional de Modificación de Conducta, Panama City, Panama, February 1979, and in "Dialectical Psychologies: Alternatives to Behaviorism" at the Benedum/Centennial Seminars, West Virginia University, Morgantown, January 1981.

REFERENCES

Amsel, A. (1958). The role of frustrative nonreward in noncontinuous reward situations. *Psychological Bulletin, 55,* 102–119.

Baer, D. M. (1970). An age-irrelevant concept of development. *Merrill–Palmer Quarterly of Behavior and Development, 16,* 238–246.

Baer, D. M. (1976). The organism as host. In H. W. Reese (Ed.), Conceptions of the "active organism" (pp. 87–98). *Human Development, 19,* 69–119.

Baltes, M. M., & Reese, H. W. (1977). Operant research in violation of the operant paradigm? In B. C. Etzel, J. M. LeBlanc, & D. M. Baer (Eds.), *New developments in behavioral research: Theory, method, and application, in honor of Sidney W. Bijou* (pp. 11–30). Hillsdale, NJ: Lawrence Erlbaum Associates.

Baltes, P. B., Reese, H. W., & Nesselroade, J. R. (1977). *Life-span developmental psychology: Introduction to research methods.* Monterey, CA: Brooks/Cole.

Bechtoldt, H. P. (1959). Construct validity: A critique. *American Psychologist, 14,* 619–629.

Beilin, H. (1981, June). *Piaget and the new functionalism.* Paper presented at the Eleventh Symposium of the Jean Piaget Society, Philadelphia.

Bergmann, G. (1951). The logic of psychological concepts. *Philosophy of Science, 18,* 93–110.

Bergmann, G. (1954). Sense and nonsense in operationism. *Scientific Monthly, 79,* 210–214. Reprinted in P. G. Frank (Ed.), (1961). *The validation of scientific theories* (pp. 46–56). New York: Collier Books.

Bergmann, G. (1956). The contribution of John B. Watson. *Psychological Review, 63,* 265–276.

Bergmann, G. (1957). *Philosophy of science.* Madison: University of Wisconsin Press.

Bergmann, G., & Spence, K. W. (1941). Operationism and theory in psychology. *Psychological Review, 48,* 1–14.

Bijou, S. W., & Baer, D. M. (1978). *Behavior analysis of child development.* Englewood Cliffs, NJ: Prentice-Hall.

Bocheński, J. M. (1963). *Soviet Russian dialectical materialism (diamat)* (N. Sollohub, Trans.; rev. after 3rd ed. by T. J. Blakeley). Dordrecht, Holland: Reidel.

Brown, J. S. (1961). *The motivation of behavior.* New York: McGraw-Hill.

Burnett, A., Beach, H. D., & Sullivan, A. M. (1963). Intelligence in a restricted environment. *Canadian Psychologist, 4ª,* 126–136.

Cellerier, G. (1972). Information processing tendencies in recent experiments in cognitive learning—Theoretical implications. In S. Farnham-Diggory (Ed.), *Information processing in children* (pp. 115–123). New York: Academic Press.

Chin, R., & Chin, Ai-li S. (1969). *Psychological research in communist China: 1949–1966.* Cambridge, MA: M.I.T. Press.

Cole, M., & Scribner, S. (1978). Introduction. In L. S. Vygotsky, *Mind in society: The development of higher psychological processes* (pp. 1–14; M. Cole, V. John-Steiner, S. Scribner, & E. Souberman, Eds.). Cambridge, MA: Harvard University Press.

Dallenbach, K. M. (1953). The place of theory in science. *Psychological Review, 60,* 33–39.

Davydov, V. V. (1977). Major problems in developmental and educational psychology at the present stage of development of education. *Soviet Psychology, 15*(4), 73–95.

Davydov, V. V. (1981). The category of activity and mental reflection in the theory of A. N. Leont'ev. *Soviet Psychology, 19*(4), 3–29.

Day, W. (1983). On the difference between radical and methodological behaviorism. *Behaviorism, 11,* 89–102.

Dewey, J. (1896). The reflex arc concept in psychology. *Psychological Review, 3,* 357–370.

Dollard, J., & Miller, N. E. (1950). *Personality and psychotherapy: An analysis in terms of learning, thinking, and culture.* New York: McGraw-Hill.

Etzel, B. C., LeBlanc, J. M., & Baer, D. M. (1977). Preface. In B. C. Etzel, J. M. LeBlanc, & D. M. Baer (Eds.), *New developments in behavioral research: Theory, method, and application, in honor of Sidney W. Bijou* (pp. xv–xvi). Hillsdale, NJ: Lawrence Erlbaum Associates.

Farrant, R. H. (1977). Can after-the-fact designs test functional hypotheses, and are they needed in psychology? *Canadian Psychological Review, 18,* 359–364.

Ferguson, G. A. (1954). On learning and human ability. *Canadian Journal of Psychology, 8,* 95–112.

Ferguson, G. A. (1956). On transfer and the abilities of man. *Canadian Journal of Psychology, 10,* 121–131.

Furth, H. G., & Wachs, H. (1974). *Thinking goes to school: Piaget's theory in practice.* New York: Oxford University Press.

Goetz, E. M., & Baer, D. M. (1973). Social control of form diversity and the emergence of new forms in children's blockbuilding. *Journal of Applied Behavior Analysis, 6,* 209–217.

Goss, A. E. (1961). Verbal mediating responses and concept formation. *Psychological Review, 68,* 248–274.

Guess, D., Sailor, W., & Baer, D. M. (1974). To teach language to retarded children. In R. L. Schiefelbusch & L. L. Lloyd (Eds.), *Language perspectives—Acquisition, retardation, and intervention* (pp. 529–563). Baltimore: University Park Press.

Holman, J., Goetz, E. M., & Baer, D. M. (1977). The training of creativity as an operant and an examination of its generalization characteristics. In B. C. Etzel, J. M. LeBlanc, & D. M. Baer (Eds.), *New developments in behavioral research: Theory, method, and application, in honor of Sidney W. Bijou* (pp. 441–471). Hillsdale, NJ: Lawrence Erlbaum Associates.

Hull, C. L. (1943). *Principles of behavior: An introduction to behavior theory.* New York: Appleton–Century–Crofts.

James, W. (1907). *Pragmatism: A new name for some old ways of thinking.* New York: Longmans, Green.

Keller, F. S., & Schoenfeld, W. N. (1950). *Principles of psychology: A systematic text in the science of behavior.* New York: Appleton-Century-Crofts.

Kendler, H. H. (1967). Kenneth W. Spence: 1907–1967. *Psychological Review, 74,* 335–341. Reprinted in H. H. Kendler & J. T. Spence (Eds.), (1971). *Essays in neobehaviorism: A memorial volume to Kenneth W. Spence* (pp. 1–8). New York: Appleton-Century-Crofts.

Kessel, F. S. (1969). The philosophy of science as proclaimed and science as practiced: "Identity" or "dualism"? *American Psychologist, 24,* 999–1005.

Kohlberg, L. (1968). Early education: A cognitive-developmental view. *Child Development, 39,* 1013–1062.

Krapfl, J. E. (1977). Dialectics and operant conditioning. In N. Datan & H. W. Reese (Eds.), *Life-span developmental psychology: Dialectical perspectives on experimental research* (pp. 295–310). New York: Academic Press.

Krechevsky, I. (1938). A study of the continuity of the problem-solving process. *Psychological Review, 45,* 107–133.

Kuhn, T. S. (1970). The structure of scientific revolutions (2nd ed.). *International Encyclopedia of Unified Science, 2*(2). Chicago: University of Chicago Press.

Kvale, S. (1977). Dialectics and research on remembering. In N. Datan & H. W. Reese (Eds.), *Life-span developmental psychology: Dialectical perspectives on experimental research* (pp. 165–189). New York: Academic Press.

Lakatos, I. (1978). The methodology of scientific research programs. In I. Lakatos, *Philosophical papers* (J. Worrall & G. Currie, Eds.; Vol. 1). Cambridge: Cambridge University Press.

Lamal, P. A. (1983). A cogent critique of epistemology leaves radical behaviorism unscathed. *Behaviorism, 11,* 103–109.

Langenscheidt's German–English English–German dictionary (rev. ed.). (1970). New York: Pocket Books.

Laudan, L. (1977). *Progress and its problems: Toward a theory of scientific growth.* Berkeley: University of California Press.

Leontyev, A. N. (1974). The problem of activity in psychology. *Soviet Psychology, 13*(2), 4–33. (From *Voprosy filosofii,* 1972, No. 9, 95–108; E. Berg, Trans.). Reprinted in J. V. Wertsch (Ed. & Trans.), (1981). *The concept of activity in Soviet psychology* (pp. 37–71). Armonk, NY: Sharpe.

Leontyev, A. N. (1981a). The psychological principles of preschool play. In A. N. Leontyev, *Problems of the development of the mind* (pp. 366–390). Moscow: Progress. (Trans. from Russian paper in *Sovetskaya Pedagogika,* 1944, *4*)

Leontyev, A. N. (1981b). A contribution to the theory of the development of the child's psyche. In A. N. Leontyev, *Problems of the development of the mind* (pp. 391–416). Moscow: Progress. (Trans. from Russian paper in *Sovetskaya Pedagogika,* 1945, *4*)

Lessing, A. (1968). Marxist existentialism. In J. H. Gill (Ed.), *Philosophy today no. 1* (pp. 158–183). New York: Macmillan.

Luria, A. R. (1976). *Cognitive development: Its cultural and social foundations* (M. Lopez-Morillas & L. Solotaroff, Trans.; M. Cole, Ed.). Cambridge, MA: Harvard University Press.

MacCorquodale, K. (1970). On Chomsky's review of Skinner's *Verbal Behavior. Journal of the Experimental Analysis of Behavior, 13,* 83–99.

MacCorquodale, K., & Meehl, P. E. (1948). On a distinction between hypothetical constructs and intervening variables. *Psychological Review, 55,* 95–107.

Mao Zedong. (1965a). On contradiction. In *Selected works of . . .* (Trans. of 2nd Chinese ed.; Vol. 1, pp. 311–347). Peking: Foreign Languages Press.

Mao Zedong. (1965b). On practice. In *Selected works of . . .* (Trans. of 2nd Chinese ed.; Vol. 1, pp. 295–309). Peking: Foreign Languages Press.

Mapel, B. M. (1977). Philosophical criticism of behaviorism: An analysis. *Behaviorism, 5*(1), 17–32.

Margolis, J. (1976). In defense of "mental states." *Behaviorism, 4*(2), 223–230.

Marx, K. (1976). Theses on Feuerbach. In K. Marx & F. Engels, *Collected works* (Vol. 5, pp. 6–9). London: Lawrence & Wishart. (Notes originally written in 1845; edited by F. Engels)

Meacham, J. A. (1977). Soviet investigations of memory development. In R. V. Kail, Jr. & J. H. Hagen (Eds.), *Perspectives on the development of memory and cognition* (pp. 273–295). Hillsdale, NJ: Lawrence Erlbaum Associates.

Overton, W. F. (1984). World views and their influence on psychological theory and research: Kuhn-Lakatos-Laudan. In H. W. Reese (Ed.), *Advances in child development and behavior* (Vol. 18). New York: Academic Press.

Overton, W. F., & Reese, H. W. (1973). Models of development: Methodological implications. In J. R. Nesselroade & H. W. Reese (Eds.), *Life-span developmental psychology: Methodological issues* (pp. 65–86). New York: Academic Press.

Paivio, A. (1971). *Imagery and verbal processes.* New York: Holt, Rinehart, & Winston.

Pap, A. (1953). Does science have metaphysical presuppositions? In H. Feigl & M. Brodbeck (Eds.), *Readings in the philosophy of science* (pp. 21–33). New York: Appleton-Century-Crofts.

Parker, F. (1977). *What can we learn from the schools of China?* Bloomington, IN: Phi Delta Kappa Educational Foundation.

Payne, T. R. (1968). *S. L. Rubinstejn and the philosophical foundations of Soviet psychology.* Dordrecht, Holland: Reidel.

Peirce, C. S. (1923). How to make our ideas clear. In C. S. Peirce, *Chance, love and logic: Philosophical essays* (M. R. Cohen, Ed.; pp. 32–60). New York: Harcourt, Brace. (Original work published in *Popular Science Monthly,* 1878)

Pepper, S. C. (1942). *World hypotheses: A study in evidence.* Berkeley, CA: University of California Press.

Piaget, J. (1952). *The origins of intelligence in children* (M. Cook, Trans.). New York: International Universities Press.

Piaget, J. (1963). *The psychology of intelligence* (M. Piercy & D. E. Berlyne, Trans.). Paterson, NJ: Littlefield, Adams.

Piaget, J. (1970). *Science of education and the psychology of the child* (D. Coltman, Trans.). New York: Orion.

Piaget, J. (1972). Intellectual evolution from adolescence to adulthood. *Human Development, 15,* 1–12.

Piaget, J. (1973). *The child and reality: Problems in genetic psychology* (A. Rosin, Trans.). New York: Grossman.

Piaget, J. (1977). Chance and dialectic in biological epistemology: A critical analysis of Jacque Monod's theses. In W. F. Overton & J. M. Gallagher (Eds.), *Knowledge and development. Vol. 1. Advances in research and theory* (pp. 1–16). New York: Plenum.

Planty-Bonjour, G. (1967). *The categories of dialectical materialism: Contemporary Soviet ontology* (T. J. Blakeley, Trans.). New York: Praeger.

Proceedings of the twenty-first annual meeting of the American Psychological Association, Cleveland, Ohio, December 30 and 31, 1912, and January 1, 1913. (1913). *Psychological Bulletin, 10,* 41–84.

Proceedings of the twenty-second annual meeting of the American Psychological Association, New Haven, Connecticut, December 29, 30 and 31, 1913. (1914). *Psychological Bulletin, 11,* 29–72.

Proceedings of the twenty-third annual meeting of the American Psychological Association, Philadelphia, Pennsylvania, December 29, 30, 31, 1914. (1915). *Psychological Bulletin, 12,* 45–81.

Razran, G. (1978). Systematic psychology and dialectical materialism: A Soviet story with non-Soviet imports. *Behaviorism, 6,* 81–126.

Reese, H. W. (1962). Verbal mediation as a function of age level. *Psychological Bulletin, 59,* 502–509.

Reese, H. W. (1971). The study of covert verbal and nonverbal mediation. In A. Jacobs & L. B. Sachs (Eds.), *The psychology of private events: Perspectives on covert response systems* (pp. 17–38). New York: Academic Press.

Reese, H. W. (1976a). Discussion. In H. W. Reese (Ed.), Conceptions of the "active organism" (pp. 108–119). *Human Development, 19,* 69–119.

Reese, H. W. (1976b). Models of memory development. *Human Development, 19,* 291–303.

Reese, H. W. (1979). Gedachtnisentwicklung im Verlauf des Lebens: Empirische Befunde und theoretische Modelle (W. Karny, Trans.). In L. Montada (Ed.), *Brennpunkte der Entwicklungspychologie* (pp. 90–102). Stuttgart: Kohlhammer.

Reese, H. W. (1986). On the theory and practice of behavior analysis. In H. W. Reese & L. J. Parrott (Eds.), *Behavior science: Philosophical, methodological, and empirical advances* (pp. 1–33). Hillsdale, NJ: Lawrence Erlbaum Associates.

Reese, H. W., & Overton, W. F. (1970). Models of development and theories of development. In L. R. Goulet & P. B. Baltes (Eds.), *Life-span developmental psychology: Research and theory* (pp. 115–145). New York: Academic Press.

Reese, H. W., & Parnes, S. J. (1970). Programming creative behavior. *Child Development, 41,* 413–423.

Riegel, K. F. (1973). Developmental psychology and society: Some historical and ethical considerations. In J. R. Nesselroade & H. W. Reese (Eds.), *Life-span developmental psychology: Methodological issues* (pp. 1–23). New York: Academic Press.

Riegel, K. F., & Meacham, J. A. (1978). Dialectics, transaction, and Piaget's theory. In L. Pervin & M. Lewis (Eds.), *Perspectives in interactional psychology* (pp. 23–47). New York: Plenum.

Risley, T. R. (1977). The development and maintenance of language: An operant model. In B. C. Etzel, J. M. LeBlanc, & D. M. Baer (Eds.), *New developments in behavioral research: Theory, method, and application, in honor of Sidney W. Bijou* (pp. 81–101). Hillsdale, NJ: Lawrence Erlbaum Associates.

Robinson, D. N. (1979). *Systems of modern psychology: A critical sketch.* New York: Columbia University Press.

Rozeboom, W. W. (1956). Mediation variables in scientific theory. *Psychological Review, 63,* 249–264.

Rychlak, J. F. (1976). Psychological science as a humanist sees it. In W. J. Arnold (Ed.), *Nebraska symposium on motivation 1975* (Vol. 23; pp. 205–279). Lincoln: University of Nebraska Press.

Ryle, G. (1949). *The concept of mind.* London: Hutchinson's University Library.

Sánchez Vázquez, A. (1977). *The philosophy of praxis* (M. Gonzalez, Trans.). London: Merlin Press. (Original work published in 1966)

Schumaker, J., & Sherman, J. A. (1970). Training generative verb usage by imitation and reinforcement procedures. *Journal of Applied Behavior Analysis, 3,* 273–287.

Skinner, B. F. (1945). The operational analysis of psychological terms. *Psychological Review, 52,* 270–277.

Skinner, B. F. (1953). *Science and human behavior.* New York: Free Press.

Skinner, B. F. (1957). *Verbal behavior.* New York: Appleton–Century–Crofts.

Skinner, B. F. (1969). *Contingencies of reinforcement: A theoretical analysis.* New York: Appleton–Century–Crofts.

Skinner, B. F. (1974). *About behaviorism.* New York: Knopf.

Spence, K. W. (1940). Continuous versus non-continuous interpretations of discrimination learning. *Psychological Review, 47,* 271–288. Reprinted in K. W. Spence (1960). *Behavior theory and learning: Selected papers* (pp. 308–325). Englewood Cliffs, NJ: Prentice-Hall.

Spence, K. W. (1956). *Behavior theory and conditioning.* New Haven: Yale University Press.

Spence, K. W. (1960). The roles of reinforcement and non-reinforcement in learning. In K. W. Spence, *Behavior theory and learning: Selected papers* (pp. 91–112). Englewood Cliffs, NJ: Prentice-Hall.

Spiker, C. C. (1977). Behaviorism, cognitive psychology, and the active organism. In N. Datan & H. W. Reese (Eds.), *Life-span developmental psychology: Dialectical perspectives on experimental research* (pp. 93–103). New York: Academic Press.

Spiker, C. C., & McCandless, B. R. (1954). The concept of intelligence and the philosophy of science. *Psychological Review, 61,* 255–266.

Stokes, T. F., & Baer, D. M. (1977). An implicit technology of generalization. *Journal of Applied Behavior Analysis, 10,* 349–367.

Tilley, M. P. (1950). *A dictionary of the proverbs in England in the sixteenth and seventeenth centuries: A collection of proverbs found in English literature and the dictionaries of the period.* Ann Arbor: University of Michigan Press.

Vygotsky, L. S. (1962). *Thought and language* (E. Hanfmann & G. Vakar, Eds. & Trans.). New York: Wiley.

Vygotsky, L. S. (1978). *Mind in society: The development of higher psychological processes* (M. Cole, V. John-Steiner, S. Scribner, & E. Souberman, Eds.). Cambridge, MA: Harvard University Press.

Watson, J. B. (1913). Psychology as the behaviorist views it. *Psychological Review, 20,* 158-177.

Watson, J. B. (1925). *Behaviorism.* New York: Norton.

Watson, J. B. (1928a). Feed me on facts. *Saturday Review of Literature, 4,* 966-967.

Watson, J. B. (1928b). *The ways of behaviorism.* New York: Harper.

Watson, J. B. (1930). *Behaviorism* (rev. ed.). New York: Norton.

Watson, J. B. (1936). John Broadus Watson. In C. Murchison (Ed.), *A history of psychology in autobiography* (Vol. 3; pp. 271-281). Worcester, MA: Clark University Press.

Wertsch, J. V. (1979). From social interaction to higher psychological processes: A clarification and application of Vygotsky's theory. *Human Development, 22,* 1-22.

Wertsch, J. V. (1981). The concept of activity in Soviet psychology: An introduction. In J. V. Wertsch (Ed. & Trans.), *The concept of activity in Soviet psychology* (pp. 3 36). Armonk, NY: Sharpe.

White, S. H. (1970). The learning theory tradition and child psychology. In P. H. Mussen (Ed.), *Carmichael's manual of child psychology* (3rd ed., pp. 657-701). New York: Wiley.

White, S. H. (1976). The active organism in theoretical behaviorism. In H. W. Reese (Ed.), Conceptions of the "active organism" (pp. 99-107). *Human Development, 19,* 69-119.

Wicksteed, P. H., & Cornford, F. M. (1929). General introduction. In Aristotle, *The physics* (Vol. 1; P. H. Wicksteed & F. M. Cornford, Trans.). London: Heinemann.

Wozniak, R. H. (1975). Dialecticism and structuralism: The philosophical foundation of Soviet psychology and Piagetian cognitive developmental theory. In K. F. Riegel & G. C. Rosenwald (Eds.), *Structure and transformation: Developmental and historical aspects* (pp. 25-45). New York: Wiley.

Yendovitskaya, T. V., Zinchenko, V. P., & Ruzskaya, A. G. (1971). Development of sensation and perception. In A. V. Zaporozhets & D. B. Elkonin (Eds.), *The psychology of preschool children* (J. Shybut & S. Simon, Trans.; pp. 1-64). Cambridge, MA: M.I.T. Press.

Zivin, G. (Ed.). (1979). *The development of self-regulation through private speech.* New York: Wiley.

8 The Humanistic and Scientific View of Human Behavior

Frances Degen Horowitz
The University of Kansas

In an era of exploding technology and large advances in our knowledge about human behavior and development there is, understandably, concern and anxiety over the relationship between a science of human behavior and human values in a humanistic context. In this chapter I have set the task as one in which there is an attempt to consider the role of the humanistic view of human behavior at a time when the power of science has taken hold of both the fears and imaginations of large numbers of people, and when the visions called up by Huxley's *Brave New World* and Orwell's *Nineteen Eighty Four* raise questions about the destiny of human relationships in modern society.

This task takes up the challenge of reconciling what the humanistic approach could stand for in our society, while plumping for an unregenerate picture of the eventual power of behavioral science to account for much that is lawful in human behavior. The title of this chapter ("The Humanistic and Scientific View of Human Behavior") might occasion a variety of tongue-in-cheek comments from friendly readers: "I hope you won't do a snow job"; or "Don't leave it go on for too long"; or as a New Yorker might have said, "It should be a trilling lecture"—obvious punster references to the two cultures controversy that had its origins in the rise of the modern scientific era and in the debate between Matthew Arnold (1903–04) and Thomas Huxley in the last century and C. P. Snow and F. R. Leavis in this century. As Lionel Trilling (1962) pointed out, C. P. Snow's 1959 Cambridge University Rede lecture was directly antedated by Arnold's 1882 Rede lecture. Matthew Arnold had claimed that the facts of science, however interesting, could never satisfy the need for guidance of good

197

conduct or the need to be in contact with beauty; Huxley (1898), however, defended the relevance of science, claiming "nature is the expression of a definite order with which nothing interferes . . . the chief business of mankind is to learn that order and govern themselves accordingly." Huxley saw science as an appeal "not to authority . . . but to nature," and even though "all our interpretations of natural fact are more or less imperfect and symbolic," we are bid to "seek truth not among words but among things." Such a view, Huxley said, "warns us that the assertion which outstrips the evidence is not only a blunder but a crime" (p. 150).

Unfortunately, the Snow–Leavis point–counterpoint was considerably more diffuse in drawing the issues. Snow addressed the problem of communication across what he termed *two cultures;* Leavis and Yudkin (1962) railed at what he supposed was the thought that material wealth could be confused with intrinsic well-being. This latter point of view is instructive only in that it is not unlike current reactions to the use of M & M candies or token reinforcers with children and the fear that such extrinsic rewards will somehow blunt the development and power of intrinsic rewards. But, our discussion does not dwell upon the two cultures issue except by indirection. Instead, the focus is one of exploring the nature of the enterprise of behavioral science, the knowledge that has resulted from it, the implications of that understanding for the point of view that one might take with regard to what has been called "the law of necessity" or the issue of determinism and free will, and the role and relationship of the efforts that comprise the humanities with respect to a world view that must accommodate the facts of behavioral science.

Let us begin our discussion of behavioral science by making reference to Thomas Kuhn's notions of paradigm in science wherein a community of scientists functions according to a common set of shared rules and practices (Kuhn, 1970). One might question whether it is possible to characterize behavioral science today in terms of a paradigm. Leaving aside the many issues that are called forth by the question, it is probably valid to say that the social sciences involve many different paradigms. Even within the narrower realm of what we call the behavioral sciences, one still finds a variety of paradigms, some of which are in conflict not only methodologically but philosophically (see Koch, 1981). For our purposes here, the definition of behavioral science derives from the set of traditions and paradigms typically embodied in behaviorism — behaviorism as it is descended from John B. Watson and Clark Hull and B. F. Skinner into the modern functioning of applied behavior analysis so fully exemplified by my own colleagues in the Department of Human Development at the University of Kansas. But, I am taking a slightly different tack into a channel I think of as biobehavioral psychology that involves both an evolutionary and a developmental point of view. I want to sketch, briefly, the picture I believe is most supported by the data currently available as regards the behavioral development of the human organism.

Human Behavioral Development

When the egg and the sperm unite to form the beginnings of the human organism, there is represented there not only the immediate hereditary patterns of the contributing parents but the evolutionary history of the human species in which the genetic expression has been honed by eons of adaptive processes, thereby setting the organism on a highly probable course of structural and functional development. It has become quite apparent that this evolutionary and genetic expression is, from the beginning, subject to environmental influences; by the time birth occurs, the organism has a 9-month history of experience in a restricted but developmentally important environment.

It is now clear that at birth the human infant possesses a rather remarkable range of behavioral responses and is not simply a bundle of reflexes. The newborn infant responds to patterns of visual and auditory stimuli, to olfactory and tactile stimuli, and can engage in interactive behavior with other human beings. There is a rapid course of behavioral development over the first 2 years of life that is at once highly regular and individually variable. The regularity in part reflects the finely sculptured evolutionary patterns that have led to a determination of probable responses to common stimulus conditions. The human infant's behavioral course is thought to be highly canalized; that is, according to Scarr-Salapatek (1976), it is influenced by "a genetic predisposition for the development of a certain form of adaptation, guided along internally regulated lines". The terms *predisposition* and *guided* are critical here because human behavioral development does not automatically unfold; it cannot occur in a vacuum. Understanding the processes by which the environment actualizes behavioral development is a major focus in behavioral science.

The basic processes, clearly established with animals, and demonstrable in infants, children, and adults, involve elemental forms of conditioning. The acquisition of these responses can be partially understood as a function of the occurrence and repetition of given sets of stimulus conditions, responses, and reinforcing or consequent events. These processes appear to be subject, in both lower and higher animals, to certain neurological and genetic parameters that make it highly probable that the specific behavior acquired is species typical behavior. Thus, the normal child acquires spoken language, the cat and the dog not.

Language, the gross topography of motor development, and aspects of cognitive development all appear to occur universally in normal individuals across many different environments. Universality has led some behavioral scientists to reject basic conditioning as an underlying process of complex behavior. Awed by the universality of a phenomenon, they lose sight of the fact that the description of a recurring event as universal does not explain how the event comes to be, or what factors control the process that is responsible for its occurrence. Rain may be a universal phenomenon, but the description of regularity does not necessarily illuminate the processes by which rain is formed nor how it functions. Similarly, the identification of universals in human behavior still leaves us to work out an understanding of the basic processes that can account for the acquisition of the behaviors and how they function. The basic processes of conditioning are of central importance in accounting for human development.

It would seem an elementary matter—this understanding that for every behavioral domain there must be a set of processes that accounts for the acquisition of the behavior. The infant is born with a set of basic behaviors. These behaviors undergo rapid change and complex development, culminating, in the normal individual, in complex adult behavior that appears to function under given rules and conditions. However, some of the more simple conditioning paradigms do not appear to adequately account for complex adult behavior—another reason to question whether conditioning can serve as a cornerstone to account for behavioral development. But, one can be easily misled by focusing largely upon a well-developed domain of adult behavior. Just as the analysis of the late mature work of a writer, artist, or musician may fail to reveal the developmentally more simple artistic patterns evident in early work, complex processes in adults may have so fully subsumed simpler basic processes that the basic processes are difficult to reveal by looking at advanced, well-formed behavior. From just such an error did Noam Chomsky conclude too much with respect to the observation of seemingly universal characteristics in adult language behavior. He reasoned backwards that the process that would account for language acquisition in the child could not be found in a configuration of the child interacting with environmental factors, and that learning or conditioning principles could not account for language acquisition. Instead, he posited a genetic "language acquisition device" that provided an innate understanding of complex language forms.

The evidence, however, now suggests otherwise. There appear to be powerful environmental factors and conditions that help to facilitate language acquisition in the child; further, the acquisition process may be aided by strong determining neurological factors that give high probability to the occurrence and sequencing of special processing of language stimuli. The evidence points to important learning opportunities that occur in the context of infants and children interacting with adults and that thus account for large portions of language acquisition in the child. One need not repair to innate knowledge for an explanation.

Certain forms of adult behavior increase the probability of attracting and maintaining infant attention. These behaviors appear to facilitate the processing of the information provided in the language stimulation made available to the child and to amplify the conditions that enhance learning. The evidence that now exists thus points to an account of language acquisition that involves specific opportunities to learn the nature and characteristics of the language the child is expected to acquire, opportunities that involve the principles of conditioning as they function in a normal environment. The principles of conditioning appear to be enhanced by the presence of highly probable human information-processing strategies that are likely related to some specific, perhaps language specific, neurological mechanisms. It is possible that these or other mechanisms influence the sequencing of differential salience of language-relevant environmental stimuli (Gleitman, Newport, & Gleitman, 1984.)

The example of language development is an important one, for many who consider themselves humanists and thus worry about a *science* of human behavior, are concerned with forms of language behavior. In looking at the use of language, the humanist typically deals with well-formed adult behavior. The behavioral scientist interested in the same domain from a developmental point of view deals with the process of acquisition and wants to come to an understanding of how the variables important to the process function. This calls for a different approach than, for example, John Searle's philosophical analysis of "speech acts." Searle (1969) justified a philosophical analysis, as opposed to an empirical investigation, in claiming that a reflection on one's own language use would reveal the facts recorded in linguistic characterizations. From such observations, Searle thought, it would be possible to formulate the rules that underlie linguistic characterizations, and he proceeded to do so.

Two things can be said about such a philosophical analysis, however much it turns out to be verified in tests of language use in literature or in conversation. The first is that the rules that govern adult use of language do not necessarily elucidate the process by which such rules have been acquired. Sometimes the description of adult behavior, especially when it is shown to be quite regular from person to person, encourages ignoring the fact that there is a process or processes involved in the phenomenon and that the tools of empirical investigation are necessary to the verification of process. The fact of universal characteristics does not negate the possibility that each individual goes through a process of acquisition that involves basic principles of parametrically constrained conditioning and the establishment of long chains of conditioned, complex responses.

The second observation is that any attempt at a philosophical analysis of language rests upon an assumption that language is subject to lawful functioning. Language behavior is not capricious, whether in the specific use of certain linguistic forms, in the choice of vocabulary, or in the operation of discourse. Taken to a broader view, and the one that gets us to the eventual heart of this discussion, the analyses of language, of literature, of historical events all involve the identification of patterns of consistency, the identification of relationships that permit causal inferences and the description of patterns that involve regularities in the operation of principles and events. Indeed, the philosopher, the literary critic, and the historian act in such a manner as to generally expect that, as the result of their labors, an understandable and explainable pattern of usage, of symbol, of events will be revealed that have coherence and that show that the subject under study was regulated by the operation of some consistent principles.

The analysis of language, of art, and of historical record rests upon expectations of some form of lawful relationships. These analyses are thought to serve, among other purposes, as mirrors held up to life. As such they reflect the depiction of lawful regularities in life. In the work of the humanist then, there is an assumption of lawful relationships. And, here we have come now to the central issue. Lawfulness implies both regularity and, in principle, predictability. If there is lawfulness in life's events, then an understanding of the laws should enable us to predict the future, to foretell behavior. Does this mean that human behavior, functioning according to lawful principles, is thus determinable and predictable? In such a case how much and to what degree can we claim that behavior occurs as the result of free, unfettered, and unpredictable choice? If behavior is the result of processes of conditioning, does this imply that all behavior is determined? Assertions concerning the primacy of conditioning in human behavior are often taken to imply determinism and the denial of free will. And it is the desire to claim free will for human beings that frequently forms the motivation to refuse to accept the proposition that processes of conditioning are central to an account of human development and behavior. But, in the face of existing evidence, is such a position reasonable?

Let me provide a subsummary here that bridges us over to the next section of this discussion. The evidence to date supports a picture in which behavioral development is seen as a joint function of the operation of biological and genetic parameters, evolutionarily determined, that interact with environmental experience. The interaction results in the acquisition of behavior. The account includes the notion that complex sophisticated behavior is the result of long chains of conditioned responses that are fully integrated into the fabric of the behavioral repertoire and quite different from simpler forms of functioning. Thus, for example, behaviors that were initially dependent on extrinsic reinforcers such as simple material or social rewards are, through increasingly complex forms of conditioning, shaped over to dependence on intrinsic rewards and highly complex symbolic systems.

It would, however, be misleading if the certainty of these statements resulted in an overestimation of the extent to which our current level of understanding fully accounts for human behavior. We understand some of the principles and how they operate. We can account for their functioning with animals to a greater extent than with humans; we appear to have a better understanding of their functioning with retarded and severely handicapped organisms, where there are biological limitations and these individuals are less likely to be enmeshed in the broader functioning of cultural mores. With normal adult individuals who must function within complex cultural patterns, our ability to account for behavior is presently much less successful. However, the basic processes involved in conditioning still appear to provide the most useful general scientific framework for guiding research.

Behaviorism and Determinism

Human behavior is probably the most complex phenomenon on this planet. Some behavioral scientists have become discouraged in the face of such complexity and given up the enterprise; others search for different paradigms that seem to shade into nonscientific approaches, though Kuhn might see in such the making of a scientific revolution. The arguments as to what is and is not science in psychology are fierce indeed. Most behaviorists take their cornerstone of criteria from the logical positivists, from the canons that require objective verification of lawful relationships. The scientific method sets as a goal the extraction of laws from nature. This requires that information be organized into reliable patterns and followed by proposals of the mechanisms involved in those patterns. These, in turn, are tested and verified if, when used, they continue to account for the events that occur (Bronowski, 1961, p. 89). Psychologists such as Watson and Skinner have claimed that the data of behavioral science are, in essence, no different than the data from any other phenomena subject to scientific investigation. Watson defined psychology as "that division of natural science which takes human behavior—the doings and sayings, both learned and unlearned, of people as its subject matter." Scientific understanding involves the revelation of patterns of regularity, the prediction of future events, and, ultimately, the control of the phenomena involved.

The scientific method rests upon what Bertrand Russell (1913) called an

attitude of mind that sweeps away all other desires in the interest of the desire to know—it involves suppression of hopes and fears, loves and hates, and the whole subjective emotional life, until we become subdued to the material, able to see it frankly, without preconceptions, without bias, without any wish except to see it as it is, and without any belief that what it is must be determined by some relation, positive or negative, to what we should like it to be, or to what we can easily imagine it to be. (p. 235)

Because of this objectivity, Russell considered that science therefore brings one into the closest and most intimate relation with the outer world possible.

It is the stark application of such a point of view to the study of human behavior, a point of view adopted by Watson and by Skinner, going back to Hume and Locke, that elicits both reasoned and unreasoned rejoinders. For, taken to its logical conclusion, what appears to be implied is that the dispassionate discovery of the laws of human behavior will require the denial of free will choice. If behavior is, in its lawfulness, no different from other phenomena, and if lawful relations, once set in motion, are determinable and predictable, then how can one attribute to each person responsibility for his or her actions? Shall the question be resolved by logical analysis or is it essentially an empirical question to be decided by evidence? Both the question and the manner in which it is to be answered are, today, vibrant issues in the law and in politics. These issues appear to create the seeming gulf between humanists and behavioral scientists.

The vehemence of the rejection of the tenets of behaviorism can be found in cartoon caricature as well as reasoned philosophical analysis. In a discussion of philosophy and human nature, one philosopher, Nott (1970), claimed that:

> The behaviorist allows no room for human nature even as a functional concept while he treats human behavior as an adaptable engineering product. Clearly the behavioristic psychology has no useful bearing on . . . the nature and validity of moral judgment considered as essentially dependent on individual freedom and responsibility. If you cannot locate the human person, it is impossible to give any idea how he could be responsibly free. (p. 57–58)

This philosopher's discussion ends in an inconsistent muddle. The fact that we live in a lawful world was not denied. But, because human beings engage in "questioning at various levels of conceptualization," somehow the consistency of lawful relations as they apply to human behavior were thought, by this philosopher, to be negated (Nott, 1970, p. 228). The New York Times reviewer of Skinner's book *Beyond Freedom and Dignity* was more straight forward in his conclusion—he said that although it might be all true he didn't like it.

He didn't like it because of the inevitable implications that appear to follow from admitting that human behavior is under lawful control. Some people feel that any admission of lawful functioning somehow deromanticizes the human individual. Then there is the question of freedom of the will, and the law of necessity, and the spectra of complete determinism.

If all human behavior is controlled by predetermining factors, are not the questions of moral responsibility, good and evil, and personal freedom rendered moot? Joel Feinberg (1978) describes three positions on this question. One can be thought of as "hard determinism": The notion of free will and moral responsibility is discarded and an essentially fatalistic view of the future is adopted. Many have, however, tried to preserve free will in a second position that still permits determinism to prevail. Feinberg characterizes this second point of view as soft or reconciling determinism wherein determinism is not denied, but free will is retained as an expression of common sense—"I could have done otherwise if I had chosen to do so." This argument involves the belief that free will exists as part of common parlance. Individuals are considered to have responsibility for their actions. It doesn't matter if the choice itself was caused. Finally, a third position is to claim that although human behavior is not random, at some point it is lifted out of ordinary nature and said to be subject to special kinds of explanation. Determinism in this case does not exist; free will is preserved.

There are few adherents to hard determinism and many variations of reconciling or soft determinism. Hume (1748) essentially lamented that in practice there must be a doctrine of necessity in human behavior, but he avoided the inevitable conclusion of hard determinism by arguing that if you define liberty as the power of acting or not acting according to the determinations of the will, liberty and determinism could thus coexist. One hundred and fifty years later, Bertrand Russell continued the tradition at a somewhat more sophisticated level, but no less evasively, when it came to the question of human behavior. If all events of the past can be explained by resorting to explanations of causal relations, then, Russell claimed, there was no reason to doubt that all future events would be similarly explained and therefore the future would be completely determined. If human behavior is caused, then human behavior is fully determined—a point of view that Russell acknowledges generates great trepidation, because we do not like to think of ourselves as entirely in the hands of fate and thus compelled to act as we do (i.e., accept the implications of hard determinism).

Russell's semantic escape was to argue that the only meaningful sense of free will is to put it in opposition to the concept of external compulsion. And he did so by arguing that if all is foreseen, then included are human volitions. Human volitions, he reasoned, must be the result of desire. To have volition contrary to desire is not logically possible. Therefore, the fact that future behavior is determined does not deny the existence of personal desire and volition. Thus free will, in the only sense that Russell believed it meaningful, was preserved (Russell, 1914). Free will exists not in terms of denying determinism, but in terms of rescuing the "sense" of freedom for individuals. Alvin Goldman (1978) took up a similar theme when he proposed that acknowledging human behavior as determined is analogous to claiming that for each individual there is a complete Book of Life, in which all the events between birth and death are recorded, unknown to the individual. The existence of such a book does not, Goldman argues, necessarily rob the individual of the sense of engaging in voluntary action. I am tempted to call this line of discussion "argument by illusion." Arguing determinism away by retaining the commonsense notion of freedom of the will is ultimately not very satisfactory, for it rests upon the rationale that conclusions should be drawn that have the effect of making us feel better about the world.

Interestingly, John Stuart Mill did not rely upon illusion. He preserved freedom of choice by appealing to an idea that may well stand empirical test and have foreshadowed scientific developments 125 years after his time. His argument involved the simple notion that human character is formed for and by an individual, with the individual shaping his or her own life through choices. An individual, according to Mill (1843, 1974), "has to a certain extent, a power to alter his character." Character formed for an individual "is not inconsistent with its being, in part, formed by him as one of the intermediate agents. His character is formed by his circumstances (including among these his particular organization); but his own desire to mold it in a particular way, is one of those circumstances and by no means one of the least influential" (p. 840). On the topic of absolute prediction Mill took the point of view that because human behavior was the result of circumstances in which an individual was placed, and because it was not possible to foresee the whole of the circumstances that would occur in the future, absolutely accurate prediction of the future could not occur.

But, you might argue, is not Mill's position just a more palatable form of soft determinism? If there is lawfulness, then, as Russell maintained, life in the end is all predetermined save what one wishes to salvage to make one feel more comfortable with this state of affairs. Not so, necessarily. However, a full explication of why Mill's position may be an eminently reasonable one requires us to add some concepts and to repair, finally, to some data. I argue that the question of determinism is necessarily an empirical question.

To form the argument, we must refer to Charles Peirce's discussions of probability and the concept of chance; we need to consider some of Henri Bergson's formulations; and we must, finally, bring in Schrödinger's claims that inexactitude may be an intrinsic character of nature. Charles Peirce, reputed father of pragmatism, did not doubt that scientific observations reveal the element of regularity in nature. But he claimed that such evidence for regularity did not necessarily forbid the possibility of chance occurrence. Whereas the laws of nature are immutable, they are the products of evolution and also subject to evolution (Peirce, 1962). For

Peirce there was nothing metaphysical about such an idea. However, Henri Bergson formed his metaphysics by exempting all of organic life from predeterminism in asserting that regularity in the form of repetition was ultimately a fiction. Bergson (1944) claimed that all of life was subject to processes of adaptive evolution involving the "continual creation of new forms succeeding others" (p. 96). Though this formulation has not become part of the mainstream of philosophical analysis nor been of central interest in speculations in science, short of the metaphysics involved, there are some interesting ideas in Bergson that deserve attention.

Peirce's theme leads to the proposal that the reign of law is inherently limited because of the element of chance or spontaneity operative in the world. A.J. Ayer takes this up and notes that even in causal laws there are chance elements in how factors act within a specified function (Ayer, 1968). He and others have noted that the idea that some laws are irreducibly statistical finds support in modern science. The idea that inexactitude of measurement is thus not only a function of the error of measurement but is contributed to by an intrinsic statistical phenomenon, was further developed by Schrödinger (1935), who suggested that probabilistic outcomes may be an inherent characteristic of nature. This is an increasingly prevailing view among some scientists.

The issue of intrinsic inexactitude has immediate and obvious implications with respect to prediction; and it has relevance to the discussion of free will and determinism in human behavior. As such, it is a dangerous concept if employed carelessly, a very important concept if used with sophistication. The question is at what level of minuteness and complexity of a phenomenon is there inexactitude of measurement, and to what extent a probabilistic element in prediction will hold. It is clear from the degree of orderliness we encounter in our physical world that we are not talking about the gross features of causal relationships. Water does boil when sufficient levels of heat are applied, and it is possible to predict how long it will take to bring water to the boiling point with some degree of accuracy, taking error of measurement into account. One needs to know the intensity of the heat, its degree of dispersion, all the relevant characteristics of the pot, the nature of the chemical composition of the water, and the altitude. In addition to error of measurement, there may also be an intrinsic inexactitude at the level of specifying specific movement of molecules and thus contributing to error in the exactness of the prediction.

Those who find the basic idea of prediction of human behavior an uncomfortable one may be tempted to seize upon the notion of intrinsic inexactitude to discredit the entire idea of prediction as it relates to human behavior and thereby eliminate the problem of determinism and questions of moral responsibility. It is not that I wish to hang on at whatever cost to the proposition that human behavior is lawfully regulated and, in principle, subject to prediction. But I think the idea of unpredictability in human behavior requires very careful consideration in the face of mounting evidence that there are orderly processes that can account for human behavior. Under limited and controlled conditions, relatively high levels of prediction are possible. Even under natural and complex conditions, we often have a sufficient understanding of some of the larger controlling variables to make some predictions. It is important to retain this perspective because it has some moral consequences for how we deal with children and adults who have problems and need help. Any belief system that abrogates a basic tenet that human development and human behavior are lawfully governed leads to the consequence that there is no meaningful intervention possible to ameliorate individual or group problems. In fact, it is probably not practically possible to relinquish a belief in the orderliness of human behavior. In the everyday world of interactions and expectations, we base large proportions of our own behavior on the belief that other individuals will act in an orderly and predictable manner.

No, the question of inexactitude and chance cannot become a logical basis for obviating the idea that behavior is lawfully controlled. On the other hand, inexactitude and chance may be an important factor in the operation of causal relationships by requiring that we think of laws in an essentially probabilistic form, which may have special relevance for organisms at the edge of the evolutionary process in a manner that calls up some of Bergson's notions, but at a more molecular level and with greater individual specification. The importance of this point is that an intrinsic impossibility of absolute predictability may set the limitations of a scientific account of any phenomenon. Max Black (1970) entitled one of his collections of essays *Margins of Precision*. The title was taken from a Chinese quotation: "At the margins of precision the universe wavers." Waver indeed—sometimes more than we would like, even though it is at that margin of precision that we retain probability.

However, claiming intrinsic inexactitude does not, in and of itself, rescue the concept of freedom of the will and moral responsibility. An important and related issue is the role of moral ingredient in behavioral choice. If we are claiming that human behavior is, in some degree, not entirely predictable because of the operation of intrinsic chance factors, we are not likely to want to place moral responsibility in the province of chance function. Indeed, the emotional commitment to being able to attribute moral responsibility to an individual is based on an exactly opposite notion of certainty. One can be charged as having moral responsibility only under those conditions where chance elements are said not to be dominant. Proving that a fire was set completely by chance absolves the individual of moral responsibility for the damage done as a result of the fire. Only when it becomes clear that setting the fire was the result of a lawful relationship—the individual *wanted* to set the fire or intended to set the fire, and it was that desire or intention which contributed to the fire being set—do we attribute moral responsibility.

But, you might argue, are you not involved in a logical contradiction with this example? Here moral responsibility is attributed in a situation in which determinism is said to prevail—the same determinism that often provides the grounds for denial of free will and the attribution of moral responsibility. The desire to set the fire can be said to be determined by the individual's past history. That may be true—at least past history may have increased the probability that under a given set of circumstances the individual would deliberately set the fire. That past history includes not only the external environmental conditions that the individual experienced—parental treatment, reinforcement for the use of fire as an aggressive tool, accumulated anger as the result of negative experiences, but also the behavior of the individual, including the individual's acquired knowledge about right and wrong, the individual's choice in weighting the relative importance of one variable over another. It is not just a matter of saying that the person could have done otherwise had he chosen to do so. The claim I make now is that, in fact, the choice is not entirely predetermined by the past. At the point of choice there is, if you will, the edge of precision, there is the margin of the undetermined—the measure of uncertainty. There is the volition that is partly determined by the past and partly determined at the moment of choice by the individual's election of how to weight the relevant ingredients that determine choice. If the question of right and wrong stands strongly in past history, and if I choose to give it the greatest weight at the moment of choice, a given behavior will result in an instance of creative adaptation. Can you predict with absolute certainty what behavior will result? Probably not? With a high probability? Yes, if you know the variables and their weighting sufficiently. But, the high probability reflects that margin of uncertainty (chance) plus the momentary occurrence of choice behavior. If one accepts the concept of creative adaptation, not only for the larger scale phenomena accounted for by principles of evolution, but also at the individual level of behavioral growth and adaptation, then at what might be called an individual microevolutionary level, there is an element of the undetermined in each choice. The factors in past history, especially those that reflect value orientations and moral commitments or their lack, weigh heavily but do not completely determine the choice at the moment it is made.

The preponderance of evidence for the reasonableness of this point of view is stronger than the evidence against it. Our understanding of techniques of self-modification of behavior and recent information concerning the role of behavioral function in modifying neurological structure are relevant. All of which is to say that John Stuart Mill's somewhat colloquial claim for the "formation of character" being influenced by the individual's own behavior may have a strong analog in what we are beginning to understand about the interaction of behavioral and biological functioning, about feedback loop effects of behavior on neurological structure, and the subsequent influence of the modified structure on behavior.

The Humanities and Behavioral Science

We have, so far, said little about the humanities directly, nor talked of the humanistic view of human behavior—the other component of the title of this chapter. As one who is not a professionally trained humanist, I think it best to tread tentatively into this domain. However, there are a number of humanists whose observations are pertinent. The late Charles Frankel claimed that it is the business of humanistic disciplines to comment on and appraise activities; to reflect on meaning and clarify judgment (Frankel, 1981). Walter Kaufmann (1977) identified four goals in the humanistic enterprise: the conservation and cultivation of the greatest works of the human spirit; the cultivation of reflection on goals, giving attention to alternative visions; the cultivation of a critical spirit; and, the teaching of vision. These responsibilities assigned to the humanistic enterprise do not necessarily intersect with the scientific view of human behavior, so you might wonder at the relationship between the two.

The relationship resides in the sometimes veiled and sometimes not so veiled rivalry between behavioral science and the humanities. Though it was more frequently encountered in past years than now, the claim is still abroad that the humanities provide the most significant and fundamental understanding of human nature. Indeed, one major objection to behaviorism is that it does not take sufficient cognizance of human nature, what with all this talk about conditioning, stimuli and responses, response chains, and reinforcement.

There are two attitudes with respect to humanist views of human behavior vis-a-vis behavioral science. One is that somehow the discussion of human behavior in terms of responses, conditioning, and stimulus conditions deromanticizes people. It is an attitude that ought to be easily countered. Gustav Bergman, the philosopher and University of Iowa guru to behaviorists, was fond of saying that just because one can analyze the chemistry and physics of very hot running water does not mean that when one puts one's hand into the water, the person will not still say "ouch." Similarly, because a late Beethoven quartet can be described in mathematical and structural terms, one is not therefore prevented from having an emotional and aesthetic experience when hearing it played beautifully. Indeed, the issue of analysis as somehow robbing the emotional and aesthetic dimension is dispelled even within the humanities, where literary criticism and analysis can sometimes account in more complete detail for the structure of a piece of fiction than we can successfully account for a domain of human behavior. One can still enjoy both the meaning and the beauty of the work. I would venture a hypothesis that the more one knows about the structure of a complex literary work or a musical composition, the greater is the potential for its emotional and aesthetic impact upon insight and appreciation. Thus, short of claiming that it is the business of the humanist to engage in uncritical impressionism, the very fact of analysis ought not to put the humanist off when it comes to behavioral science.

The second attitude separating the humanist and the behaviorist, and by far the more serious one, brings us back to the question of moral responsibility, free will, and determinism. As we have already noted, if all of behavior is determined, then it is not possible to ascribe moral responsibility to an individual for his or her choice. For the humanist trained to analyze a work of fiction or poetry not only in its structural terms but in relation to the values and morals exemplified in the literature, a belief in total determinism could render the tuitional value of such activity irrelevant. Yet, as we have seen, the best hypothesis at the present time concerning human behavior is that it is not completely determined. Further, there is considerable evidence that values and moral positions are themselves the result of learning. Learned values, in turn, influence subsequent behavior. Different diets of moral milieus have different consequences for not only the behavior of individuals, but for the behavior of groups and cultures. The operation of a culture tends to perpetuate systems that reflect the values of the culture. Indeed, numerous analyses by quite radical behaviorists have been directed at discussions of the possible mechanisms involved in the functioning of different cultures. Central to these analyses is the idea that cultures evolve to different kinds of functioning as the result of differential contingencies. The contingencies involve not only primary reinforcers such as food and water, but complex secondary reinforcers such as approval and disapproval and, ultimately, contingencies as depicted in the abstract and symbolic representations of good and evil, truth and falsity, the moral and the immoral. One might even argue, from the point of view of the behavioral scientist, that in affluent societies where primary reinforcers are in abundance, there is more dependence on the functioning of abstract and symbolic contingencies than is true for societies closer to the edge of physical survival.

Many modern postindustrial societies are not stressed by the scarcity of food and water. Their travails are more deeply and complexly rooted in the weakness with which contingencies operate in relation to moral values, in the consensus or lack of functional consensus as to what constitutes good and what constitutes evil.

Therefore, the role of the humanities in proffering a view of human behavior is not to counter the horrid mechanisms of conditioning and the behavioristic view, but to provide the content against which the moral choice is to be made, to illuminate through the analysis of literature and art, through the analysis of the use of language, and through the documentation of the past, the kinds of choices available and some of the consequences of those choices in relation to both the professed values of our society, and the value choices we might consider. You might say that this argument rests too strongly upon a rejection of complete determinism. What if it should turn out to be the case that all is determined? My answer is that in such an instance, one would choose between fatalism and the development of arguments that avoid fatalism, a la Russell and others. But, in thinking about the "what if" question, I am reminded of the title that was chosen for the volume of selected lectures from the first 2 years of the University of Kansas Humanities lecture series. It was published in 1949 and entitled *The Humanities for Our Time* (Lind, 1949). We must think in terms of the humanities for *our* time, not for some future time when the assumptional base may be different. The humanities for our time must be related to our current best perspective about human behavior and to our current best understanding of the laws that govern human behavior. If there should be a radical change in that understanding, the humanities for that time may have a different function. In our time, the past is constantly interpreted and reinterpreted in the light of the present, and the ideas in philosophy and literature have ever meaningful but evolving significance in each age.

The claim that one should study literature is not made only because of the sheer delight in the progress of a story, though at times that may be momentary justification enough simply for reading. Requiring the study of literature in the curriculum is done because such study is seen as a vehicle for the apprehension of ideas, of moral choices, of the depiction of good and evil and the consequences therefrom, whether it be by intuitive insight or critical explication. The kind of knowledge acquired becomes part of the factors that weigh in at real personal choice points. They are there at the point that is at the edge of decision. Such knowledge that is imparted in humanistic studies influences the kind of social system one supports, the kind of climate that one fosters in a home, the kind of values and ideals one imparts to one's children. What the humanities contribute, both by being a habit of mind and by presenting issues, can play a functional role in the laws that control human behavior. Values, ideals, morals are functional variables in the equation that accounts for human behavior.

The tendency on the part of some analysts to contrast the knowledge derived from science as objective and verifiable, and the knowledge derived from humanistic study as private, unverifiable, and intuitive, has done immeasurable harm, for there is the implication that scientific knowledge stands higher in the value hierarchy than humanistic knowledge. No one would dispute that the method for apprehending knowledge in science is different from that in the humanities, but I think one would be hard pressed to prove that there is a differential value of one over the other. They are different, though Polyani (1946) has been insistent in observing that there *is* intuition in science and there *are* aesthetic criteria by which we evaluate solutions to scientific problems—at least for what we label as "elegant" in science.

To depict science as positive knowledge in the public domain, and to say that because the meaning of good and evil, of joy and sorrow, of beauty and justice are private convictions and thus can in no way be transmitted from person to person, is to confuse the personal content of belief systems with how belief systems are acquired and function. It may be romantic to claim that such meanings constitute a personal store of wisdom, that each person starts from scratch, acquires his or her own wisdom from experience, and that there is thus no accumulated store of wisdom (see Hubble, 1954). But such a claim reveals an appalling lack of appreciation for our understanding of human behavior. As Northrop Frye has noted, the difference between science and the humanities is not necessarily in their subject matter; it is in the method (Frye, 1966). It is in the justification for what is accepted as evidence that the difference lies, not in the value of that evidence once it is produced.

Evidence in the humanities derives from a habit of mind that rests upon an anatomy of criticism, as Frye would have it. Thus, I would maintain that the humanities qua humanities implies no special view of human behavior, only a set of techniques related to the content of literature, art, music, history, and language, which, through analysis and intuitive insight, yields an understanding and perspective unique to these methods.

I am arguing here for the importance of knowledge related to human behavior, to moral choices, and to aesthetic experience derived from humanistic study because that knowledge and the perspectives that accompany the knowledge have, in my opinion, an important function in the behavioral equation. Bennett (1981) argued that "if . . . humanists abandon the nurture of the heritage, the recall of the desolations and the victories, the dreams, the hopes, fears, disappointments and aspirations of a people, and of all people,—then they will abandon instruction about our spiritual circumstances."

A thoughtful behaviorist does not shrink from using the terms hope, fear, spiritual enrichment, insight, and intuition, for it is known that the behavior embodied in the manner in which those entities function is lawfully governed, and that when it comes to the edge of the predictable equation, to the moment of choice, the direction of that choice will be partially controlled by how those ingredients weigh into the process. To the extent that the behavioral scientist sees the knowledge derived from science as possibly contributing to the betterment of society, and to the extent that the humanist similarly justifies the activities of the humanities, they share common cause. One need not seek reconciliation to preserve the sense of freedom and moral responsibility; it is an empirical question, and for the moment the evidence is on the side of incomplete determinism. Some indeterminism notwithstanding, much is determined in causal relationships, but the content of those causal relationships is, in turn, partially determined by knowledge that we derive from the humanistic enterprise. Whether one characterizes these two forms of knowledge as public and private, as objective and subjective, as beauty and truth, or as It and Thou, they are companions. Or, as Emily Dickinson said, beauty and truth, "Themself are One—/We Bretheren are."

ACKNOWLEDGMENT

This chapter was originally given as an invited Humanities Lecture at the University of Kansas in September, 1982. It has been revised slightly for inclusion in this book. I am grateful to the Humanities Lecture Series Committee for extending this invitation and stimulating the consideration of this issues discussed in this chapter. I hope that Charles Spiker, who is being honored by this volume, will recognize the seeds of his instruction as they have taken root, have formed the foundation upon which this lecture was built, and have been an enduring influence upon my work.

REFERENCES

Arnold, M. (1903–04). "Literature and Science." *The works of Matthew Arnold.* IV London: MacMillan.

Ayer, A. J. (1968). *The humanist outlook.* London: Pemberton.

Bennett, W. (1981). The humanities, the universities and public policy. In J. Agresto & P. Riesenberg (Eds.), *The humanist as citizen* (pp. 188-201). Chapel Hill: The National Humanities Center, University of North Carolina Press.

Bergson, H. (1944). *Creative evolution.* New York: Random House, Modern Library.

Black, M. (1970). *Margins of precision.* Ithaca, NY: Cornell University Press.

Bronowski, J. (1961). Science in human. In J. S. Huxley (Ed.), *The humanist frame* (pp. 83-94). New York: Harper.

Feinberg, J. (1978). *Reason and responsibility* (4th ed.). Encino, CA: Dickenson.

Frankel, C. (1981). Why the Humanities? In J. Agresto & P. Riesenberg (Eds.), *The humanist as citizen* (pp. 3-15). Chapel Hill: National Humanities Center, University of North Carolina Press.

Frye, N. (1966). Speculation and Concern. In T. B. Stroup (Ed.), *The humanities and the understanding of reality.* Lexington: University of Kentucky Press.

Gleitman, L. R., Newport, E. L. & Gleitman, H. (1984). The current status of the motherese hypothesis. *Journal of Child Language, 11,* 43–79.

Goldman, A. I. (1978). Actions, predictions and Books of Life. In J. Feinberg (Ed.), *Reason and responsibility* (4th ed., pp. 387-394). Encino, CA: Dickenson.

Hubble, E. P. (1954). *The nature of science and other lectures.* San Marino, CA: The Huntington Library.

Hume, D. (1955). *An inquiry concerning human understanding.* Indianapolis: Bobbs-Merrill Educational Publishing (Original essay 1748).

Huxley, T. H. (1898). "Science and Culture." In T. H. Huxley, *Collected essays. Vol. III. Science and education* (pp. 134-159). New York: D. Appleton.

Kaufmann, W. (1977). *The future of the humanities.* New York: Reader's Digest Press. Corwell.

Koch, S. (1981). The nature and limits of psychological knowledge. *American Psychologist, 36,* 257-269.

Kuhn, T. (1970). *The structure of scientific revolution.* Chicago: University of Chicago Press.

Leavis, F. R., & Yudken, M. (1962). *Two cultures? The significance of C.P. Snow.* London: Chatto & Windus.

Lind, R. L. (1949). *The humanities for our time.* Introduction. Lawrence: University of Kansas Press.

Mill, J. S. (1843; 1974). Of liberty and necessity. In *Collected works. Vol. XI. Of a system of logic rationcinature and inductive* (pp. 836-843). Toronto: University of Toronto Press.

Nott, K. (1970). *Philosophy and human nature.* London: Hodder & Stoughton.

Peirce, C. S. (1962). The doctrine of necessity. In W. Barrett & H. Aiken (Eds.), *Philosophy in the twentieth century* (pp. 122-136). New York: Random House.

Polyani, M. (1946). *Science, faith and society.* Oxford: Oxford University Press.

Russell, B. (1913). Science as an element in culture. *New Statesman,* May 31, 234-236.

Russell, B. (1922). *Our knowledge of the external world.* London: George Allen & Unwin. (Originally published 1914 by Open Court Publishing Co.)

Scarr-Salapatek, S. (1976). An evolutionary perspective on infant intelligence, species patterns and individual variations. In M. Lewis (Ed.), *Origins of intelligence* (pp. 165-197). New York: Plenum.

Schrödinger, E. (1935). *Science and the human temperament.* New York: Norton.

Searle, J. R. (1969). *Speech acts.* Cambridge: Cambridge University Press.

Snow, C. P. (1959). *The two cultures: A second look.* Cambridge: Cambridge University Press.

Trilling, L. (1962). Science, literature and culture: A comment on the Leavis-Snow controversy. *Commentary,* June, 461-477.

9

On The Teaching
of Teaching

Winifred Shepard
State University of New York College at Fredonia

In the fall of 1951, East Hall on the campus of the State University of Iowa was alive with psychological luminaries. To name just a few, Kenneth Spence and Judson Brown held sway in the Department of Psychology with Gustav Bergmann as resident philosopher, while E. F. Lindquist, Professor of Education, was completing work on his influential text on analysis of variance. The top two floors of the building housed what was then known as the Iowa Child Welfare Research Station. Directed by Boyd McCandless, the faculty included such distinguished veteran researchers into child development as Beth Wellman, Orvis Irwin, and Howard Meredith. There was also a very young faculty member named Charles Spiker who, even in the midst of this formidable array of colleagues, dazzled the incoming group of graduate students with the clarity of his thought, dedication to data, and contagious conviction that there was order and system out there in the world waiting to be revealed to those who sought it with appropriate methodology.

Those of us who would spend the next few years learning from Charlie were in for a difficult, exciting, occasionally stressful, and, ultimately, invaluable experience.

There is probably no way to specify completely or adequately evaluate the influence of any teacher. What are appropriate criterion measures? When should they be assessed? Some impacts are immediate and obvious, others are delayed but obvious, and still others become so enmeshed in the web of ensuing life experiences that they are difficult to tease out. There are also, no doubt, always multiple interactions with such variables as subject matter, type and level of educational institution, and student characteristics. It is also true that just as Mark Twain claims to have realized in his early adulthood that his father had matured greatly in the previous 10 years, many students do not realize until years later what they had learned from a particular teacher. Nevertheless, each of us remembers some—a very few—teachers whom we know with personal, if not statistical, certainty made an enormous difference in our lives.

A glance at the contents of this volume attests to the fact that Charlie was a catalyst for many impressive and productive research careers. What's probably not so obvious is the impact that he had on his students' teaching activities and, through them, on thousands of students he never met and never will meet. I'm fairly certain that he wasn't consciously preoccupied with the fact that he was teaching teachers. Indeed, as one who has been primarily a full-time teacher, I'd never consciously thought extensively about the ways in which the years at Iowa with Charlie shaped my teaching philosophy and practice until I began to write this chapter. Now, having taken the time to reflect, I clearly and certainly recognize enormous valuable and enduring influences. The following personal and unscientific recollections, based on the period 1951–1955, try to make explicit the messages about teaching that Charlie conveyed through his own teaching behaviors—what he did and did not do. Despite the tenuous nature of this data base, I'm confident that these experiences were not unique.

Teaching is an extremely important activity in any society and ought to be taken seriously. This shouldn't be a surprising message for any teacher to convey, except that Iowa was, notably, a research institution. Both in the Station and in the Department of Psychology downstairs, there was general agreement that psychology was a science and psychologists should be continuously engaged in contributing to it. Charlie certainly shared that view. He was, himself, heavily engaged in research and was an active director and participant in the research activities of his students.

It's no secret in higher education that, where there is strong faculty commitment to research, there is danger of giving short shrift to teaching, suggesting in subtle ways that it is a secondary activity and that the time spent on it is begrudged. In institutions with heavy stress on research and a publish or perish atmosphere, undergraduates complain about being turned over to teaching assistants and not having enough access to the professors, while graduate students often are made to feel that their primary task is not so much to learn as to enhance their professors' reputations. That was not Charlie's way.

Genuinely concerned that his students learn, this young instructor was scrupulous about details. Classes met regularly and there were none of those embarrassing early dismissals occasioned by an instructor's failure to gauge how much material was needed for the allotted class time, assuming no interruptions by student questions. Evening after evening when students were in their offices working or commiserating with each other, Charlie was in his office typing out material for the next day. Moreover, tests and feedback from them were frequent. He graded his own tests and no one had to wait half a semester to find out how s/he was doing.

Beyond these quantifiable measures were others, less tangible but at least as important. We knew that Charlie really cared whether or not we learned. If an idea didn't come across as originally stated, I remember his working hard to rephrase it in a way that would ensure understanding. Often, it seemed to me, this would involve him in retracing his own thinking, making explicit, first to himself and then to us, those assumptions or states in the development of an argument that had become automatic, "given," to him, but which did not yet have that status with his students. It's hard to know if this was a deliberate technique on his part, but he did it and most effectively. He wanted us to understand. By taking the time and making the effort to analyze carefully what he was teaching, he made it possible for us to understand and, at the same time, modeled excellence in an important aspect of teaching.

While classroom teaching utilized primarily lecture format, individualized one-on-one teaching was handled very differently. Those of us who were trying to design independent study or thesis projects were led, through a kind of Socratic technique, to a realization of which of our ideas were potentially productive and which were heading into blind alleys. This skill in shifting pedagogical gears as instructional situations change is not easy to come by. Charlie was good at it.

Students need to have their efforts recognized and reinforcement for good performance was generous and individualized. It was not a matter of a perfunctory or patronizing "very good" or "that's right" for each correct response, but rather a comment in class or on a paper or during a meeting in the hallway that took cognizance of the difficulty of the task or the usefulness of the response. When student performance was not top notch he reacted in a way that did not so much express disappointment as encourage future improvement. There was, for example, the day he returned a particularly rough test to a tension-filled group and diffused the tension by remarking, before handing out the papers, that he was impressed by the fact that even the lowest score indicated so much progress toward mastering this very difficult material. He used, in effect, a well-designed variable reinforcement schedule that kept us working hard and striving to improve.

Speaking of hard, there were those reading lists. Charlie thought that it was better all around for students to rise to his expectations rather than for him to accommodate to theirs. I well remember the incredulity I felt after looking over the first reading list he handed out. Those articles by Bergmann, Cooley, Feigl, and Spence were impossible. "He's got to be kidding." He wasn't. There was no watering down, no mercy, no concession to the literal and figurative whimpering. He said in class one day that whatever reputation he developed he was determined that no one would ever accuse him of teaching a Mickey Mouse course. No chance! We would always be sent directly to the professional literature rather than to one of the predigested sanitized texts many of us were used to. The material he assigned was the background we needed to understand the course and certainly it was possible if you were willing to expend the time and effort. Most of us eventually found out it was possible, albeit painful, and our self-respect rose in direct relationship to our understanding of this impossible stuff. That's been a useful experience to reflect on in the face of years of pressure to modify demands and to assign superficially relevant materials written, unblushingly, in "readable" prose.

Undoubtedly, for me, the most important and valuable course I ever took was Charlie's course on Research Methodology, which students were required to take during their first semester. Formally this course included units on definition, causation, logic, probability, psychophysical measurement, and theory. Pretty heavy stuff and much of it, I thought, had nothing to do with people. Fresh from an undergraduate experience that emphasized, although it did not clearly articulate, a diametrically opposed orientation to knowledge in general and psychology in particular, I was at first appalled. After awhile, however, it became apparent that we were being taught some fundamentally useful principles. Basically, Charlie was letting us know what it was possible for scientists of human behavior to accomplish and what was impossible. We were led to a convincing awareness of the difference between fact and value, the probabilistic nature of empirically derived scientific knowledge, the danger of generalizing beyond the limitations of specific data, the necessity of guarding against the always present temptation to impute natural language implications and connotations to scientific concepts, and the importance of formulating and critically evaluating higher order conceptualizations. Teachers of psychology who manage to convey these ideas have accomplished a great deal indeed.

Recently, in leafing through the now fragile and yellowed notes taken over 30 years ago, it was surprising to see what a slim packet of papers they were. It shouldn't have been surprising. Ideas that have been carefully thought through and distilled to the essence don't need padding. Clear and devoid of obfuscating embroidery, the ideas Charlie communicated in that introduction to graduate training have withstood the test of time—transcending changes in subject-matter preference and the particulars of the individual research and teaching careers of his students.

Communication—unambiguous and succinct—is of the essence in the educational process and it has to be two-way. Students have a right to expect it from their teachers and an obligation to strive for it themselves. As previously mentioned, Charlie consistently worked at rephrasing ideas in the clearest possible fashion, but he was equally demanding of his students. His unrelenting insistence on precise expression often elicited frustration and exasperation, but no lesson was more worthwhile to anyone who would go on to be a teacher. During my first year at Iowa I recall that I would often utter some deathless gem only to be responded to with something like "What you might mean by. . . . " I wasn't overjoyed and, moreover, sometimes what he said I "might mean" was not what I meant. Avoidance learning, however, does occur and, eventually, it became clear that if I didn't want anyone telling me what I might mean, I'd better say it clearly myself and that if I was clear about the message, the words could be found. In the classroom nothing forces a teacher to formulate an idea more carefully than the recognition that students are not getting it and nothing is more rewarding than success in finding the right words. By the same token, nothing is less convincing than the often repeated refrain "I know what I mean, but I can't say it." Those students who do learn the importance of clear communication recognize its worth and, sometimes, even say so.

Lest the preceding conjures up an incredible picture of some kind of annoying, inhuman paragon of pedagogical virtue, it should be noted that such was not the case. Charlie was irritated when students wouldn't follow advice that he thought was in their own or the program's best interest and, without overt berating, he showed it, although I don't remember anyone ever permanently falling from grace. Moreover, he conveyed the belief, prevalent at Iowa in that heyday of behaviorism and logical positivism, that there really was only one right way. Although this may be an inevitable part of the evolution of paradigms, it raised some hackles and elicited some reactance. At the same time, however, it did not diminish and even sometimes enhanced the salience of his viewpoints and the integrity of his commitment.

Looking at educational experience from a life-span developmental perspective, the graduate school years stand out as peculiarly intense. There are, for the students, great investments of time, money and effort, and, more subtly, a pervasive moment-of-truth atmosphere. With perhaps unnecessary rigidity, there is a feeling that choice and commitments have been made. No more stalling or vacillating can be indulged in and one must now acquire the skills to ensure that the choices and commitments were good ones. The importance of instructors, major professors particularly, is enormous. In fact, many students are left with a form of intellectual dependency that takes some time to overcome. In such a milieu the need for excellent teaching is highlighted. Those of us who had Charlie Spiker as a teacher, mentor, and model during our graduate training were fortunate indeed. I am—we are—grateful.

10 Closeness to Parents and Siblings: Developmental and Gender Effects

Kathryn Norcross Black
Purdue University

INTRODUCTION

Children are typically born into a family and over the course of time develop an attachment to other family members. At one time both professionals and laypersons assumed that the first and major attachment would be to the mother who was, of course, the primary caretaker. The newer view that fathers may care for children as well as mothers, and that children need not be primarily attached to their mother, is reflected in both recent child psychology textbooks (e.g., Hall, Lamb, & Perlmutter, 1982; Santrock & Yussen, 1984; Tomlinson-Keasey, 1985) and in present law in child custody cases (Cantor & Drake, 1983, Chapter 5). We have also begun to focus on the influence of other family members and especially on the effects of the presence of siblings and their interactions with one another. Furthermore, it is clear that not all family relationships are positive ones. For example, research on infants has found that attachment may be either secure, anxious resistant, or anxious avoidant (Ainsworth, Blehar, Waters, & Wall, 1978). Further, a distressing incidence of abuse by parents of their children has not only been suggested by newspaper reports but documented by professionals. Belsky, Lerner, and Spanier (1984), for example, briefly review some literature and conclude that, depending on the definition of level of mistreatment used, from 1.7 to 6.5 million children are abused each year. The concept of sibling rivalry is one frequently made use of by the general public, and research with siblings has necessarily measured both prosocial and aggressive/domineering kinds of behaviors. (This literature has been summarized by Dunn, 1983.)

As developmental psychologists, we are committed to the notion that behaviors and other psychological responses are likely not only to show individual differences but also are manifested differently over time. As Maccoby and Martin (1983) have noted, there are enormous developmental changes in children that force parents to change in the way they deal with socialization activities such as child care, discipline, and joint activities. We know a fair amount about such educational activities or particular parental styles and their consequences over time. However, the state of empirical knowledge concerning family relationships, especially over time, is surprisingly limited. We know about variables affecting mother–child attachment in infancy and that adolescents are not necessarily at odds with their parents. Research on sibling interactions is increasing but is primarily cross-sectional or concerned with only a time-span of a few years.

This chapter reports on some research concerned with the relationships between family members—between parents and children and between siblings—at various times in life. This study measured the perceptions, retrospective and present, of college students who had left home. The present report considers the variables of individual differences, of developmental factors, and of sex differences.

Method

After the usual subject consent procedures, students at Purdue University filled out an anonymous questionnaire. After reporting their own sex, age, and race, they listed information about their family. They noted their parent's ages and marital situation and listed the sex and ages of all siblings. They then used a 7-point scale to rate the closeness of their relationship with family members at three times. The three times were first, during elementary school, second, during junior high and high school and, finally, at the present time. The bottom score of the scale, 1, was labelled, "We just don't get along at all," whereas the top score of 7 was labelled, "We're extremely close." Troll and Bergston (1982) have previously suggested that the quality of a relationship can be described in terms of closeness. Use of the concept of closeness is supported by the findings of Ross and Milgram (1982), who concluded on the basis of interviews and questionnaires that the "most complex, elusive, and somewhat abstract concept to emerge from our study of adult sibling relationships was that of closeness. Closeness was perceived both as an attribute of the family as well as a descriptor of the relationships between siblings" (p. 227).

Additional information gathered on the questionnaire included a written statement from each respondent as to why they thought changes in ratings from one time to another had occurred. Finally, if remarriage had occurred after parental divorce or death, information was obtained for not only the family of origin, but also for stepparents and stepsiblings.

Results

The present chapter reports only the ratings data for offspring from white families where the parents are both alive and still married. Complete protocols were obtained from 842 white respondents from intact families. There were 432 males and 410 females. These respondents ranged in age from 18 to 31 with an overall mean age of 20.1 years. The average age of males was 20.4 and of females 19.8. This 6-month difference was statistically significant because of the large sample size. Analyses were done of the actual ratings after examination of data plots for normality of distribution.

Parent–Offspring Relationships. Information concerning ratings of parent–respondent relationships is first presented. Table 10.1 shows, separately for the sexes, means and standard deviations for ratings at the three time spans. These data are plotted in Fig. 10.1. It is clear that the average rating is more positive than negative (that is, greater than 4), which matches my impression that the undergraduates at Purdue most often express warmth when talking about their parents. Of course, the particular rating values are likely to be specific to this population, or at least to college students. In general, the sexes did not differ in mean ratings. The one exception was the rating for present relationship with mother, where the female mean of 6.2

TABLE 10.1
Means and Standard Deviations of Student Ratings
of Parents at Three Times, for White Respondents,
Separately by Gender
(*N* = 432 Males and 410 Females)

	Elementary School	Junior, Senior High School	Present
Mother Ratings			
Males Means	5.7	5.4	6.0
S.D.	1.0	1.2	1.0
Females Means	5.7	5.3	6.2
S.D.	1.0	1.3	1.0
Father Ratings			
Males Means	5.2	5.0	5.8
S.D.	1.2	1.3	1.2
Females Means	5.3	4.9	5.9
S.D.	1.2	1.3	1.2

was significantly higher than the male mean of 6.0. However, visual examination suggests, and statistics confirmed, that for both sexes the mean ratings for mother are higher than those for father. Finally, it can be seen that there appears to be a time-span effect for the ratings by both sexes and for both parents, with the highest ratings occurring at the present time and the lowest ratings occurring during the period of junior and senior high school. Again, all of these points in time are statistically different from one another.

These findings are congruent with a study by Hunter and Youniss (1982), who had offspring rate certain aspects of relationships with both parents and friends at four points in time. Subjects were 4th, 7th, and 10th graders and college undergraduates. They asked questions designed to assess perceived behavioral control, intimacy, and nurturance. Findings relevant here were that nurturance was rated higher for mothers than for fathers, and that intimacy ratings for both parents dipped at 10th grade and rose again at college.

Means and standard deviations are, of course, generalizations about distributions, and more accurate information about the extent of individual differences can be obtained from an examination of frequency distributions.

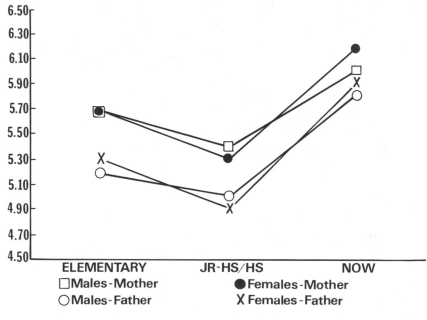

MEANS of PARENT RATINGS at THREE TIMES

FIG. 10.1.

Table 10.2 presents distributions of ratings over the seven points given in percentages calculated for the sexes and parents separately. Examination of these distributions enables the following generalizations. For fathers, at every time, ratings cover the entire range possible. In contrast, for mothers there were no ratings of 1 given at either the "elementary" or "now" times. For the first two time periods, when children were at home, the modal rating for fathers was a 5 whereas the modal rating for mothers was a 6. Clearly, although the means are significantly lower at the second time, the majority of offspring still report positive relations with their parents. While they are in college, a modal rating of 6 is given by both sexes for the father and by males for their mother. Remarkably, 48.8% of females gave a top and modal rating of 7 to describe their relationship with their mother.

With the information presented, it might seem that one could make the generalizations that mothers have closer relationships with their offspring than do fathers, and that parent–child relationships are lowest in adolescence and closest when the children have left home. In fact, such generalizations would be misleading at best and in part erroneous. An examination of the patterns within individuals shows the limits of such generalizations.

Table 10.3 presents the information indicating the percentage of individuals for whom mother ratings were higher than fathers, mother and father ratings were equal, or father ratings were higher than mother ratings. The modal situation for both sexes and at all three time periods is for the parent ratings to be identical. Although the second most frequent pattern is for the ratings for mothers to be higher than those for fathers, at all times there are groups who gave a higher rating to their relationship with their father (the range is from 8.3 to 16.8%). Overall, the correlation between the parent ratings is significant and ranges between .45 and .47 for the various subsets of data.

Table 10.4 presents information about the individual patterns of changes in relationship ratings over time. Again, it can be seen that although mean ratings were statistically significantly lower at the second period than the first, the modal response is again one of equivalence. More than half of these offspring report that their relationship with their parents during junior and senior high school is as good as, or better than, it was during elementary school. There is some proportion, ranging from 34 to 39%, who show a decreased rating of closeness, and it is this group that brings about the statistically significant mean decrease. It should also be noted that there is another group for which relationships were closer at this time than they were earlier. Respondents were asked to briefly note "why" changes in relationships had occurred and these responses were then categorized. The largest category associated with drops in ratings at adolescence had to do with the issue of control, with the typical respondent indicating that parents were trying to control their lives more than they felt justified.

TABLE 10.2
Percentage Distributions of Student Ratings by Gender
(*N* = 842)

| | Father | | Mother | |
	Male	Female	Male	Female
		Elementary School		
7	15.5	16.3	24.5	25.6
6	23.1	31.0	36.3	36.1
5	35.0	31.0	28.5	28.5
4	18.3	15.6	8.3	7.6
3	6.3	3.4	1.4	2.0
2	1.2	2.0	.5	.5
1	.7	.7	.5	0.0
		Junior and Senior High School		
7	5.7	5.1	18.5	19.8
6	25.5	23.2	33.1	30.5
5	30.3	33.9	27.1	26.8
4	21.5	19.8	14.8	12.7
3	7.2	8.3	3.2	6.8
2	3.2	2.4	3.0	2.0
1	1.2	2.0	.2	1.5
		Present Time		
7	28.7	31.0	31.0	48.8
6	39.6	43.9	45.6	35.9
5	19.0	14.4	15.0	9.3
4	7.6	5.4	5.6	3.4
3	3.0	2.4	1.4	1.5
2	1.2	2.0	1.2	1.2
1	.9	1.0	.2	0.0

Interestingly, Hunter and Youniss (1982) reported that their respondents rated parents highest on the behavioral control factor at grades 7 and 10 and that there was a notable drop for the college undergraduates. In the present data, those college undergraduates who reported an increase in closeness primarily gave reasons relating either to their perceptions of lessened control or to changes in their own perceptions as

TABLE 10.3
A Comparison Within Individuals of Parent Ratings
at Three Times, Separately by Gender

	Elementary School	Junior, Senior High School	Present
Males			
Mother > Father	41.9	36.8	23.6
Mother = Father	49.8	49.5	62.5
Mother < Father	8.3	13.7	13.9
Females			
Mother > Father	37.8	39.8	32.9
Mother = Father	49.8	43.4	56.1
Mother < Father	12.4	16.8	11.0

to what their parents had been doing. Research by Steinberg (1981) may also be relevant here. Steinberg found that the control relationship between mothers and sons changed with changes in the son's physical maturity at adolescence.

In contrast to the differences between generalizations based on means and those resulting from examination of individual patterns, it does appear that one can generalize that relationships between parents and college offspring will most often be as good as, or better than, previously.

Sibling Relationships.   Other family members, the siblings of the rater are now considered with respect to their influence on the parental relationship. The number of siblings ranged from none to thirteen. The average number of siblings was 2.5—another example of how one must be careful in interpreting means as accurately reflecting real life. There were 1.4 male and 1.2 female siblings.

The first question asked was whether or not the number of children in the family was related to the parent ratings. Simple correlations yielded no effects. Multiple regressions were then calculated for each rating time, taking into account the variables of sex of respondent, age of respondent, and total number of siblings. One weak relationship was found for the ratings of fathers at the elementary school period. At that time period, paternal ratings tended to be lower when the family size was larger. However, family size does not appear to be related in an important way to relationships with parents.

I now consider some findings concerning the rated relationship with siblings. Table 10.5 gives means and standard deviations for ratings of sibling relationships combined over family sizes and varying family constellations.

TABLE 10.4
Comparing Patterns of Change in Parent Ratings
(*N* = 432 Males and 410 Females)

	Father	Mother
Males		
Jr/Hi School > Elem	24.3	16.4
Jr/Hi School = Elem	41.4	48.6
Jr/Hi School < Elem	34.3	35.0
Females		
Jr/Hi School > Elem	18.0	20.7
Jr/Hi School = Elem	44.6	40.2
Jr/Hi School < Elem	37.3	39.0
Males		
Now > Jr/Hi School	54.9	44.7
Now = Jr/Hi School	35.6	45.6
Now < Jr/Hi School	9.5	9.7
Females		
Now > Jr/Hi School	62.7	58.5
Now = Jr/Hi School	32.4	35.4
Now < Jr/Hi School	4.9	6.1

Means were calculated separately for male and female raters and for male and female siblings. The sample sizes for each of these combinations naturally vary. These scores are plotted in Fig. 10.2.

Visual examination of Table 10.5 suggests that the ratings for siblings are more positive than negative, as was also true for the parent ratings. Parents did receive significantly higher average ratings than did siblings. Further, there was a difference between the two sets of ratings in the pattern of change over time. Although both the relationships were highest at the present time, the sibling relationship was lowest at the elementary school period. T-tests confirmed for all dyads involving males a pattern of increasing mean scores; however, this increasing pattern did not occur for females rating females. The latter finding appears to be due to the fact that at elementary school the female dyad had been rated as closer than the male dyad. Although statistically significant, this difference at elementary school level is of course extremely small. Individual difference data related to these generalizations is now examined.

TABLE 10.5
Means and Standard Deviations of Sibling Ratings
at Three Times by Gender Separately

	Elementary School	Junior, Senior High School	Present
Males rating males	(N = 566)	(N = 584)	
Means	4.7	4.8	5.5
S.D.	1.4	1.3	1.2
Males rating females	(N = 517)	(N = 526)	
Means	4.7	4.9	5.5
S.D.	1.4	1.4	1.3
Females rating males	(N = 585)	(N = 594)	
Means	4.6	4.8	5.6
S.D.	1.4	1.4	1.3
Females rating females	(N = 466)	(N = 477)	
Means	4.8	4.8	5.8
S.D.	1.4	1.5	1.2

Note: N's indicate the number of raters who provided scores for particular siblings at the first two times and at the last two times.

Tables 10.6 and 10.7 show the distribution, in percentages, of sibling ratings at the three times, for the sexes considered separately. It is clear that the greatest number of negative ratings occurs during the elementary school period, although a cumulative proportion of ratings 1, 2, and 3 does not rise above 20.4. The cumulative proportion of positive ratings (5, 6, and 7) steadily increases and varies around 85% for the present time. The extent to which this is true for individuals can be seen by an examination of Table 10.8, which gives information about individual patterns of change. These numbers reveal that the modal situation for ratings at the first two time periods is for there to be no change. However, there is considerable change in both directions, with the statistically significant increases in means resulting from a greater number of upward than downward shifts. The situation concerning shifts from the second to the third rating period is different. The modal situation is for an increase in closeness from the junior/senior high school period to the present time, whereas the proportion of downward changes varied around 10%; that is, like the relationship with parents, the relationship with siblings is closest at the present time when the rater is in college and no longer at home.

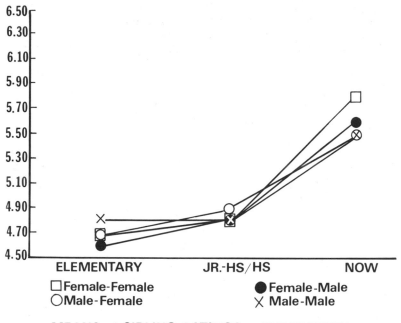

MEANS of SIBLING RATINGS at THREE TIMES

FIG. 10.2.

TABLE 10.6
Distribution of Sibling Ratings at Three Times
for the Sexes Separately, for Male Raters

| Rating | Elementary School | | Junior, Senior High School | | Present | |
	Males for Males	Males for Females	Males for Males	Males for Females	Males for Males	Males for Females
7	10.6	8.1	9.6	10.8	20.9	23.1
6	19.6	22.8	23.3	26.4	38.7	35.6
5	27.3	27.3	29.5	28.1	23.3	25.9
4	23.3	25.0	23.1	20.5	11.8	8.7
3	12.5	10.1	5.1	4.2	2.4	2.7
2	4.9	5.0	.7	1.9	1.5	2.7
1	1.8	1.7	.2	0.0	.2	0.0

TABLE 10.7
Distribution of Sibling Ratings at Three Times
for the Sexes Separately, for Female Raters

	Elementary School		Junior, Senior High School		Present	
Rating	Females for Males	Females for Females	Females for Males	Females for Females	Females for Males	Females for Females
7	9.9	12.7	10.4	11.7	25.3	31.6
6	15.9	18.7	22.8	24.9	35.6	36.8
5	27.2	29.6	28.5	26.6	24.3	17.8
4	26.7	21.5	18.8	20.1	7.6	8.6
3	12.8	12.0	5.9	6.5	4.5	2.8
2	5.5	5.2	1.3	2.1	1.3	2.1
1	2.1	.4	0.0	0.0	0.0	0.0

Parent Versus Sibling Closeness.   Visual examination of Figs. 10.1 and 10.2 suggests, and t-tests confirm, that at all times children are closer to their parents than to their siblings, with this difference especially true for mothers. Table 10.9 gives information related to this question. For those situations where a sibling rating was available at all three times, a comparison was made of each sibling rating with the rating given to the parents at the same time. Table 10.9 presents this information separately for each parent at each rating time, separately for male and female raters, but with the sex of the sibling ignored. For both sexes, the modal situation at all times is for the parent rating to be higher than the sibling rating. As the means suggested, this is even more true for mothers than for fathers. The likelihood of a differential rating in favor of the parent decreases steadily over time, with a notable increase in the proportion of instances of equal ratings for siblings and parent.

This finding that college-aged offspring are still more likely to be closer to their parents than to their siblings may at first appear to be in disagreement with findings reported by Cicirelli (1980). Cicirelli found that female college students tended to feel closer to siblings than to parents. However, his measure of closeness was based on a composite of 10 items that included not only feelings of closeness but also such things as similarity of views, feeling understood, and feeling relaxed with the family member.

A number of investigators have considered the possible interaction between the parent situation and sibling relationships. Bank and Kahn

TABLE 10.8
Patterns of Change in Ratings of Sibling Relationships

	Rating Males	Rating Females
Males		
Jr/Hi School > Elem	32.5	39.5
Jr/Hi School = Elem	43.5	37.1
Jr/Hi School < Elem	24.0	23.4
Females		
Jr/Hi School > Elem	35.6	33.7
Jr/Hi School = Elem	40.2	36.9
Jr/Hi School < Elem	24.3	29.4
Males		
Now > Jr/Hi School	52.2	47.7
Now = Jr/Hi School	38.5	40.5
Now < Jr/Hi School	9.2	11.8
Females		
Now > Jr/Hi School	57.1	58.5
Now = Jr/Hi School	33.7	31.0
Now < Jr/Hi School	9.3	10.5

(1982), in their investigation of the sibling bond and sibling loyalties, have suggested that one factor fostering sibling closeness would be a lack of a good parental relationship. Their hypothesis is not unlike that of Bossard and Boll (1956), who interviewed adults from large families. Bossard and Boll attributed the closeness to siblings in such families in part to the difficulty of getting enough attention from parents. Levy (1937) earlier had found an inverse relationship between sibling rivalry and large families in preschool-aged children. He suggested that children had intensified their rapport with one another because of the dilution of relationships with parents. The present data demonstrated a relationship for family size and parental closeness only at elementary school, when children from large families tended to report a less close relationship with their fathers. However, it is still possible that there is an effect of family size or parental closeness upon the sibling relationship.

In order to take into consideration not only sibling characteristics but also other variables associated with the family, a multiple regression was

TABLE 10.9
A Comparison of Ratings of Parents and Siblings
at Three Times, Separately by Gender

	Elementary School	Junior, Senior High School	Present
Male Raters			
Mother > Sib	65.0	53.4	46.3
Mother = Sib	24.4	26.2	36.9
Mother < Sib	10.6	20.5	16.8
Father > Sib	48.4	40.0	39.8
Father = Sib	27.9	28.4	38.8
Father < Sib	23.7	31.6	21.4
Female Raters			
Mother > Sib	63.3	51.0	46.6
Mother = Sib	24.0	24.3	37.2
Mother < Sib	12.7	24.7	16.2
Father > Sib	52.7	39.8	38.6
Father = Sib	26.6	27.4	37.5
Father < Sib	20.7	32.8	23.8

computed for the sibling ratings at each of the three rating periods. Variables included were: sex of respondent, sex of sibling, respondent age, total number of siblings, mother rating at that time period, and father rating at that time period.

There were two, and only two, of these variables that significantly predicted sibling ratings at all three time periods. For both mother and father, ratings entered separately, it was found that a better parent relationship was related to better sibling relationships. The empirical finding that there is a positive relation between parent and sibling ratings is in disagreement with the theoretical predictions, discussed previously, that there would be an inverse relationship such that children would develop a closer relationship with their siblings in reaction to a lack of a satisfying parental relationship. One possible interpretation of this finding is that it is not a "real" one but rather results from a rating response bias in which some individuals tend either to rate everything high, whereas alternatively or simultaneously, others tend to rate everything at other levels. This same interpretation may also explain the finding that the parent ratings were correlated. There is no way to test for this interpretation using the available data, but such a possibility is likely to weigh heavily with anyone who already has concerns about the validity of the questionnaire and rating methods. I am presently gathering new data designed to give more information about this possibility.

Nonetheless, it would seem profitable to consider the possibility that there is indeed an apparent contagion for warmth and closeness in a family. Perhaps the characteristics and behaviors of a parent that bring about a good parent–child relationship also serve as a model for the offspring, who then are more likely to develop good relationships among themselves. Perhaps the parents who have good relationships with children are also more likely to have the skills to manage sibling relationships—whatever these skills may be! Another possible hypothesis is that parents who have close relationships with children spend more time with them, and this negates sibling rivalry or bad feelings between siblings. That the situation is a complex one may be inferred from the next finding discussed.

The variable of family size entered into the multiple regression for sibling ratings at two time periods. During the elementary school years, respondents from larger families were more likely to report closeness to siblings. The finding that sibling relations are better in a large family may be surprising, both because there was a negative relationship between family size and father ratings, and because this finding runs counter to the intuitive idea that with a larger family there will be less parental time with each child, resulting in bad feelings between the children. Whatever the interpretation, it must be a mechanism that is specific to the elementary years, as this particular relationship was not found at the two later times. Family size was not a contributing variable at all at junior/senior high school. However, it again contributed to the present ratings of these college students, but in an inverse fashion! Now those students from smaller families were more likely to report that they were close to their siblings. An elaborate hypothesis as to why this occurs would probably be appropriate only when these results are confirmed.

In confirmation of previous analyses, the variables of sex of respondent and sex of sibling did not enter into the regression equation. However, the variable of age of respondent did enter at the final rating period. Specifically, older college students were more likely to rate sibling relations less highly than did younger college students. Examination of individual data suggested that this was particularly true for respondents over age 22. We should consider the possibility that although sibling relationships do improve when one first leaves home, the overall later relationship is a curvilinear one such that with increasing time, and perhaps distance, siblings again lose some of their closeness. Other demographic data concerning this population has shown that older students are more likely to be married and to have children of their own. Perhaps these additional emotional attachments have resulted in decreased closeness to siblings. It is also possible that those older students who did not complete college in the usual time are a group with different background experiences and family relationships.

Overview

When one considers the results of analyses of mean differences, the following summary conclusions may be made. Male and female respondents generally do not differ in their ratings. This population of college students has a more positive than negative relationship with parents. They reported themselves to be closest to both parents at the present time and least close during the adolescent period. Offspring rate themselves as closer to mothers than to fathers.

However, with these data, as I suspect with most samples, means fail to convey the great individual variability. Examination of score distributions and patterns lead to the following additional information. There are some individuals at all levels of closeness. The adolescent decrease in closeness with parents results from lowered ratings for only about 35% of the population and there are some who reported greater closeness at this time. The modal situation is for parents to receive identical ratings of closeness, and the mean difference results from a greater proportion who were closer to their mother than were closer to their father.

The particular numbers reported here are probably specific to this white population from intact-families, about 75% of whom claim residence in the state of Indiana. Analyses of similar data from other subgroups have shown mean differences for groups that differ in racial background or whose family history includes parental death or divorce.

This collection of data, like most, leads to more questions than it answers. One would like to know, for example, more about the factors that lead to the individual variability as well as more about when any change occurs at adolescence. Present plans include additional data collection with both this population and in another country, including the use of additional variables such as information concerning the employment history of both parents.

Coda

There has recently been considerable attention paid to the *mentor* relationship. This term has been operationalized by some as the major professor and defined by others as a relationship with "a person who took a personal interest in your career and who guided or sponsored you." Levinson et al. (1978) have suggested that the mentor serves as a mixture of parent and peer and fosters young adult's development by believing in and sharing a dream. They and others suggest that the mentor relationship lasts for only a brief period of time, but that it has long-term effects on one's career.

I believe that it was no accident that when I was asked by Lew and Joan, both of whom were among my peers while I was in graduate school, to contribute to a book in honor of Charles Spiker, that what came to my mind was a presentation of data on family closeness. Charles Spiker was my advisor and major professor while I was a graduate student at the University of Iowa from 1954 to 1957. Charles was a model of the committed professional. His courses were always carefully organized and one expected class lectures that were prepared and thoughtful. Only later as a college professor myself did I realize what an accomplishment this was. Charles believed in the usefulness of a logical analysis of psychological questions and their empirical investigation. Although his profession was a central focus of his life, he was humble as to his role in the acquisition of the knowledge that he considered so important. I remember that he once told me that he would consider his life a success if he were to be included in a footnote in a book detailing the history of psychology in the latter half of this century.

Levinson et al. found that in their sample of males, the mentoring relationship was often ended with conflict and hurt feelings on both sides. That this is not so in our case is probably in part due to the fact that Charles did in fact serve as an analog of the "good parent" and did not insist that his students follow in his footsteps. I, and other fellow students, became interested in variables and questions that were very different from those that were of concern in my Iowa training, and I suspect that Charles often did not agree with the value we placed on what involved us. He would never volunteer that information. At no time in my career have I thought that I would have been better off if I had been trained elsewhere. It was in graduate school and as a student of Charles Spiker that I learned how to think with what I believe is rigor, and by doing so found that the world of psychology offered continual intellectual challenge. I can only hope that this chapter conveys something of the fascination and pleasure I have found as a result.

ACKNOWLEDGMENTS

I gratefully acknowledge the assistance of Diane Villwock with data analysis and of Michael Botts, Regina Good, and Kate Burton with data transcription. Portions of this chapter were presented at colloquia at Kent State University and Ball State University. Comments from various people there were helpful to my thinking. I appreciate the suggestions of Thomas Berndt and Joan Cantor who read an early draft of this chapter.

REFERENCES

Ainsworth, M., Blehar, M., Waters, E., & Wall, S. (1978) *Patterns of Attachment: Psychological study of the strange situation.* Hillsdale, NJ: Lawrence Erlbaum Associates.

Bank, S., & Kahn, M. D. (1982) Intense sibling loyalties. In M. E. Lamb & B. Sutton-Smith (Eds.), *Sibling relationships: Their nature and significance across the life span.* Hillsdale, NJ: Lawrence Erlbaum Associates.

Belsky, J., Lerner, R. M., & Spanier, G. B. (1984) *The Child in the family.* Menlo Park, CA: Addison-Wesley.

Bossard, J. H. S., & Boll, E. S. (1956) *The large family system.* Philadelphia: University of Pennsylvania Press.

Cantor, D. W., & Drake, E. A. (1983) *Divorced parents and their children.* New York: Springer.

Cicirelli, V. G. (1980) A comparison of college women's feelings toward their siblings and parents. *Journal of Marriage and the Family, 42,* 95-102.

Dunn, J. (1983) Sibling relationships in early childhood. *Child Development, 54,* 787-811.

Hall, E., Lamb, M. E., & Perlmutter, M. (1982). *Child psychology today.* New York: Random House.

Hunter, F. T., & Youniss, J. (1982) Changes in function of three relations during adolescence. *Developmental Psychology, 18,* 806-811.

Levinson, D. J., Darrow, C. N., Klein, E. B., Levinson, M. H., & McKee, B. (1978) *The seasons of a man's life.* New York: Knopf.

Levy, D. M. (1937). Sibling rivalry. *American Orthopsychiatric Association Research Monographs, No. 2.*

Maccoby, E. E., & Martin, J. A. (1983) Socialization in the context of the family: Parent–child interaction. In E. Mavis Hetherington (Ed.), *Socialization personality and social development* (Vol. IV).

Ross, H. G., & Milgram, J. I. (1982) Important variables in adult sibling relationships: A qualitative study. In M. E. Lamb & B. Sutton-Smith (Eds.), *Sibling Relationships: Their nature and significance across the life span.* Hillsdale, NJ: Lawrence Erlbaum Associates.

Santrock, J. W., & Yussen, S. A. (1984) *Children and adolescents.* Dubuque, IA: Brown.

Steinberg, L. D. (1981) Transformations in family relations at puberty. *Developmental Psychology, 17,* 833-840.

Tomlinson-Keasey, C. (1985) *Child development.* Homewood, IL: Dorsey.

Troll, L., & Bergston, V. (1982) Intergenerational relations throughout the life span. In B. Wolman (Ed.), *Handbook of developmental psychology* (pp. 890-911). Englewood Cliffs, NJ: Prentice-Hall.

11

Predicting Individual Differences in Reaction Time from Variable Criterion Theory: Extension of the Hull-Spence Approach

Victor Alan Spiker
Anacapa Sciences, Inc.
Santa Barbara, California

INTRODUCTION

This chapter discusses the conceptual underpinnings of a comprehensive theory of information processing, Variable Criterion Theory, and describes its application to the study of individual differences in disjunctive reaction time. Developed and nurtured by G. Robert Grice, Variable Criterion Theory (VCT) has addressed an impressive array of sensory, motivational, and associative phenomena using the paradigms of human eyelid conditioning, simple and complex auditory reaction time, and simple visual reaction time. Conceptually, VCT enjoys a kinship with the theoretical approach adopted by Hull (1943, 1952) and Spence (1936, 1937, 1956). Mathematically, VCT has close ties with Thurstonian scaling theory (Thurstone, 1925, 1928), McGill's (1963) stochastic decision model, and signal detection theory (Green & Swets, 1966).

In a larger sense, though, this chapter is intended to underscore the explanatory insight and personal satisfaction that result from applying a comprehensive quantitative theory to behavior. As we pay tribute to Professor Charles Spiker in this festschrift volume, it is especially appropriate that we acknowledge the benefits of using psychological theory in conjunction with a cogent philosophy of science. Throughout his productive and distinguished career, Professor Spiker has written eloquently on the characteristics of a good psychological theory and on the importance of using theory to guide research (e.g., Spiker, 1963, 1977). In discussing the concepts and principles of VCT, this author attempts to evaluate the theory using the same criteria that have characterized Professor Spiker's own theoretical work: clearly defined concepts, quantitative lawful relationships between concepts, novel predictions based on derivations of theorems from theoretical concepts and axioms, parsimonious explanation, and comprehensive scope (Bergmann, 1957; C. Spiker, this volume).

This chapter is presented in four sections. The first section describes the development of VCT, focusing on its relationship to the Hull–Spence approach, its treatment of stimulus intensity effects, and its application to simple reaction time. The second section discusses the VCT analysis of disjunctive reaction time, including the procedural relationship to simple reaction time, the additional theoretical processes required to interpret disjunctive reaction time data, and the emergence of qualitative individual differences in disjunctive reaction time performance. The third section describes the results of an auditory disjunctive reaction time experiment designed to test the theory's analytic ability to interpret individual differences in processing strategies. The fourth section concludes with an evaluation of the present status of VCT, and a final personal note.

DEVELOPMENT OF VARIABLE CRITERION THEORY

Legacy of the Hull–Spence Approach

In a thoughtful analysis of the reasons behind the decline in popularity of the Hull–Spence approach, Professor Spiker (1977) carefully distinguished between two aspects of behaviorism that together characterize this landmark in psychological theory. First, following Watson, its philosophy of science was based on methodological behaviorism, in which a theory's undefined primitive terms are couched in the same language as the physical sciences. Second, the axioms were derived from classical conditioning, marking the approach as a conditioning theory. As Professor Spiker (1977) has astutely noted, one may reject the latter approach as a theoretical ideal without abandoning the former philosophical position.

This distinction provides a convenient framework for comparing VCT to the Hull–Spence approach. Although following the philosophical tenets of this approach, and even expanding on some of its concepts, VCT is not a "conditioning theory" in the Hull–Spence sense, as many of its key concepts are rooted in information processing terminology. There are, nevertheless, five objectives of the Hull–Spence approach that capture much of the conceptual spirit of VCT: clearly defined concepts, use of time-based process laws, association of quantitative parameters with observable variables, categorization of experimental variables by theoretical process, and application of the theory to diverse research paradigms. Each topic is discussed briefly in turn.

Clearly defined concepts were ever present in the Hull–Spence approach, receiving their most formal treatment in Hull's (1943) *Principles of Behavior.* Many definitions were quantitative, leaving little room for ambiguity. Thus, habit was defined as an exponential function of number of conditioning trials, drive was a complex mathematical function of the various relevant and irrelevant sources of motivation in the situation, reactive inhibition was a positively accelerated function of the amount of work involved in performing the response, and so forth. By today's standards, Hull's presentation of these terms seems unnecessarily formal, an obvious attempt to mimic the more mature physical sciences. Nevertheless, this dedication to rigorous definition is a hallmark of the Hull–Spence approach, and it has served as a useful model for other theoretical efforts (Hilgard & Bower, 1966).

In contrast to the static cross-sectional laws of the introspectionists (Bergmann, 1956), the Hull–Spence approach applied a number of time-based "process" laws (Bergmann, 1957) to the analysis of conditioning behavior. Notable examples include the equation for delay of reward (Hull, 1943) and the stimulus trace interpretation of the interstimulus interval in classical conditioning (Hull, 1952). These process laws allow the theorist to address the dynamic nature of behavior occurring within conditioning trials, and importantly, set the stage for bridging the gap between trial-based accounts of learning and time-based interpretations of information processing (Logan, 1977).

A more subtle aspect of the Hull–Spence approach was its attempt to relate the parameters of its mathematical functions to variations in experimental conditions. Not only do such associations embue parameters with "psychological meaning," they impose systematic constraints on curve-fitting activities. In Hull's (1943) treatise, much of this activity was relegated to the theoretical notes at the end of each chapter. Still, they serve as a valuable model for increasing the rigor of the parameter estimation process. For example, such an approach was used to relate the growth of habit strength, H, to delay in reward. Hull defined H as: $m' - m' \times 10^{-kN}$, where N equals trial number and m' is the upper limit on habit growth. Yet, m' was itself assumed to decline exponentially with time since delivery of reward. Though not carried out, this latter function could be integrated into the expression for habit, thereby eliminating the need for the m' parameter altogether.

A fourth and all-too-frequently-forgotten virtue of the Hull–Spence approach was its categorization of experimental variables by their predicted effects on theoretical processes. Often these classifications were quite straightforward, as in postulating that food deprivation potentiates responding through increasing drive, or reward magnitude facilitates learning by raising the upper limit on habit strength. Occasionally, though, the theory was used to interpret the consequences of more problematic experimental variables. In the 1950s, Spence exploited this strategy in a series of ingenious aversive conditioning studies designed to delineate the theoretical role of unconditioned stimulus intensity (e.g., Spence, Haggard, & Ross, 1958). Through a novel procedure of employing presentations of the unconditioned stimulus by itself between regular trials, Spence untangled the drive-inducing properties of the unconditioned stimulus from its effects on habit. As we see, Grice used a similar strategy in applying VCT to the analysis of stimulus intensity effects.

A fifth legacy of the Hull–Spence approach was its development of a broad data base to encompass diverse paradigms and procedures. Historians still marvel at the variety of paradigms that were embraced by the Hull–Spence approach, including: classical conditioning, discrimination learning, social behavior, abnormal behavior, stimulus generalization, and avoidance conditioning (Hilgard & Bower, 1966). Present-day attempts at theoretical scope are more modest, with many theories content to explain the behavior of a single procedure. As the following sections hopefully show, the advances in VCT made by Grice and his students have attempted to buck this trend by expanding the theory's scope from initial investigations of human eyelid conditioning and simple auditory reaction time, to include more complex reaction time procedures.

VCT's Initial Treatment of Stimulus Intensity Effects

VCT first appeared as a methodological solution to a problematic finding in classical conditioning: In contrast to results from animal conditioning preparations, variation in intensity of the conditioned stimulus (CS) in human eyelid conditioning did not affect rate of conditioning (Kimble, 1961). Whereas some theorists attributed this difference to the greater cognitive capacity of humans (Kimble, 1961), Grice and his students suspected that the results were unique to the between-subjects nature of the experimental designs typically employed, and that larger effects would be observed if CS intensity were varied within subjects. Grice and Hunter (1964) confirmed this hypothesis in a three-group human eyelid conditioning experiment, and extended these findings to include simple RT as well. An early interpretation in terms of Helson's (1964) sensory adaptation-level theory was quickly abandoned, as it became clear that a much broader and more dynamic principle of response evocation was needed.

Whereas less quantitative than its later forms, the initial version of VCT (Grice, 1968) laid down a lasting conceptual foundation. Three simple, yet powerful, assumptions were made that provided an integrated account of stimulus intensity effects in both conditioning and RT, and allowed the flexibility to add other postulates when addressing other phenomena.

In the first assumption, and following McGill (1963), stimulus onset was assumed to trigger a series of impulses that accrued linearly over time. The slope of this linear function, corresponding to sensory recruitment, was assumed to increase directly with signal intensity. Consistent with the notion of an "irreducible minimum" (Woodworth & Schlosberg, 1954), sensory recruitment was not assumed to begin until after a fixed amount of time, usually 100 msec., had occurred.

In its second assumption, VCT became a decision theory by the incorporation of a principle of response evocation that assumed that responding occurs once sensory growth exceeds a preset threshold or criterion. The setting of this criterion was assumed to reflect the joint effects of a host of internal and external factors. One factor influencing the criterion level was assumed to be stimulus intensity, with more intense stimulation producing a higher overall criterion. Another factor was assumed to be unpredictability in either the timing or intensity of the stimulus, with greater uncertainty serving to raise an individual's criterion.

In the third assumption, trial-to-trial variation in responding was addressed by assuming that the criterion fluctuates randomly according to a normal distribution. Responses will be more likely (or faster) on trials when the criterion is set low, and less likely (or slower) when it is set high. Grice's assumption of a subject-based fluctuating criterion contrasts with that of McGill's (1963) stochastic latency model and signal detection theory (Green & Swets, 1966), both of which attribute response variability to fluctuating sensory impulses. Whereas all three positions are similar mathematically, Grice's assumption provides a broader context for interpreting behavioral variability outside the realm of stimulus intensity manipulations.

Grice (1968) needed only the first two assumptions to deduce the design-dependent nature of the stimulus intensity effect. These assumptions are represented in Fig. 11.1, which shows that presenting two different stimulus intensities, such as a loud tone and a soft tone, produce two distinct and diverging sensory recruitment lines. Importantly, the same two recruitment lines result whether each subject receives both intensities or different subjects receive the two intensities.

Further inspection of the figure reveals that the type of research design affects the number and placement of the mean criterion lines. Between-subject variation in stimulus intensity produces two criterion lines, L and S, with a higher criterion set for the loud stimulus group. In contrast, within-subject designs produce one criterion, L–S, with this line raised above the L line to reflect the greater stimulus uncertainty in the latter design.

The lower part of the figure shows the predicted effects of stimulus

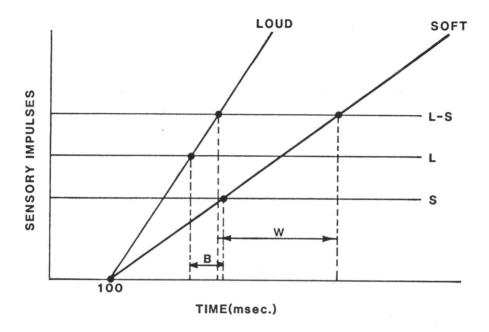

FIG. 11.1.   VCT representation of the design-dependent effects of stimulus intensity on simple response evocation.

intensity. The difference in mean RT to the two stimuli is represented by
the length of the two lines, with the within-subject intensity difference, W,
substantially larger than the between-subject difference, B. Note that the
size of the design effect can be varied by suitable placement of the criterion
lines. For example, the complete absence of a between-subject intensity
effect, B = O, can be predicted by either raising L or lowering S.

Although some preliminary attempts at curve fitting were included in
Grice's (1968) initial statement of VCT, it was the successful derivation of
the design-dependent nature of the stimulus intensity effect that marked
the theory's first major success. Whereas subsequent applications of the
theory followed different tracks for the human eyelid conditioning and RT
paradigms, the remainder of this chapter is concerned exclusively with the
VCT analysis of human RT. Yet, it is important to note that the theory has
been successfully applied to a wide range of classical conditioning proce-

dures and variables, including differential conditioning (Grice, 1972a), and the effects of variation in stimulus intensity, drive, and length of the interstimulus interval (Grice, 1977).

Application of VCT to Simple Reaction Time

As the most basic RT task, simple RT (SRT) was the logical starting point to expand the quantitative scope of VCT. But before discussing the specifics of the VCT analysis of SRT, a brief background describing the goals of RT theories in general is needed.

Historically, the RT task has been the mainstay of information-processing analyses of behavior (Woodworth & Schlosberg, 1954). Since Donders' initial stage theory approach to RT, an explicit theoretical goal has been to infer the internal processes that intervene between onset of the signal and initiation of the response. Early attempts at introspecting for these mental events eventually gave way to more respectable mathematical detective analyses using the moments of a distribution of observed RTs (Boring, 1950). Current conceptions assume that the shape of the RT distribution, obtained over a long series of trials under constant conditions of stimulation, is a more or less valid representation of the internal processes that were controlling responding during any given trial. Because the RT is the theorist's only clue, simply plotting the moments of the distribution as a function of some independent variable will not reveal the time course of each theoretical process. Instead, the entire RT distribution must be employed and a mathematical fit attempted. The analytic challenge, then, is to determine which combination of mathematical functions gave rise to the empirical RT distribution, subject to the constraint that these postulated functions be consistent with existing knowledge of how people process information.

The typical SRT distribution is positively skewed, resembling a gamma or F-distribution. Because variations in signal intensity profoundly influence the shape of the distribution, this variable has received the most study in SRT. Relative to strong signals, weaker signals produce distributions with a longer mean, greater positive skew, larger variance, as well as a slower rise to the mode (McGill, 1963). Superimposing several intensity distributions on the same graph yields a series of overlapping curves with the lower intensity distributions successively displaced to the right. The overlapping nature of these distributions implies that on any given trial the RT to a stronger signal need not be faster than to a weaker signal, suggesting that the detection process may contain a random component (Christie & Luce, 1956).

Many theories of SRT have adopted this stochastic point of view by working directly with the RT distribution to uncover the particular statistical processes that gave rise to the empirical distribution (e.g., Christie &

Luce, 1956; Hohle, 1965; McGill, 1963). Though similar mathematically, these theories employ surprisingly diverse underlying concepts, ranging from neural counts (McGill, 1963) to engineering analogs based on processes in convolution (Christie & Luce, 1956).

Despite the mathematical sophistication of these stochastic SRT models, most did not permit derivation of reliable parameter estimates for their functions nor an accurate fit to an entire SRT distribution (Luce & Green, 1972). Instead, only limited assumptions of the models could be tested, such as that specifying an intensity-independent response movement time (McGill, 1963). This failure stemmed mainly from the inability to generate stable parameter estimates of complex probability distributions using standard numerical analytic methods (Luce & Green, 1972). Nevertheless, several stochastic models were successfully fit to an entire SRT distribution, most notably LaBerge's (1962) stimulus sampling theory and Hohle's (1965) convolution model. However, neither approach was pursued beyond its initial development.

In contrast with these stochastic models, stimulus detection is viewed in VCT as a deterministic process, recruiting in exactly the same way on each trial. As the theory matured, the assumption of a linear recruitment of detection information was abandoned in favor of a more mathematically tractable curvilinear function (Grice, 1972b; Grice, Hunt, Kushner, & Morrow, 1974). Also in contrast to the stochastic approach, VCT analyses are based on the cumulative form of the RT distribution, thus simplifying mathematical analyses and parameter estimation.

In VCT, SRT is considered to be a joint function of two processes, sensory growth ($V(t)$) and the criterion (C). Sensory growth is the detection component of the theory, and is mathematically represented by:

$$V(t) = m' - me^{-at}, \tag{1}$$

where m' is the asymptote of the function and m and a are rate parameters. Graphically, $V(t)$ is a negatively accelerated function of time whose form resembles the traditional learning curve. The parameters of the growth function are assumed to reflect the dynamogenic properties of the trial stimulus, such as signal intensity, rise time, duration, and signal-to-noise ratio.

As noted earlier, the criterion is the workhorse of the theory as it specifies that a response will occur whenever the recruited value of $V(t)$ exceeds the criterion level set for that trial. Values of C are assumed to randomly vary over trials according to a normal distribution with a given mean μ and standard deviation σ. Algebraically, the two processes combine in the following way to determine responding:

$$E(t) = V(t) - C, \tag{2}$$

where $E(t)$ or excitatory potential represents the cumulative distance from the criterion mean scaled in the σ-units of the criterion distribution. This fact is indicated more clearly by integrating the criterion parameters into Equation 2 to yield the following expression:

$$E(t) = (1/\sigma)(V(t) - \mu). \tag{3}$$

The assumption of a negatively accelerated growth function and a normally distributed decision criterion permits Thurstone's (1925) powerful scaling techniques to be used for parameter estimation. From Equations 11.1 and 11.3, VCT may be represented as a five-parameter model, three from the $V(t)$ function, m', m, and k, and two from the criterion, μ and σ. Accepting Thurstone's original assumption that the normal distribution has an underlying interval scale, one of the observed SRT distributions may be arbitrarily selected to have a criterion distribution with $\mu = 0$ and $\sigma = 1$. This distribution then becomes the "reference" condition against which all others are compared.

To illustrate how the Thurstonian technique is used within VCT, suppose that an SRT experiment was conducted using two different foreperiods, defined as the time interval between the warning signal and the signal to respond. Over trials, two distinct empirical SRT distributions would be generated. Each distribution would then be transformed into z-scores in accordance with the assumption of a normal criterion, producing an $E_x(t)$ and $E_y(t)$ distribution, respectively. These two distributions could then be plotted as (x,y) coordinates at comparable time intervals, say every 10 msec. Such plots are called Response Evocation Characteristics or RECs (Grice, 1971), and an example plot is shown in Fig. 11.2. The distributions begin in the lower left quadrant, with time incrementing by 10 msec. for each successive point.

Grice (1971) has used the Thurstone (1925) scaling procedure to expand VCT's analytic power by showing that linear RECs, as in Fig. 11.2, imply that a common $V(t)$ process produced the two $E(t)$ distributions. On the other hand, significant and systematic departures from linearity indicate that the variable influenced one or more of the parameters of $V(t)$. This aspect of the scaling methodology is a truly powerful one, as it allows experimental variables to be classified according to their putative influence on sensory growth, the criterion, or both.

Besides indicating which component of the model is affected by experimental manipulations, the REC analysis also provides parameter estimates of the criterion distribution. Specifically, the slope of the line is the ratio of the criterion standard deviations (σ_y/σ_x) and the intercept is the mean criterion difference scaled in σ_x-units $((\mu_x - \mu_y)/\sigma_x)$. These estimates can be simplified by arbitrarily selecting the x-condition as the reference

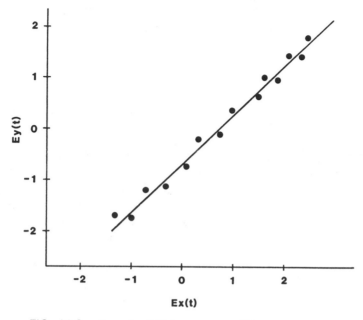

FIG. 11.2. Example REC between two different simple reaction time
distributions.

distribution, with the slope and intercept providing direct estimates of σ_y
and μ_y, respectively (Grice, 1971).

To date, VCT analyses of SRT have shown that, with the exception of
signal intensity, the effects of all other variables are localized in the parameters of the criterion distribution. Confidence in these findings is heightened
by the high degree of linearity in the RECs, with r^2 in excess of .99, and in
the accuracy of the distribution fits, with 98–99% of the variance typically
explained. The variables studied thus far include the effects of instructions,
deadlines, catch trials, as well as individual differences (Grice, 1972b;
Grice, et al., 1974). This latter finding is particularly noteworthy as it
implies that a common sensory growth function can be used to describe the
data for all subjects given the same signal intensity. The large between-
subject differences in overall RT frequently observed in these studies can
be completely accounted for by differences in the criterion distribution,
with slower subjects having higher criterion means and larger criterion
variances (Grice, Nullmeyer, & Spiker, 1982).

VCT ANALYSIS OF DISJUNCTIVE RT

Procedural Aspects of Disjunctive RT

Although providing valuable data on the time course of detection and the dynamics of criterion changes, the SRT procedure does not address one of the more interesting aspects of information processing, stimulus differentiation. To this end, Grice and his students (Grice, et al., 1974; Grice, Hunt, Kushner, & Nullmeyer, 1976) soon applied VCT to the theoretically more challenging task of disjunctive RT (DRT). In the typical DRT task, subjects receive presentations of an imperative signal, $S+$, randomly interspersed with presentations of a second signal, $S-$, to which the subject is instructed to withhold responding.

Procedurally, SRT and DRT can be placed on a continuum defined by the type of $S-$ that is used. On one end is the pure form of SRT in which an imperative signal occurs on every trial. Next is the more traditional SRT procedure that inserts periodic blank "catch" trials as the $S-$, forcing subjects to distinguish the imperative signal from no signal. On the other end of the continuum is the typical DRT paradigm that replaces the catch trials with presentations of a second stimulus. This $S-$ might be in a different modality from $S+$ or it might differ from $S+$ along the same physical dimension. Because mean DRT increases with the degree of similarity between $S+$ and $S-$ (e.g., Grice et al., 1974), any serious theory of DRT must be able to delineate the discrimination processes responsible for this increase.

In Donders' original stage theory analysis, the DRT task played an important role in inferring the durations of different processing stages (Taylor, 1966). In this analysis, SRT was assumed to consist of one processing stage, detection. DRT was assumed to require two stages, detection and stimulus differentiation. A third task, choice RT, was presumed to involve detection and stimulus differentiation, plus a third stage, response choice. Estimates of the stimulus differentiation and response choice stages were obtained by subtracting, respectively, average SRT from DRT and DRT from choice RT.

As interest in stage analysis waned, interest in DRT also diminished as it became viewed merely as an inefficient method for collecting choice RT data (Taylor, 1966). Not surprisingly, renewed interest in the paradigm has coincided with the resurgence of the processing stage methodology represented in the work of Sternberg (1969) and others. But regardless of whether one adopts a strict stage point of view, DRT is a useful information-processing task, as it allows the theorist to study the processes involved in stimulus differentiation without the analytic complexities involved in having a second response. As such, it is a procedure that will continue to play an important role in future theoretical analyses of information processing (LaBerge, 1971).

Theoretical Processes

For several reasons, the VCT analysis of DRT is necessarily more complex than for SRT. One, some process of stimulus differentiation is needed to account for subjects' ability to discriminate between $S+$ and $S-$. Two, on some occasions this process may fail, giving rise to an error distribution that must also be modeled.

Employing an analysis originally applied to differential eyelid conditioning (Grice, 1972b), Grice et al. (1976) decomposed the DRT distribution of correct responses into three components:

$$E_c(t) = V(t) + A(t) - C. \qquad (4)$$

As in SRT, $E_c(t)$ is the transformation of the cumulative probability of responding by time, t, into the corresponding z-score. The growth of sensory information, $V(t)$, is estimated from a SRT condition in which the same stimulus intensity was used as $S+$. The criterion, C, again represents the subject's readiness to respond as a normal distribution with specified mean and variance. The new process in this analysis is $A(t)$, representing the cumulative amount of associative information that has accrued by time t.

The presence of an associative process in DRT is inferred from several lines of evidence. Graphically, the onset of $A(t)$ is seen as a very slight acceleration or inflection in the $E_c(t)$ function of the DRT distribution, in contrast to the smooth noninflected functions found in SRT. $A(t)$ may be more easily inferred from the nonlinear REC that results between the $E_c(t)$ function in DRT and the corresponding SRT distribution. A typical REC is exemplified in Fig. 11.3, with the x-axis of the REC representing the SRT distribution and the y-axis the $E_c(t)$ function from DRT. The lowest point on the REC line corresponds to a time value of 250 msec. for each distribution, with each succeeding point in the graph representing an increment of 10 msec.

Representative of many of the RECs that have been produced over the years, the one shown in Fig. 11.3 plots linearly during the early portions of the distributions and becomes curvilinear after 300 msec. The linear segment corresponds to that portion of the DRT distribution based solely on detection information, with its slope and intercept giving the criterion parameters of the DRT condition in the scale units of the SRT condition.

Using this REC information, it is then possible to derive the $A(t)$ contribution to the DRT function. First, the entire SRT function is converted to the scale units of DRT by: $(1/\sigma)(V(t) - \mu)$. Letting $\mu = 0$ and $\sigma = 1$, then $E_x(t) = V(t)$ and $E_y(t) = E_x(t) + A(t)$. Subtracting $E_x(t)$ from $E_y(t)$ at each

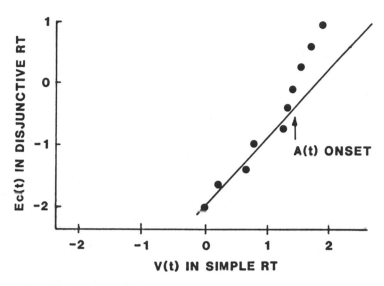

FIG. 11.3. Example REC between a simple reaction time distribution (x-axis) and a disjunctive reaction time distribution (y-axis).

point in time yields the $A(t)$ function. For the data in Fig. 11.3, this difference will be zero until 300 msec., after which $A(t)$ will show a positive acceleration followed by a negative acceleration. Mathematically, $A(t)$ can usually be described by a Gompertz growth function (Lewis, 1960) of the form:

$$A(t) = vg^{h^t}, \tag{5}$$

where v is the asymptote, g is the intercept, and h is the rate parameter. Intuitively, it is reasonable that this associative information should not accrue until after considerable detection information has recruited, because the identification of the stimulus presupposes that it has been detected. Although the DRT variables affecting the time course of $A(t)$ have not been as extensively studied as those determining $V(t)$, several studies have shown that a major determinant is stimulus similarity, in which the growth rate and asymptote of $A(t)$ both decrease with increasing similarity (Grice et al., 1982).

A somewhat different analysis is required for the error distribution in DRT, $E_e(t)$. Like correct RTs, the $E_e(t)$ function exhibits a slight acceleration after $V(t)$ onset, suggesting the presence of a second process. Because this inflection occurs considerably sooner than $A(t)$ onset, generalization of the $A(t)$ process from $S+$ can be ruled out as the responsible process. Instead, Grice et al. (1976) have interpreted the second process as inhibitory, denoted by $I(t)$ for associative inhibition. Mathe-

253

matically, the effects of this $I(t)$ process are integrated into the full expression for $E_e(t)$ by:

$$E_e(t) = V(t) - I(t) - C. \tag{6}$$

The specific form of this inhibitory function can be derived from an REC analysis similar to that performed for the correct RT distribution. In this case, however, the REC plots values of the $E_e(t)$ function on the y-axis against $V(t)$-values derived from an SRT experiment with an $S-$ stimulus intensity as the x-axis. Such plots exhibit systematic departures from linearity after 150–200 msec., marking the appearance of the inhibitory process. The time course of the process can be determined by analyzing the residuals in much the same way as was done for $A(t)$. These analyses show $I(t)$ to be a negatively accelerated function, having the same mathematical form as $V(t)$.

The rapid growth of $I(t)$ allows subjects to efficiently withhold responding to $S-$ and roughly corresponds to recognition of the negative stimulus. That subjects can rapidly inhibit responding is given empirical support from studies in which a countermand to the "Go" signal, interspersed with trials without the countermand, only slightly increased RT (Lappin & Eriksen, 1966). In addition, this inhibitory process accounts for the accurate DRT performance of most subjects. The full expression for the error distribution specified in Equation 6 is:

$$E_e(t) = (1/\sigma)(V(t) - I(t) - \mu). \tag{7}$$

Thus, an error occurs whenever $V(t) - I(t) > \mu$. The presence of $I(t)$ on S-trials therefore reduces the probability of an error, given a reasonably high criterion, because $P(V(t) - I(t) > \mu) < P(V(t) > \mu)$. The inhibitory process has also been identified in the two-response choice RT paradigm (Grice, Nullmeyer, & Spiker, 1977), with a similar interpretation provided.

Response Strategies in Disjunctive Reaction Time

The go/no-go response requirement in DRT makes the interplay between the $A(t)$ and $I(t)$ processes theoretically quite interesting. This occurs because, procedurally, the absence of a second response in the task induces a qualitative distinction in the performance on $S-$ and $S+$ trials; that is, in VCT, a no-response trial can occur only if the criterion has not been exceeded during the trial, with less information required to inhibit responding to $S-$ than to associate an overt response to $S+$.

The invariant stimulus–response relationship in DRT allows the subject to use the inhibitory process efficiently, and importantly, permits two distinct performance strategies to be derived from VCT. From a theoretical standpoint, this distinction comes about because in DRT there are two different stimulus recognition processes, $A(t)$ for $S+$ and $I(t)$ for $S-$, yet only one overt response is required. Thus, one method would use the $A(t)$ process described previously, with the subject responding once sufficient $S+$ associative information has accrued to exceed the criterion. Concurrently, he would inhibit responding on $S-$ trials. Alternatively, however, the single-response nature of the DRT procedure permits subjects to produce acceptable performance by relying on $I(t)$ as the sole recognition process. On $S+$ trials, the subject would respond once detection information had exceeded the criterion ($V(t) > C$). On $S-$ trials, the inhibitory process would prevent the growth of $S-$ sensory information from exceeding the criterion.

Casually speaking, use of the first (associative) method implies a "set to withhold responding" prior to $A(t)$ onset whereas the second (inhibitory) method indicates a "set to respond" unless and/or until $S-$ inhibitory information dictates otherwise. Theoretical interest in these alternative response strategies developed when it was discovered (Grice et al., 1976) that, under identical conditions, some subjects employed the associative method whereas other subjects used the inhibitory method.

Graphically, the two strategies can be identified by the different correct RT distributions that they produce. Inhibitory subjects generate noninflected $E_c(t)$ functions analogous to those in SRT whereas associative subjects produce functions with a slight acceleration at the point of $A(t)$ onset. The correct RT distribution produced under the inhibitory strategy is represented by $E_c(t) = (1/\sigma)(V(t) - \mu)$ and the associative strategy by $E_c(t) = (1/\sigma)(V(t) + A(t) - \mu)$, so an REC comparison with SRT will indicate the type of strategy being used. Specifically, subjects employing the associative strategy will have nonlinear RECs, with the point of nonlinearity indicating the time of $A(t)$ onset. Inhibitory subjects have linear RECs, with the intercept showing a higher mean criterion relative to SRT.

The error distributions for the two strategies are qualitatively similar as both can be represented by Equation 7. Grice et al. (1976), however, noted that the temporal characteristics of $I(t)$ are different for the two strategies. For inhibitory subjects, the $I(t)$ function rises slowly and reaches a high asymptote after about 400 msec. In contrast, the inhibitory process for associative subjects grows rapidly but reaches a low asymptote by 250 msec. Consistent with the relative timing of these asymptotes, associative subjects make most of their errors before 250 msec. whereas errors for inhibitory subjects occur in the 200–400 msec. range.

The presence of two distinct response strategies, although heightening theoretical interest in DRT, is also unsettling unless their occurrence can be tied to specific features of either the subject or the task. Because subjects are unable to verbalize these strategies, nor are they even aware of their existence (Grice et al., 1982), a more productive research approach would be to study the task conditions influencing the relative likelihood of the two strategies.

Whereas little research has been devoted explicitly to this purpose, three lines of evidence can be identified suggesting that strategy use is not solely a function of the subject, but is also influenced by experimental conditions. One source of evidence stems from the Grice et al. (1976) interpretation of a DRT study conducted by LaBerge (1971). In that study, five groups of subjects received the same five tone frequencies as $S+$ (1300–1700 Hz in steps of 100). They differed in their $S-$ stimulus, receiving either blank catch trials (Group Nothing), a red square (Group Red), a burst of white noise (Group Noise), 900 and 2100 Hz tones (Group Far), or 1100 and 1900 Hz tones (Group Near). Plotting mean RT as a function of $S+$ frequency yields a discrimination gradient, whose steepness indicates the degree of control exerted by the frequency dimension. Groups Nothing and Red, receiving $S+$ and $S-$ in different modalities, displayed flat $S+$ frequency gradients, indicating that frequency information was not needed to recognize a tone $S+$. This absence of frequency control may be interpreted as evidence for the pure inhibitory strategy, with $A(t)$ not required for $S+$ recognition. Subjects receiving auditory stimulation as $S-$ exhibited frequency gradients of varying degrees of sharpness, corresponding to increasing reliance on the associative strategy. Overall, these results suggest that similarity between $S+$ and $S-$ is a likely determinant of strategy use, with higher degrees of similarity promoting the associative strategy.

Data from Grice's own laboratory implicate task instructions as a second factor influencing strategy use. In an auditory DRT task requiring a frequency discrimination, REC analyses revealed greater use of the inhibitory strategy when instructions emphasized speed rather than accuracy. This finding suggests that forcing subjects to adopt a lower criterion will increase reliance on the inhibitory strategy.

A third assessment of strategy use comes from a DRT experiment (Kushner, 1977) in which discriminations were based on tone intensity. Several factors were examined in this study, but the comparison of most interest is between a group receiving a loud tone as $S+$ and a softer tone as $S-$, and a group for whom the contingencies were reversed. In this context, Kushner (1977) noted that the inhibitory strategy was more likely for subjects receiving a loud tone as $S+$. A similar result has been reported by Grice et al. (1982). Taken together, these findings suggest that an important determinant of strategy use is stimulus intensity, with reliance on the inhibitory strategy increased when the contingencies dictate responding to the more intense stimulus.

The next section reports the results of an auditory DRT experiment designed to influence strategy use directly by varying the difficulty of the task demands. Using an intensity discrimination task, the variables

(1) relative stimulus intensity and (2) stimulus similarity were orthogonally varied in a 2 × 3 between-subjects design. Specifically, with tone intensities of either 65, 80, or 90 dB, the three possible intensity pairs were factorially combined with a counterbalancing of the response contingency to produce the six experimental groups. In this arrangement, positive relative intensity is defined by the three conditions in which the louder tone is the $S+$, whereas negative relative intensity is represented by the three conditions for whom the weaker tone is $S+$. On the other hand, a high degree of stimulus similarity is produced in the conditions where $S+$ and $S-$ intensities are close together (i.e., 65 vs. 80 db; 80 vs. 90 dB) and low similarity is represented in the two extreme intensities (65 vs. 90 dB).

Using the research design described earlier, the present experiment addressed the following questions. One, is strategy use generally susceptible to experimental influence, showing systematic relations to either relative stimulus intensity, stimulus similarity, or both? Two, are the temporal parameters of the associative and inhibitory processes affected by either or both of the experimental variables? Three, does the use of one strategy or the other lead to uniformly better task performance, or does the advantage depend on the difficulty of the task involved?

DISJUNCTIVE REACTION TIME EXPERIMENT

Method

A total of 108 female undergraduates, distributed equally across six groups, served as subjects. All subjects received identical treatment except for the intensities of their respective $S+$ and $S-$ tones. For Group $90+80-$, a 90 dB tone served as $S+$ and an 80 dB signal was $S-$. Group $80+90-$ received the same two intensities, but with the response contingencies reversed. Groups $90+65-$ and $65+90-$ were exposed to 90 and 65 dB tones, with the former group receiving a 90 dB $S+$ and the latter group a 65 dB $S+$. Groups $80+65-$ and $65+80-$ received 80 and 65 dB tones, with Group $80+65-$ receiving 80 dB $S+$ signals and Group $65+80-$ receiving 65 dB $S+$ signals.

Tones were 1000 Hz in frequency with a rise time of 10 msec. They were presented through a pair of Grason–Stadler earphones, with programming and data collection controlled by BRS solid state logic and associated relays. To respond, subjects depressed a telegraph key that controlled input to a BRS/LVE digital accumulator. RTs were recorded to the nearest msec.

A .5 sec. white light served as the warning signal, preceding the tone by either 1.5, 2.0, or 2.5 sec. The tone remained on for either 1.5 sec. or until the subject depressed the key. On $S-$ trials, a response produced a red error light located below the warning signal. Each subject received 324 trials, with the last 300 providing the RT data for analysis. The sequence of intensities was random subject to the constraints that each intensity could not occur more than three times in a row and was presented equally often within a block of 30 trials.

Empirical Results

The left frame of Fig. 11.4 depicts the mean of the individual subject correct RT medians for each group. The data are plotted with the three levels of stimulus similarity on the x-axis and relative intensity (loud tone as $S+$ or soft tone as $S+$) as a parameter. The similarity conditions were ordered according to Stevens' (1956) sone scale of perceived loudness, yielding values of 15.6, 22.0, and 37.6 sones for the 80-65, 90-80, and 90-65 combinations, respectively.

Figure 11.4 indicates a rather large difference in correct RT due to relative intensity, with similarity exerting a smaller effect. Moreover, the parallel nature of the curves suggests that the two variables influenced RT in an additive fashion. These observations were substantiated by analysis of

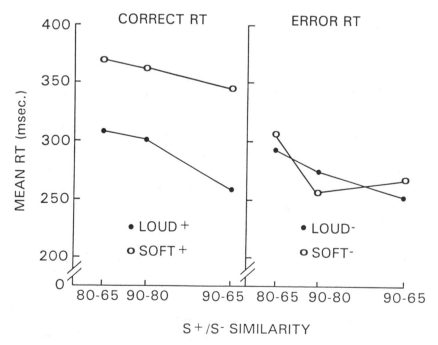

FIG. 11.4.   Group means of the individual subject median RTs for correct and error trials.

variance, which showed significant effects for the main effects of relative intensity (F = 62.09, df = 1/102, p < .001) and similarity (F = 6.07, df = 2/102, p < .005) and a nonsignificant interaction (F = 0.63, df = 2/102). A Newman–Keuls test on the similarity factor indicated that Groups 90+65– and 65+90– were significantly faster (p < .01) than the other four groups.

The right frame of Fig. 11.4 shows the group means of the individual subject median error RTs. The overlapping and horizontal nature of the curves suggests that this measure was fairly insensitive to either variable, and analysis of variance showed all effects to be nonsignificant. A similar analysis of overall error rate also proved nonsignificant, with the group rates ranging between 3.8 and 8.0%. However, as is shown later, the invariance of these summary measures of error performance did not imply that the underlying distributions were indifferent to similarity and intensity variations.

Theoretical Measurement of Strategy Use

Response strategies were classified by an REC analysis of the $E_c(t)$ functions for each subject. These functions were formed by placing the 150 RTs to $S+$ from each subject into a separate distribution and converting the cumulative probabilities, computed at every 10 msec., into the corresponding z-score. To obtain each subject's REC, $E_c(t)$ was plotted, at every 20 msec., against the corresponding $V(t)$-values based on the appropriate $S+$ intensity. The $V(t)$ functions for the three intensities were derived from a previous SRT study that used different subjects (Spiker, 1978). The three $V(t)$ curves are plotted in Fig. 11.5 and are defined by the following equations:

$$V_{90}(t) = 2.188 - 21.378e^{-.01215t}, \tag{8}$$
$$V_{80}(t) = 1.996 - 18.052e^{-.01082t}, \tag{9}$$
$$V_{65}(t) = 2.053 - 21.171e^{-.01116t}. \tag{10}$$

Recall that strategy identification hinges on the degree of linearity of the REC plot. For inhibitory subjects, their entire $E_c(t)$ distribution should be linearly related to the corresponding SRT distribution. For associative subjects, on the other hand, only the initial segment of the REC, that prior to A(t) onset, will be linear. However, there is no hard and fast rule that specifies when a plot is linear, so two alternative methods of strategy measurement were tested. The first method treats strategy as a continuum, with high amounts of REC linearity, as measured by the r^2 goodness of fit, indicating greater reliance on the inhibitory strategy. Alternatively, strategy can be treated in the more traditional way as a dichotomy, defined in terms of a cutoff value from the distribution of individual r^2. The results of both strategy measurement procedures are described later.

To assess the continuum method of strategy measurement, the r^2 from

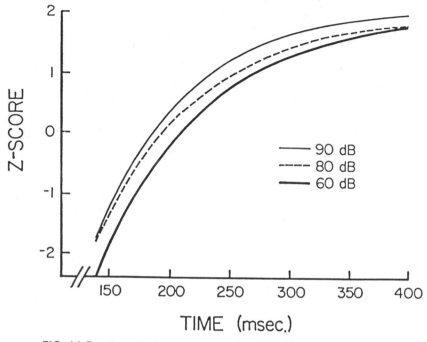

FIG. 11.5.   Growth of sensory information ($V(t)$) for three levels of stimulus intensity in simple RT.

each subject's REC was computed, and a mean value calculated for each of the six groups. These means have been plotted in the upper portion of Fig. 11.6. Note that the trend conforms to the pattern observed previously for correct RT medians, as relative intensity and similarity both exert substantial effects on mean r^2, with higher $S+$ intensities and lower similarity increasing r^2. Analysis of variance on the individual subject r^2 substantiated this interpretation, with both main effects statistically significant ($p < .05$) whereas their interaction was not. Follow-up testing showed that the two 90–65 groups relied more on the inhibitory strategy, as defined by higher r^2 relative to the other groups.

The measurement of strategy use as a dichotomy was performed as follows. The cutoff value of r^2 for classifying strategy was obtained by placing the r^2 values for all 108 subjects into a single distribution, and then identifying the most prominent inflection point. This determination was easy, as a distinct plateau in the frequency distribution was observed between .985 and .99. Thus, subjects with r^2 less than .99 were classified as associative whereas those with values greater than .99 were classified as inhibitory. Based on this classification, the total number of inhibitory subjects in each group is plotted in the lower part of Fig. 11.6. For the most

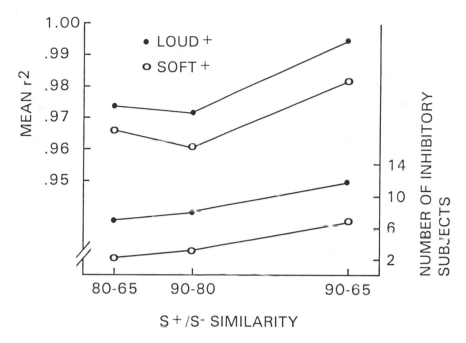

FIG. 11.6.   Group mean r^2 based on individual subject RECs with simple RT (top) and number of inhibitory subjects per group (bottom).

part, the pattern mirrors the plot of mean r^2, with relative intensity and similarity both exerting marked and additive effects on strategy use. The consistency between these two types of analyses supports the validity of r^2 as a measure of strategy. But because a dichotomous view of strategy is more amenable to theoretical analysis, the results of this second method of analysis are followed in the remainder of the chapter.

Analysis of Associative and Inhibitory Processes

With each subject's strategy identified, it is then possible to combine the distributions for subjects using the same strategy to estimate the time course of the associative and inhibitory processes produced under each condition. The analysis of associative information processing was, by necessity, restricted to those subjects employing the associative strategy. Because these subjects initially had been classified on the basis of a nonlinear (i.e., $r^2 < .99$) REC with $V(t)$, their slopes and intercepts were recalculated, using only the initial linear segment, to provide valid estimates of the criterion parameters. For each subject, this linear segment was determined by finding the best fitting line for the first three points, the first four, and so forth until r^2 fell below .99. At this point, the recalculation process stopped and the slope and intercept of the last analysis were used as estimates of σ and μ, respectively. In addition, the time value of this last point defines the point of $A(t)$ onset for that subject. The group means for the two criterion parameters and the average time of $A(t)$ onset are shown in the left portion of Table 11.1.

Because of substantial within-group variability in $A(t)$ onset time, analyses based on group distributions were not attempted. Nevertheless, several insights regarding the aspects of the associative process may be inferred from the onset time data. In particular, it is apparent from Table 11.1 that two classes of onset times exist, with Groups 90+65− and 90+80− exhibiting considerably faster $A(t)$ onset. The proximity of the other four group means shows that similarity had little effect on $A(t)$ onset, suggesting that absolute $S+$ intensity is the major determinant. This interpretation was substantiated by analysis of variance, in which the two 90 dB $S+$ conditions produced significantly faster $A(t)$ onset ($F = 10.40$, $df = 1/61$, $p < .01$) than the other conditions.

In keeping with previous theoretical work (Grice, Spiker, & Nullmeyer, 1979), estimates of $I(t)$ were restricted to the error distributions of subjects using the inhibitory strategy. Because these subjects' RECs with $V(t)$ had been linear initially, their slope and intercept provide valid estimates of the criterion parameters and thus did not require recalculation. For each group, $E_e(t)$ was obtained by combining the error RTs across subjects within a group, converting to cumulative probabilities, and then transforming into z-scores. The distributions for Groups 65+80− and 80+90− were not analyzed, as these conditions produced only two and three inhibitory subjects, respectively. Once each group's $E_e(t)$ function was determined, Equation 7 was rewritten as:

$$I(t) = V(t) - (\Sigma E_e(t) + \mu). \tag{11}$$

TABLE 11.1
Group Means of Selected Theoretical Parameters
by Type of Strategy

		Associative Strategy		Inhibitory Strategy	
Group	$A(t)$ onset (msec.)	μ	σ	μ	σ
90 + 65 −	293	1.290	.730	.991	.741
90 + 80 −	292	1.868	.827	1.397	.651
80 + 65 −	320	1.576	.756	.994	.608
65 + 90 −	328	1.645	.593	1.538	.394
80 + 90 −	333	1.910	.587	1.580	.385
65 + 80 −	344	1.748	.610	1.538	.453

Group estimates of μ and σ were obtained from the corresponding correct RT trials according to the following conventions: (1) μ was defined as the mean of the individual inhibitory subjects' criterion means, and (2) σ was defined as SQRT($S_c^2 + \frac{\Sigma}{N} \sigma^2/N$), where S_c^2 is the variance of the criterion means and N is the number of inhibitory subjects for that group (Grice et al., 1977).

The $I(t)$ functions for each of the four groups are plotted in Fig. 11.7. For each group, $I(t)$ begins in the vicinity of 180 to 200 msec. and shows a negatively accelerated growth rate. Comparison of the curves indicates that stimulus similarity and absolute stimulus intensity both affect the time course of $I(t)$. Specifically, $I(t)$ grows rapidly toward a high asymptote under conditions of low similarity and low $S-$ intensity (Group 90+65$-$). Yet, when $S-$ intensity and similarity are both high (Group 90+80$-$), $I(t)$ grows more slowly toward a low asymptote. In the intermediate case of low similarity but high $S-$ intensity, represented by Group 65+90$-$, $I(t)$ exhibits a slow approach to a reasonably high asymptote.

Effects of Strategy on Overall RT

Because subjects using the two strategies differentially rely on the associative and inhibitory processes, it is possible to make an additional prediction about the effects of strategy use on overall RT. Specifically, prior investigations of VCT have shown that the time course of sensory information, $V(t)$, is not influenced by the effects of stimulus similarity whereas the growth of $A(t)$ is quite sensitive to the effects of this variable. On the other hand, the rate of growth and asymptote of the inhibitory process is profoundly influenced by the absolute intensity of the stimulus (Grice et al., 1982). Taken together, these results suggest that overall RT for subjects employing the associative strategy—and hence relying on the associative process—these should be more sensitive to variation in stimulus similarity, whereas RTs for inhibitory subjects should show a greater effect of the stimulus intensity variation.

This prediction was tested by separately computing the mean correct RTs for subjects in each strategy category for each of the six conditions. These RTs are plotted in Fig. 11.8, with similarity comprising the x-axis and relative intensity as a parameter. The right frame of Fig. 11.8 shows that the mean RT for associative subjects increases with stimulus similarity. In contrast, the left frame of Fig. 11.8 shows RT to be a flat function of similarity for inhibitory subjects. Additionally, the greater distance between the two relative intensity curves for the inhibitory subjects confirms the theory's prediction that subjects employing this strategy are more sensitive to variations in stimulus intensity.

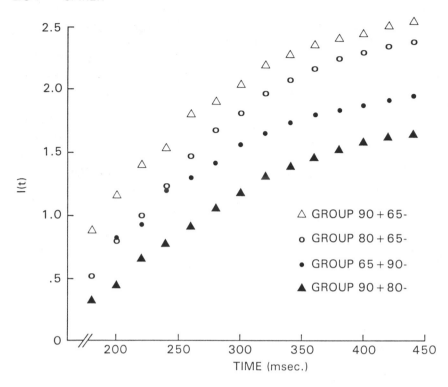

FIG. 11.7.   Growth of inhibition ($l(t)$) for four of the six conditions, plotted at every 20 msec.

Discussion

The results of the present experiment demonstrate that, to a large extent, adoption of the inhibitory or associative strategy depends on the task demands imposed by the similarity and intensity relations between $S+$ and $S-$. This finding replicates and extends previous work suggesting that, in general, reliance on the inhibitory strategy is more likely under lighter task demands, as defined by low stimulus similarity and/or positive relative intensity. In addition, the temporal characteristics of the inhibitory and associative processes were influenced by these experimental variables. Onset of $A(t)$ occurred sooner for associative subjects in the loudest $S+$ intensity conditions. On the other hand, $I(t)$ was influenced by both similarity and relative intensity, growing more slowly to a lower asymptote under conditions of high similarity and negative relative intensity.

Despite the sensitivity of strategy to both variables, it must be noted that

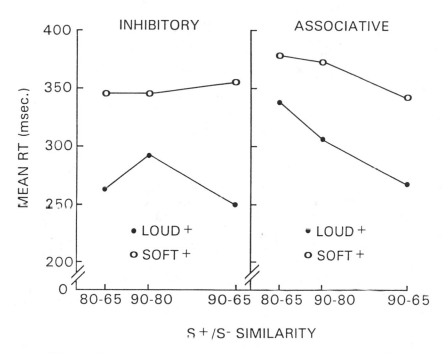

FIG. 11.8. Group means of the individual subject median correct RTs, plotted separately for inhibitory and associative subjects.

no condition produced complete reliance on either strategy. Even the least demanding condition, Group 90+65−, produced only 12 inhibitory subjects out of 18, suggesting that the subject's own pre-experimental disposition will play a major role in strategy selection. The extent to which some objectively definable measure of personality may be used to predict this susceptibility, however, remains a topic for future study.

Grice and Spiker (1979) have shown that considerable insight into the processing dynamics of the RT paradigm can be gained by comparing the values of the theoretical parameters produced under the different experimental conditions. In this regard, the present experiment offers new information with respect to three aspects of processing.

First, examination of the group criterion means in Table 11.1 indicates that, for each condition, the criterion mean was higher for subjects employing the associative strategy compared to their counterparts using the inhibitory strategy. This trend is consistent with the view that, if a subject is to use the associative strategy effectively, he must wait until $A(t)$ has accrued sufficient information about the identity of $S+$. Inhibitory subjects, on the other hand, have no such requirement because they are basing their differential responding on the fast rising inhibitory process. As shown in Fig. 11.8, inhibitory subjects were faster than their associative counterparts in all conditions except 65+90−. The size of the difference, however, was generally larger when task demands are light (e.g., 80+65−, 90+80−, 90+65−). On the other hand, imposition of more difficult task conditions, as in conditions 80+90− and 65+80−, greatly diminished the advantage of the inhibitory strategy.

A second finding of interest, and some surprise, was the inverse relationship between time of $A(t)$ onset and intensity of the $S+$ tone (see Table 11.1). Similar observations have not been made in choice RT (Grice et al., 1982) and suggest that different processing dynamics may be involved in the two tasks. The present study suggests that recruitment of associative information begins only after a fixed amount of detection information has accumulated, with the particular point of $A(t)$ onset directly related to the growth of $V(t)$. In this regard, the comparable $A(t)$ onset times noted for the groups receiving either a 65 dB or 80 dB tone $S+$ is consistent with this hypothesis, because by 300 msec., the $V(t)$ functions produced by these two intensities have converged (see Fig. 11.5). One interpretation is that associative subjects in DRT use two criteria, with the second criterion determining the amount of detection information that must be accrued before initiation of the associative process. The marked between-subject variability in $A(t)$ onset times observed in the present experiment suggests that considerable variability may exist in the setting of this criterion.

Third, the present results, like those of previous VCT analyses (e.g., Grice & Spiker, 1979; Grice, Spiker, & Nullmeyer, 1979), indicate that substantially different processing is used in withholding responding as opposed to making an overt response. This is most evident in the consistent differences between the temporal parameters (see Fig. 11.7) and environmental influences (see Fig. 11.8) of the inhibitory ($I(t)$) and associative ($A(t)$) processes. The decision to inhibit responding can be made quickly, as shown by the rapid onset and recruitment of $I(t)$. Its major nemesis is the absolute intensity of the negative stimulus ($S−$), although factors such as high similarity may also retard its growth. In contrast, active recognition of a positive stimulus seems to accrue more slowly, being less a function of the dynamogenic properties of the stimulus, and more a function of the associative factors acquired through learning and influenced by context.

CONCLUSIONS

Evaluation of VCT

With the presentation of VCT complete, it is appropriate at this point to evaluate the theory's present status in terms of the five objectives listed at the outset. To reiterate, these criteria are: using clearly defined concepts, specifying principles as functions of time, tying theoretical parameters to observable variables, categorizing variables by theoretical process, and applying the theory to different research paradigms.

In keeping with its Hull–Spence roots, all the concepts in VCT are unambiguously defined. Although not always explicit, the definitions and measurement operations are, so to speak, "available upon demand." For example, the concept of an internal response criterion, whereas somewhat vague when expressed verbally, can be precisely defined in Thurstonian scaling terms as the first and second moments of a cumulative probability distribution converted to z-scores. Moreover, like Donders' stage theory, a task-based procedure is used to define the growth of sensory information as the cumulative distribution produced in SRT. Likewise, the temporal characteristics of the inhibitory and associative processes are defined by a signal detection theory-type analysis in which the $E(t)$ distribution for either correct or error RTs are compared to the corresponding $E(t)$ distribution from SRT. Even the notion of a response strategy is specified quantitatively by the degree of linearity in an REC plot between DRT and SRT. Whereas each concept and process within VCT may be discussed in loose terms that facilitate spoken discourse, all have a precisely defined counterpart based on standardized measurement procedures.

VCT has also been quite successful in that many of its principles are stated as functions of time. Indeed, a unique aspect of the theory is the analysis of the dynamic interplay among the sensory, associative, and inhibitory processes. In this regard, it is ironic that the most powerful concept in the theory, the criterion, is not represented as process but is assumed to take on a single value at the start of each trial. Yet, it is not inconceivable that a dynamic role may eventually be given the criterion such that its value fluctuates along a specified path over time. For example, one could conceive of the criterion decreasing systematically during the interval between the warning cue and onset of the imperative signal. Such an approach will remain speculative, however, until an explicit procedure is derived for determining how the moments of the distribution change over time.

Additionally, considerable strides have been made in associating VCT parameters to values of experimental variables. Most notable in this regard is the specification of the criterion distribution parameters, μ and σ, as reflecting the subject's current motivational or attentional state. Receiving less study have been the growth rate and asymptotic parameters of the associative and inhibitory processes, $A(t)$ and $I(t)$, whose rate and asymptotes have been shown to vary with stimulus similarity and stimulus intensity. Yet, further work in this area is clearly needed. For example, it would be informative to plot the specific values obtained for previous estimates of the growth rate parameter of $V(t)$, m, as a function of specific values of stimulus intensity. If fitted mathematically, such a plot would provide a psychophysical function indicating the appropriate growth rate parameter to use in any future SRT study. Not only would this approach economize parameter estimation, it also might provide additional insight into the dynamics of the sensory process itself. Similar psychophysical analyses could be performed for the parameters in the other theoretical processes.

Regarding the fourth objective, VCT represents a continuation of the Hull–Spence tradition of using theory to untangle the complex effects of variables on behavior. For instance, sources of variation not amenable to experimental manipulation, such as subject trait variables, measurement error, and so forth have been conveniently combined to reflect fluctuations in the criterion distribution. Further, it has been shown that the effects of stimulus intensity are quite complex. Initial application of VCT to SRT indicated that intensity affects both criterion and sensory growth, making its study theoretically challenging and useful. Further work in the disjunctive and choice RT paradigms has shown that discriminations based on stimulus intensity require considerable analysis to delineate their complex effects on the criterion and sensory growth, as well as the associative and inhibitory processes. In all these efforts, a commitment to classifying variables by process has been vital to furthering our understanding of the processing dynamics involved in the RT task. Such an approach has also allowed the prediction of previously untested combinations of variables, as seen in the initial studies on the design-dependent effects of stimulus intensity and in the present study of individual differences in response strategies.

The final point concerns the theory's current predictive scope and the likelihood for advances in the future. On both counts, there is cause for optimism. Theoretical scope is difficult to define in an absolute sense but can be gauged in comparison to other theories in the area. In this latter sense, the predictive scope of VCT has been quite impressive. In few extant theories has the general area of RT been covered in as much depth as in VCT. Whereas some accounts can be considered theories of SRT (e.g., Luce & Green, 1972) or DRT (e.g., LaBerge, 1971) or choice RT (e.g., Link, 1975), they have yet to bridge the gap between paradigms. In this regard, an attempt has been made in VCT to replace Donders' stage theory integration of the RT paradigms with a process-oriented account of the relationships between the paradigms. In recent applications of VCT (e.g., Grice et al., 1979, 1982), the attempt has been made quite explicit by using SRT to estimate the $V(t)$ process, DRT to estimate the $I(t)$ process, and choice RT to provide estimates of $A(t)$ and several other theoretical processes.

On the horizon, extending the VCT approach to other paradigms looks promising. For example, preliminary analyses of visual SRT have been accomplished (Grice, Nullmeyer, & Schnizlein, 1979), with a similar account to that of auditory RT provided. As mentioned earlier, a substantive theoretical base of work has already been achieved with human eyelid conditioning (Grice, 1977), with possibilities for additional work in this frequently neglected area seemingly limitless. Moreover, expansion of the VCT approach into more complex realms of information processing, such as the letter-matching paradigm of Posner (1973) and the same–different memory judgments of Sternberg (1969), is a definite possibility and one that will hopefully materialize in the coming years.

In his characteristically modest fashion, Grice has described the current status of VCT as "a measurement operation," which must precede the "development of a more comprehensive theory" having "deductive and integrative capacity" (Grice et al., 1982). Yet, as one reflects on the conceptual foundations of the theory, laid down by the integrative work of Hull–Spence and the mathematics of Thurstone, it could be argued that VCT has already taken great strides toward the organization of research that characterizes a more mature theory. It is indeed the belief and hope of this author that VCT will continue to exert an integrative influence in information processing research for many years to come.

Final Note

As we pay tribute to Charles Spiker in these pages, it is especially difficult for me to express my feelings about a man who has so profoundly shaped the course of my professional and personal life. Yet, this chapter would not be complete, nor would the entire purpose of this volume be served, without a few words on this topic.

The influence of Charles Spiker on this author's career has been extremely positive, manifesting itself in ways that are not always visible to the casual observer. Besides his always highly valued counsel, Charles Spiker has served to inspire a strong work ethic, an appreciation of scientific theory, a fascination with new ideas and new ways of thinking, and above all, a genuine love of knowledge and the desire to live a life of never-ending learning.

From a personal standpoint, of the many things a father can give his son, I feel I have received them all. A strong inner core of self-respect, a desire to serve society, a commitment to honest labor, and a belief in things bigger than myself are all parts of an inner world that this son wishes to thank his father for.

Besides the professor and the father, though, there is the man himself. Men and women with clear vision, strong values, and a pure dedication to their ideals are all too rare in our society. All who know Charles Spiker know him to be such a man. Whereas respect for such people comes easy, an appreciation of their virtues usually comes much later, often too late. It is therefore especially appropriate that we now acknowledge the contribution of Charles Spiker to our discipline, as a man who has dedicated his entire life to advancing the scientific knowledge of human behavior through the setting and achieving of high standards of scholarship, teaching, and research.

ACKNOWLEDGMENTS

This research was supported by PHS Grant MH 16400 from the National Institute of Mental Health to G.R. Grice and was based on a doctoral dissertation submitted to the University of New Mexico. The author wishes to thank Dr. Grice for his comments on an earlier version of this chapter.

REFERENCES

Bergmann, G. (1956). The contribution of John B. Watson. *Psychological Review, 63,* 265–276.
Bergmann, G. (1957). *The philosophy of science.* Madison: University of Wisconsin Press.
Boring, E. G. (1950). *A history of experimental psychology.* New York: Appleton-Century-Crofts.
Christie, L. S., & Luce, R. D. (1956). Decision structure and time relations in simple choice behavior. *Bulletin of Mathematical Biophysics, 18,* 89–112.
Green, D. M., & Swets, J. A. (1966). *Signal detection theory and psychophysics.* New York: Wiley.
Grice, G. R. (1968). Stimulus intensity and response evocation. *Psychological Review, 75,* 359–373.
Grice, G. R. (1971). A threshold model for drive. In H. H. Kendler & J. T. Spence (Eds.), *Essays in neobehaviorism.* New York: Appleton-Century-Crofts.
Grice, G. R. (1972a). Conditioning and a decision theory of response evocation. In G. H. Bower (Ed.), *Psychology of learning and motivation* (Vol. 5). New York: Academic Press.
Grice, G. R. (1972b). Application of variable criterion model to auditory reaction time as a function of the type of catch trial. *Perception & Psychophysics, 12,* 103–107.
Grice, G. R. (1977). Information processing dynamics of human eyelid conditioning. *Journal of Experimental Psychology: General, 106,* 71–93.
Grice, G. R., Hunt, R. R., Kushner, B. A., & Morrow, C. W. (1974). Stimulus intensity, catch trial effects, and the speed–accuracy tradeoff in reaction time A variable criterion theory interpretation. *Memory and Cognition, 2,* 758–770.
Grice, G. R., Hunt, R. R., Kushner, B. A., & Nullmeyer, R. T. (1976). Associative processes and strategies in disjunctive reaction time. *Memory and Cognition, 4,* 443–445.

Grice, G. R., & Hunter, J. J. (1964). Stimulus intensity effects depend upon the type of experimental design. *Psychological Review, 71,* 247-256.

Grice, G. R., Nullmeyer, R. T., & Schnizlein, J. M. (1979). Variable criterion analysis of brightness effects in simple reaction time. *Journal of Experimental Psychology: Human Perception and Performance, 5,* 303-314.

Grice, G. R., Nullmeyer, R. T., & Spiker, V. A. (1977). Application of variable criterion theory to choice reaction time. *Perception & Psychophysics, 22,* 431-449.

Grice, G. R., Nullmeyer, R. T., & Spiker, V. A. (1982). Human reaction time: Toward a general theory. *Journal of Experimental Psychology: General, III,* 135-153.

Grice, G. R., & Spiker, V. A. (1979). Speed-accuracy tradeoff in choice reaction time: Within conditions, between conditions, and between subjects. *Perception & Psychophysics, 26,* 118 126.

Grice, G. R., Spiker, V. A., & Nullmeyer, R. T. (1979), Variable criterion analysis of individual differences and stimulus similarity in choice reaction time. *Perception & Psychophysics, 25,* 353-370.

Helson, H. (1964). *Adaptation-Level theory.* New York: Harper & Row.

Hilgard, E. R., & Bower, G. H. (1966). *Theories of learning.* New York: Appleton-Century-Crofts.

Hohle, R. H. (1965). Inferred components of reaction times as functions of foreperiod duration. *Journal of Experimental Psychology, 69,* 382-386.

Hull, C. L. (1943). *Principles of behavior.* New York: Appleton-Century-Crofts.

Hull, C. L. (1952). *A behavior system: An introduction to behavior theory concerning the individual organism.* New Haven: Yale University Press.

Kimble, G. A. (1961). *Hilgard and Marquis' conditioning and learning.* New York: Appleton-Century-Crofts.

Kushner, B. A. (1977). *Disjunctive reaction time: A variable criterion approach.* Unpublished doctoral dissertation, University of New Mexico.

LaBerge, D. A. (1962). A recruitment theory of simple behavior. *Psychometrika, 27,* 375-396.

LaBerge, D. A. (1971). Effect of type of catch trial upon generalization gradients of reaction time. *Journal of Experimental Psychology, 88,* 225-228.

Lappin, J. S., & Eriksen, C. W. (1966). Use of a delayed signal to stop a visual reaction-time response. *Journal of Experimental Psychology, 72,* 805-811.

Lewis, D. (1960). *Quantitative methods in psychology.* New York: McGraw-Hill.

Link, S. W. (1975). The relative judgment theory of two choice response time. *Journal of Mathematical Psychology, 12,* 114-135.

Logan, F. A. (1977). Hybrid theory of classical conditioning. In G. H. Bower (Ed.), *The psychology of learning and motivation.* New York: Academic Press.

Luce, R. D. & Green, D. M. (1972). A neural timing theory for response times and the psychophysics of intensity. *Psychological Review, 79,* 14-57.

McGill, W. J. (1963). Stochastic latency mechanisms. In R. D. Luce, R. R. Bush, & E. Galanter (Eds.), *Handbook of mathematical psychology.* New York: Wiley.

Posner, M. I. (1973). *Cognition: An introduction.* Glenview, IL: Scott, Foresman.

Spence, K. W. (1936). The nature of discrimination learning in animals. *Psychological Review, 43,* 427-449.

Spence, K. W. (1937). The differential response in animals to stimuli varying within a single dimension. *Psychological Review, 44,* 430-444.

Spence, K. W. (1956). *Behavior theory and conditioning.* New Haven: Yale University Press.

Spence, K. W., Haggard, D. F., & Ross, L. E. (1958). UCS intensity and the associative (habit) strength of the eyelid CR. *Journal of Experimental Psychology, 55,* 404-411.

Spiker, C. C. (1963). The hypothesis of stimulus interaction and an explanation of stimulus compounding. In L. P. Lipsitt & C. C. Spiker (Eds.), *Advances in child development and behavior* (Vol. 1). New York: Academic Press, 233-264.

Spiker, C. C. (1977). Behaviorism, cognitive psychology, and the active organism. *Life-Span Developmental psychology.* New York: Academic Press.

Spiker, V. A. (1978). *Effects of stimulus intensity and intensity differences on simple and disjunctive reaction time: A variable criterion theory analysis.* Unpublished doctoral dissertation, University of New Mexico.

Sternberg, S. (1969). The discovery of processing stages: Extensions of Donders' method. *Acta Psychologica, 30,* 276-315.

Stevens, S. S. (1956). Calculation of the loudness of complex noise. *The Journal of the Acoustical Society of America, 28,* 807-832.

Taylor, D. A. (1966). Latency components in two-choice responding. *Journal of Experimental Psychology, 72,* 481-487.

Thurstone, L. L. (1928). Scale construction with weighted observations. *Journal of Educational Psychology, 19,* 441-453.

Thurstone, L. L. (1925). A method of scaling psychological and educational tests. *Journal of Educational Psychology, 16,* 433-451.

Woodworth, R. S., & Schlosberg, H. (1954). *Experimental psychology revised edition.* New York: Holt.

Appendix
Bibliography of
Charles C. Spiker

PUBLICATIONS

Spiker, Charles C., & Irwin, Orvis C. (1950). The relationship between IQ and indices of infant speech sound development. *Journal of Speech and Hearing Disorders, 15,* 335–343.

Cantor, Gordon N., & Spiker, Charles C. (1954). Effects of nonreinforced trials on discrimination learning in preschool children. *Journal of Experimental Psychology, 47,* 256–258.

Spiker, Charles C., & McCandless, Boyd R. (1954). The concept of intelligence and the philosophy of sciences. *Psychological Review, 61,* 255–266.

Spiker, Charles C., & Terrell, Glenn. (1955). Factors associated with transposition behavior of preschool children. *Journal of Genetic Psychology, 86,* 143–158.

McCandless, Boyd R., & Spiker, Charles C. (1955). Experimental research in child psychology. *Child Development, 27,* 75–80.

Spiker, Charles C. (1956). Effects of stimulus similarity on discrimination learning. *Journal of Experimental Psychology, 51,* 393–395.

Spiker, Charles C. (1956). Experiments with children on the hypotheses of acquired distinctiveness and equivalence of cues. *Child Development, 27,* 253–263.

Spiker, Charles C. (1956). Stimulus pretraining and subsequent performance in the delayed reaction experiment. *Journal of Experimental Psychology, 52,* 107–111.

Spiker, Charles C. (1956). The effects of number of reinforcements on the strength of a generalized instrumental response. *Child Development, 27,* 37–44.

Spiker, Charles C. (1956). The stimulus generalization gradient as a function of the intensity of stimulus lights. *Child Development, 27,* 85–89.

Spiker, Charles C., Gerjuoy, Irma R., & Shepard, Winifred O. (1956). Children's concept of middle-sizedness and performance on the intermediate size problem. *Journal of Comparative and Physiological Psychology, 49,* 416–419.

Norcross, Kathryn J., & Spiker, Charles C. (1957). The effects of type of stimulus pretraining on discrimination performance in preschool children. *Child Development, 28,* 79–84.

Norcross, Kathryn J., & Spiker, Charles C. (1958). Effects of mediated associations on transfer in paired-associate learning. *Journal of Experimental Psychology, 55,* 129–134.

Spiker, Charles C., & Holton, Ruth B. (1958). Associative interference in motor paired-associate learning as a function of amount of first-task practice. *Journal of Experimental Psychology, 56,* 123-132.

Spiker, Charles C., & White, Sheldon H. (1959). Differential conditioning by children as a function of effort required in the task. *Child Development, 30,* 1-7.

Harms, Irene E., & Spiker, Charles C. (1959). Factors associated with the performance of young children on intelligence scales and tests of speech development. *Journal of Genetic Psychology, 94,* 3-22.

Spiker, Charles C. (1959). Performance on a difficult discrimination following pretraining with distinctive stimuli. *Child Development, 30,* 513-521.

Spiker, Charles C., & Holton, Ruth B. (1959). Similarity of stimuli and of responses in the successive discrimination problem. *Child Development, 30,* 471-480.

Spiker, Charles C. (1960). Associative transfer in verbal paired-associated learning. *Child Development, 31,* 73-87.

Spiker, Charles C. (1960). Research methods in children's learning. In P. H. Mussen (Ed.), *Handbook of research methods in child development* (pp. 374-420). New York: John Wiley and Sons, Inc.

White, Barbara N., & Spiker, Charles C. (1960). The effect of stimulus similarity on amount of cue-position patterning in discrimination learning problems. *Journal of Experimental Psychology, 59,* 131-136.

White, Sheldon H., & Spiker, Charles C. (1960). The effect of a variable conditioned stimulus upon the generalization of an instrumental response. *Child Development, 31,* 313-319.

White, Sheldon H., Spiker, Charles C., & Holton, Ruth B. (1960). Associative transfer as shown by response speeds in motor paired-associate learning. *Child Development, 31,* 609-616.

Spiker, Charles C., & Norcross, Kathryn J. (1962). Effects of previously acquired stimulus names on discrimination performance. *Child Development, 33,* 859-864.

Lipsitt, L. P., & Spiker, Charles C. (Eds.). (1963). *Advances in child development and behavior* (Vol. 1). New York: Academic Press.

Spiker, Charles C. (1963). The hypothesis of stimulus interaction and an explanation of stimulus compounding. In L. P. Lipsitt & C. C. Spiker (Eds.), *Advances in child development and behavior* (Vol. 1, pp. 233-264). New York: Academic Press.

Spiker, Charles C. (1963). Verbal factors in the discrimination learning of children. In J. C. Wright & J. Kagan (Eds.), *Basic cognitive processes in children* (Monographs of the SRCD, Vol. 28, No. 2, pp. 53-71).

Spiker, Charles C., & Lubker, Bonnie J. (1964). Experimental tests of the hypothesis of stimulus interaction. *Journal of Experimental Child Psychology, 1,* 256-268.

Lipsitt, L. P., & Spiker, Charles C. (Eds.). (1965). *Advances in child development and behavior* (Vol. 2). New York: Academic Press.

Spiker, Charles C., & Lubker, Bonnie J. (1965). The relative difficulty for children of the successive and simultaneous discrimination problems. *Child Development, 36,* 1091-1101.

Lubker, Bonnie J., & Spiker, Charles C. (1966). The effects of irrelevant stimulus dimensions on children's oddity-problem learning. *Journal of Experimental Child Psychology, 3,* 207-215.

Spiker, Charles C. (1966). The concept of development: Relevant and irrelevant issues. *Monographs of the SRCD, 31,* 39-54.

Lipsitt, L. P., & Spiker, Charles C. (Eds.). (1967). *Advances in child development and behavior* (Vol. 3). New York: Academic Press.

Price, Louis E., & Spiker, Charles C. (1967). Effect of similarity of irrelevant stimuli on performance in discrimination learning problems. *Journal of Experimental Child Psychology, 5,* 324-331.

Spiker, Charles C. (1970). An extension of Hull-Spence discrimination learning theory. *Psychological Review, 77,* 496–515.

Spiker, Charles C. (1971). Application of Hull-Spence theory to the discrimination learning of children. In H. W. Reese (Ed.), *Advances in child development and behavior* (Vol. 6, pp. 99–152). New York: Academic Press.

Spiker, Charles C., Croll, William L., & Miller, Asenath A. (1972). On the comparison of psychological theories: A reply to Professor Bogartz. *Journal of Experimental Child Psychology, 13,* 585–592.

Spiker, Charles C., Croll, William L., & Miller, Asenath, A. (1972). The effects of verbal pretraining on the multidimensional generalization behavior of children. *Journal of Experimental Child Psychology, 13,* 558–572.

Spiker, Charles C., & Cantor, Joan H. (1973). Applications of Hull-Spence theory to the transfer of discrimination learning in children. In H. W. Reese (Ed.), *Advances in child development and behavior* (Vol. 8, pp. 223–288). New York: Academic Press.

Cantor, Joan H., & Spiker, Charles C. (1976). The effects of labeling dimensional values on the setting differences in shift performance of kindergarten children. *Memory and Cognition, 4,* 446–452.

Cantor, Joan H., & Spiker, Charles C. (1977). Dimensional fixation with introtacts in kindergarten children. *Bulletin of the Psychonomic Society, 10,* 169–171.

Spiker, Charles C. (1977). Behaviorism, cognitive psychology, and the active organism. In N. Datan & H. W. Reese (Eds.), *Life-span developmental psychology: Dialectical perspectives on experimental research.* New York: Academic Press.

Spiker, Charles C. (1977). Estimation of parameters of the Grice theory of simple reaction time. *Journal of Mathematical Psychology, 15,* 102–108.

Spiker, Charles C. (1977). The estimation of parameters from systems of nonlinear questions. *Journal Supplement Abstract Service, 7,* 64.

Spiker, Charles C., & Cantor, Joan H. (1977). Intradimensional and extradimensional shifts in the rat with assessment of differential instrumental generalization. *Bulletin of the Psychonomic Society, 10,* 223–225.

Spiker, Charles C., & Cantor, Joan H. (1977). Introtacts as predictors of discrimination performance in kindergarten children. *Journal of Experimental Child Psychology, 23,* 520–538.

Cantor, Joan H., & Spiker, Charles C. (1978). The effect of change in stimuli on the transfer of dimensional pretraining to the discrimination learning of kindergarten children. *Child Development, 49,* 824–828.

Cantor, Joan H., & Spiker, Charles C. (1978). The problem-solving strategies of kindergarten and first-grade children during discrimination learning. *Journal of Experimental Child Psychology, 26,* 341–358.

Cantor, Joan H., & Spiker, Charles C. (1979). The effects of introtacts on hypothesis testing in kindergarten and first-grade children. *Child Development, 50,* 1110–1120.

Spiker, Charles C., & Cantor, Joan H. (1979). Factors affecting hypothesis testing in kindergarten children. *Journal of Experimental Child Psychology, 28,* 230–248.

Spiker, Charles C., & Cantor, Joan H. (1979). The Kendler levels-of-functioning theory: Comments and an alternative schema. In H. W. Reese & L. P. Lipsitt (Eds.), *Advances in child development and behavior* (Vol. 13, pp. 119–135). New York: Academic Press.

Cantor, Joan H., & Spiker, Charles. (1980). Factors affecting children's recognition memory for multidimensional stimuli. *Bulletin of the Psychonomic Society, 16,* 345–348.

Spiker, Charles C., & Cantor, Joan H. (1980). The effects of stimulus type, training, and chronological age on children's identification and recoding of multidimensional stimuli. *Journal of Experimental Child Psychology, 30,* 144–158.

Cantor, Joan H., & Spiker, Charles C. (1982). The effect of the temporal locus of the introtact probe on the hypothesis-testing strategies of kindergarten children. *Journal of Experimental Child Psychology, 34,* 510–525.

Spiker, Charles C., & Cantor, Joan H. (1982). Cognitive strategies in the discrimination learning of young children. In D. K. Routh (Ed.), *Learning, speech, and the complex effects of punishment.* New York: Plenum.

Spiker, Charles C., & Cantor, Joan H. (1983). Components in the hypothesis-testing strategies of young children. In T. Tighe & B. E. Shepp (Eds.), *Interactions: Perception, cognition, and development.* Hillsdale, NJ: Lawrence Erlbaum Associates.

Spiker, Charles C. (1983). Commentary: Psychophysical scaling by children. *Monographs of the Society for Research in Child Development, 48,* No. 6, 65–71.

Spiker, Charles C., & Cantor, Joan H. (1983). The dimensional analysis by children of multidimensional stimuli. *Bulletin for the Psychonomic Society, 21,* 449–452.

Cantor, Joan H. & Spiker, C. C. (1984). Evidence for long-term planning in children's hypothesis testing. *Bulletin of the Psychonomic Society, 22,* 493–496.

Spiker, Charles C., Cantor, J. H., and Klouda, Gayle V. (1985). The effect of pretraining and feedback on the reasoning of young children. *Journal of Experimental Child Psychology, 39,* 381–395.

Spiker, Charles C. (In press). An introduction to the scientific method. In J. V. Hinrichs & I. P. Levin, *Experimental Psychology.*

Spiker, Charles C. (1986). Principles in the philosophy of science: applications to psychology. In L. P. Lipsitt & J. H. Cantor (Eds.), *Experimental Child Psychologist: Essays and Experiments in Honor of Charles C. Spiker.* Hillsdale, New Jersey: Lawrence Erlbaum Associates.

PH.D. DISSERTATIONS SUPERVISED

Glenn Terrell, Jr. A study of conditions influencing discrimination learning and transposition in young children (co-directed with Prof. B. McCandless). August, 1952.

Irma E. Gerjuoy. The effect of mediated responses upon the acquisition of a motor task. August, 1953.

Gordon N. Cantor. The effects of three types of pretraining on discrimination learning in preschool children. June, 1954.

Winifred O. Shepard. Effects of verbal pretraining on discrimination learning in preschool children. August, 1954.

Ruth B. Holton. Variables affecting the change in instrumental response magnitude after reward cessation. August, 1956.

Kathryn J. Norcross. The effects of discrimination performance of the similarity of previously acquired stimulus names. August, 1957.

Sheldon H. White. Generalization of an instrumental response with variation in two attributes of the CS. August, 1957.

Hayne W. Reese. Transfer to a discrimination task as a function of amount of stimulus pretraining and similarity of stimulus names. August, 1958.

Morton Reiber. The effect of CS presence during delay of reward on the speed of an instrumental response. August, 1959.

Louis E. Price. The effect of type of verbal pretraining on transposition in children. August, 1960.

Alice S. Hawkins. Verbal identification of stimulus components in ambiguously named compounds. August, 1961.

June M. Hoyt. Conditional discrimination and serial reversal learning in children. June, 1962.

Bonnie L. Lubker. The effect of training on cue-position patterning in discrimination learning. August, 1962.

John M. Love. The effects of amount of training and an irrelevant dimension on discrimination reversal learning in children. June, 1966.

William L. Croll. Oddity discrimination learning as a function of the number of dimensions along which the correct stimulus is odd. August, 1967.

Christie J. Tragakis. The effects of irrelevant dimensions on simultaneous and successive discrimination learning. August, 1969.

Asenath A. Miller. The effects of changes in dimension-specific verbalization on children's simultaneous discrimination learning. August, 1971.

Harriette Guldmann. The effects of dimensional verbalization upon children's performance on reversal and extradimensional shift discrimination problems. February, 1972.

M.A. THESES AND
THESIS EQUIVALENTS SUPERVISED

Winifred O. Shepard. *Mediated generalization with high interstimulus similarity.* June, 1953.

Gerald Weiss. *Discrimination learning in preschool children under three levels of instruction.* August, 1954.

Ruth Hardwick. *The effect of response effortfulness on acquisition and extinction of a pulling response in young children.* June, 1955.

Kathryn J. Norcross. *The effect of mediated association on proactive facilitation and interferences in paired-associate learning.* August, 1956.

Sheldon H. White. *The effect of a variable conditioned stimulus upon the generalization of an instrumental response.* August, 1956.

Barbara E. Notkin. *The effect of stimulus similarity on amount of cue-position patterning in discrimination problems.* June, 1958.

Louis E. Price. *The effect of the similarity of irrelevant stimuli on performance in discrimination learning problems.* August, 1959.

Alice S. Hawkins. *The effects of ambiguous training with stimulus compounds on the acquisition of names for components.* August, 1960.

June M. Hoyt. *Effect of similarity of reversal cues on learning of successive stimulus reversals in children.* August, 1960.

Anne C. Weinstock. *The effect of magnitude of reward on discrimination learning in preschool children.* February, 1962.

Melinda Y. Small. *Children's performance on an oddity problem as a function of the number of values on the relevant dimension.* August, 1967.

Christie J. Tragakis. *The effects of manipulating irrelevant dimensions in successive discrimination problems.* August, 1968.

Asenath A. Miller. *Children's simultaneous discrimination learning as a function of pretraining condition* (co-directed with Prof. J. Cantor). January, 1971.

Gayle V. Klouda. *The interaction of hypothesis pretraining and locus of the probe in children's hypothesis testing* (co-directed with Prof. J. Cantor). May, 1984.

Author Index

Subject Index